DRIVING THE PACIFIC COAST

Oregon & Washington

Help Us Keep This Guide Up to Date

Every effort has been made by the author and editors to make this guide as accurate and useful as possible. However, many things can change after a guide is published—establishments close, phone numbers change, hiking trails are rerouted, facilities come under new management, and so on.

We would love to hear from you concerning your experiences with this guide and how you feel it could be made better and be kept up to date. Although we may not be able to respond to all comments and suggestions, we'll take them to heart and we'll also make certain to share them with the author. Please send your comments and suggestions to the following address:

The Globe Pequot Press
Reader Response/Editorial Department
P.O. Box 480
Guilford, CT 06437

Or you may e-mail us at:

editorial@globe-pequot.com

Thanks for your input, and happy travels!

DRIVING THE PACIFIC COAST

Oregon & Washington

Fifth Edition

Edited by
Kathy Strong

GUILFORD, CONNECTICUT

Text design by Lisa Reneson
Interior photography by Kenn Oberrecht, except where credited otherwise.

ISBN 0-7627-2492-7

Manufactured in the United States of America
Fifth Edition/First Printing

CONTENTS

INTRODUCTION

The Oregon and Washington coastlines will stun the first-time visitor with their natural beauty, drama, and diversity at every scenic turn. And those who have witnessed their awe-inspiring charm return again and again for more. The two states' consecutive coasts wind along through lush evergreen forests and pastoral fields. Wild Pacific seas billow and crash onto rugged rocks and expansive, driftwood-strewn shores. Stop to catch the sun setting slowly over a historic lighthouse. Listen to the wind howl while you curl up in front of a cozy fireplace in a cliffside cabin suspended over the hypnotizing surf. Sand dunes gleaming in the sunshine and moonshine beckon you to explore, and the quaint small-town atmosphere reigns as the only way of living. The pace is slower, friendlier, and outdoor oriented. Take the entire adventure in this book or just a portion. No matter how much you explore the area, you will definitely look forward to seeing more!

Enjoy *Driving the Pacific Coast* as a tote-along companion when you travel to the coast country. It's a carefully organized volume that's easy to follow and does not require training in advanced vector analysis. Coastal communities are arranged in the book from south to north, but it is equally useful regardless of the direction you travel.

Instead of actual rates for lodging and campgrounds and prices for meals, you will find price ranges in this book expressed as inexpensive, moderate, expensive, and so on. Keep in mind that prices change and that these ranges are general.

Lodging rates are based on two-person occupancy. Room rates up to $60 (excluding taxes) are inexpensive, from $61 to $150 moderate, $151 to $250 expensive, $251 to $500 very expensive, and more than $500 extremely expensive.

Campground and RV-park rates are based on spaces for one vehicle with water and electrical hookups. Up to $15 a day is inexpensive, $16 to $25 moderate, $26 to $40 expensive, and more than $40 very expensive.

Breakfast up to $4.00, lunch to $5.00, and dinner to $10.00 qualify as inexpensive. Breakfasts from $4.01 to $8.00, lunches from $5.01 to $9.00, and dinners from $10.01 to $20.00 are moderate. Breakfasts from $8.01 to $13.00, lunches from $9.01 to $15.00, and dinners from $20.01 to $30.00 are expensive.

Breakfasts more than $13.00, lunches more than $15.00, and dinners more than $30.00 are very expensive.

You will happily discover that major roads are well marked for general traveling. For more detailed city and county maps, write or stop by any of the chambers of commerce or visitor centers listed under Travel Information in the following pages. National forest maps, available at ranger stations, also are helpful, especially for exploring off the main highways.

Many recreational activities on the coast depend upon the tides. Beachcombers, for example, like to search for agates, Japanese glass floats, and other treasures on an ebb, or outgoing, tide. Tide-pool exploration calls for low tides. Clam diggers prefer minus tides, and crabbers usually set their gear on the flood, or incoming, tide and continue crabbing through slack high tide. Anglers have all sorts of theories as to which tide is best for catching any given species of fish. Those who hike beaches also must know the tides to avoid being stranded or endangered by rising water. A knowledge of the tides is also crucial for safe boating in salt water.

Tide table booklets, published annually, sell for less than a dollar and are available at tackle shops, marinas, and department stores along the coast.

Summers on the Northwest Coast are seldom hot. In fact, evenings and foggy or cloudy days can be chilly. Pack appropriate clothing, including a light parka or windbreaker. Winter is the rainy season, but a wet-weather front might come ashore anytime. Bring rainwear, and enjoy the coast regardless of the weather.

No matter what the weather is, ther dress is casual—more for comfort than for fashion. And if there's one thing the friendly Pacific coast inhabitants take seriously, it's recreation. So join the fun. Welcome to coast country.

> *The information and rates listed in this guidebook were confirmed at press time. We recommend, however, that you call establishments before traveling to obtain current information.*

OREGON

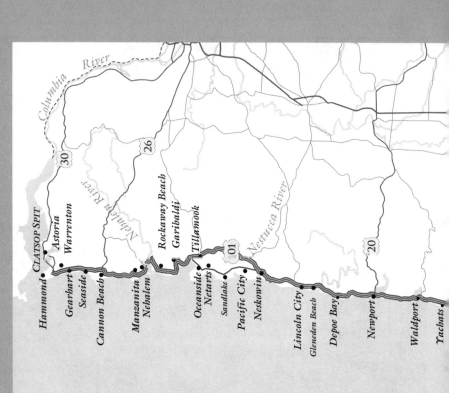

Columbia River

30

26

101

20

Nehalem River

Nestucca River

CLATSOP SPIT
Hammond •
Astoria •
Warrenton •
Gearhart •
Seaside •
Cannon Beach •
Manzanita •
Nehalem •
Rockaway Beach •
Garibaldi •
Tillamook •
Oceanside •
Netarts •
Sandlake •
Pacific City •
Neskowin •
Lincoln City •
Gleneden Beach •
Depoe Bay •
Newport •
Waldport •
Yachats •

Oregon Department of Fish and Wildlife
2501 SW First Avenue
P.O. Box 59
Portland, OR 97207
(503) 872-5310
www.dfw.state.or.us

Oregon Parks and Recreation Department
1115 Commercial Street NE
Suite 1
Salem, OR 97301
(503) 378-6305
Information: (800) 551-6949
Reservations: (800) 452-5687

Oregon Tourism Commission
775 Summer Street NE
Salem, OR 97301
(503) 986-0000
(800) 547-7842
www.traveloregon.com

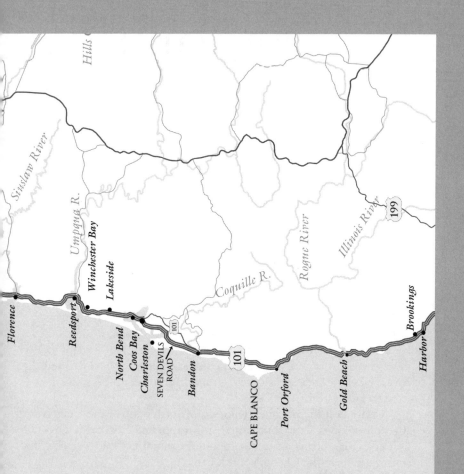

BROOKINGS
Population: 5,620

HARBOR
Population: 7,880

☆

Location: *On U.S. 101, 5 miles north of the California–Oregon state line, 110 miles south of Coos Bay. Zip: 97415.*

In the vicinity of Brookings, the coastal plain narrows as the Pacific Ocean indents eastward, and the Coast Range mountains quickly slope to the sea. The result is a countryside of spectacular beauty, with rocky headlands intruding on great sweeps of beach where surf and wind and geological upheaval have created coves, caves, sea stacks, and vertigo-inducing promontories northward to Port Orford.

Situated on the ocean and along the north bank of the Chetco River, Brookings is the southernmost incorporated city on the Oregon coast. Harbor is an unincorporated community that stretches southward from the Chetco's south bank.

Brookings was established in the early 1900s as a company town for the Brookings Lumber and Box Company. Logging and the manufacture of lumber and wood products remain the area's chief industries, although commercial fishing and agriculture are also important.

When not trolling for salmon or seining other species, the commercial fleet is moored at the busy Port of Brookings harbor on the south side of the river, where there are 281 slips for commercial boats. Visitors can watch the fleet come and go, and photographers will find many worthy subjects.

Among the cash crops here and in nearby northern California are Easter lilies. In fact, a small group of local growers produces about 90 percent of the Easter lilies sold in the United States and Canada. Many other flowers, wild and cultured, grow here in profusion, with some species or another in bloom every month of the year. The area's geology and a meteorological phenomenon known as the "Brookings Effect" keep winter temperatures warmer here than anywhere else on the Oregon coast. Ocean breezes temper the summer heat, making the climate moderate, without the seasonal extremes encountered elsewhere. In January, low temperatures are in the forties, with highs in the fifties. July offers temperatures from the low fifties to mid-sixties. Warm spells in the seventies and eighties occur in both July and January.

LODGING

Best Western Beachfront Inn, 16008 Boat Basin Road; (541) 469–7779 or (800) 468–4081. In Harbor, west of the boat basin and south of the Chetco River entrance. Cable TV, refrigerators, and microwave ovens in 102 rooms and suites with ocean-view balconies, some with in-room whirlpool tubs. Great sunset views and easy beach access to an expansive strand strewn with driftwood. The only oceanfront motel in the Brookings/Harbor area. Near boat basin, shops, and restaurants. Moderate to expensive.

Holmes Sea Cove Bed & Breakfast, 17350 Holmes Drive; (541) 469–3025 or (888) 290–0312; www.harborside.com. Just north of Harris Beach State Park. Take Dawson Road west off U.S. 101 to Holmes Drive and turn right. Two bedrooms on the lower level of Holmes house, as well as a connected guest cottage. Private baths, ocean view, beach access, trail to private park. Continental breakfast brought to rooms. Moderate.

South Coast Inn Bed & Breakfast, 516 Redwood Street; (541) 469–5557 or (800) 525–9273; www.southcoastinn.com. One block east of U.S. 101, overlooking downtown Brookings. Cable TV and shared bath. Full breakfast and evening refreshments. Dinner on request. Walk to shops, movie theater, and restaurants. Moderate.

CAMPGROUNDS AND RV PARKS

Beachfront RV Park, 16024 Boat Basin Drive; P.O. Box 848; (541) 469–5867. On the south bank of the river, west of U.S. 101. Has 134 sites: 43 full hookups, 55 electric. Showers, laundry, cable TV, minimarket, ice. On the ocean and boat basin. Fishing pier for handicapped anglers. Moderate.

Chetco RV Park, 16117 U.S. 101 South; P.O. Box 760; (541) 469–3863; www.chetcorvpark.com. South of Brookings on east side of U.S. 101. Has 121 full-hookup sites, mostly pull-through. Showers and laundry; propane, ice, and bait for sale. Near marina and within walking distance to shops. Moderate.

Driftwood RV Park, 16011 Lower Harbor Road; P.O. Box 2066; (541) 469–9089; www.driftwoodrvpark.com. South of the river, west of U.S. 101, near Port of Brookings harbor. Has 100 full-hookup sites. Cable TV, showers, and laundry. Near river and beaches. Moderate.

Harris Beach State Park, (office) 1655 U.S. 101; (541) 469–2021. Two miles north of Brookings on west side of U.S. 101. Has 155 sites: 34 full-hookup, 51 electric, 66 tent. Showers, tank dump, and firewood. Campground in a beautiful setting, typical of Oregon's coastal parks. Reservations accepted. Moderate.

FOOD AND BEVERAGES

Great American Smokehouse and Seafood Company, 15657 Highway 101 South; (541) 469–6903. Located 1.5 miles south of Brookings-Harbor Shopping Center. Monday through Saturday, 9:00 A.M. to 6:00 P.M.; Sunday, 12:30 to 6:00 P.M. Restaurant serves lunch and dinner daily. Specializes in gourmet seafoods with gift packs available. Salmon cold-smoked for three days over alder (Indian style). Custom smoking and canning. Fresh seafoods available. Restaurant offers delectable seafood in a nautical setting. For lunch try one of the great seafood sandwiches, clam chowder, bagel with smoked-salmon pâté, or old-fashioned bagels and lox. For dinner have a whole Dungeness crab, coho salmon steak, chinook salmon fillet, halibut, lingcod, prawns, scallops, oysters, lobster, or surf 'n' turf. Beer and wine. Moderate to expensive.

O'Holleran's Restaurant & Lounge, 1210 Chetco Avenue; (541) 469–9907. In Brookings on east side of U.S. 101, next to the Bonn Motel. Dinner daily. Excellent menu of steaks, chicken, and seafoods, including chinook salmon, prawns, scallops, oysters, frog legs, and abalone. Cocktails, beer, and wine. Moderate.

Smuggler's Cove Restaurant, 16011 Boat Basin Road; (541) 469–6006. The only ocean-view dining in the area, across from the Beachfront Inn. Daily breakfast, lunch, and dinner, from 7:00 A.M. to 10:00 P.M., with an ocean view. Offers all the traditional egg dishes as well as corned beef hash and eggs, pork chops and eggs with biscuit and gravy, omelettes, waffles, and pancakes. Lunch includes burgers and big deli-style and specialty sandwiches: shrimp melt, crab melt, prime rib, Reuben, chicken salad on croissant, and oyster burger. Choose from such appetizers as jumbo shrimp cocktail, crab-stuffed mushrooms, and oyster shooters. Dinner entrees include steaks, prime rib, lobster, razor clams, halibut, king crab, salmon, fish and chips, scallop scampi, chicken, and pasta dishes. Full bar. Moderate to expensive.

SHOPPING AND BROWSING

Most shops and galleries are concentrated along U.S. 101 in downtown Brookings and along the highway in Harbor, as well as in the boat-basin area on the south side of the Chetco River.

MUSEUM

Chetco Valley Historical Society Museum, 15461 Museum Road; (541) 469–6651. South of Brookings, just off the east side of U.S. 101. Memorial Day to Labor Day and some Sundays in winter; call for hours. The building was once the home of a local pioneer family. Displays of antique furniture, old photographs, gold-mining equipment, an old copper still, and many historical objects donated by families of early settlers.

BEACHES, PARKS, TRAILS, AND WAYSIDES

Beaches stretch north and south from the mouth of the Chetco River, with good access in and out of town. **Azalea Park** lies within the Brookings city limits, just off North Bank Road. The seventy-six-acre park has an abundance of native azaleas, some of which are 20 feet tall and more than 300 years old. The best time to visit the park is when the azaleas are blooming, from April through June.

Two miles north of Brookings, **Harris Beach State Park** offers camping, picnicking, hiking, beachcombing, and photographic opportunities. Just a half mile offshore from the picnic area is a bird rookery called Goat Island.

About 2 miles north of Harris Beach State Park, **Samuel H. Boardman State Park** begins and extends north for 11 miles along U.S. 101. Numerous viewpoints offer parking and opportunities for hiking, sight-seeing, beachcombing, and exploring tide pools.

Hikers and backpackers will find many trails east of Brookings in the **Siskiyou National Forest** and **Kalmiopsis Wilderness.** Trails in the Chetco Ranger District range from a fraction of a mile to 17.1 miles.

Harris Beach State Park

Those who don't wish to hike can see the district by taking a self-guided car tour that covers 42.5 miles and takes about five hours. Maps, brochures, and information are available from the Chetco Ranger Station.

WATER SPORTS AND ACTIVITIES

Fishing centers on the area's two rivers and the ocean, either from beaches and rocks or offshore from boats. With both native and migratory fish species in abundance, there's something to be caught twelve months of the year.

The Winchuck is a small river with headwaters about 15 miles inland. It empties into the ocean south of Brookings near the California–Oregon line. The upper river is good for rainbow and cutthroat trout in the spring and fall. Coho and chinook salmon enter the river in the fall, and steelhead fishing peaks in January. Perch fishing is good near the river's mouth in late winter and spring.

Although not so well known as the Rogue and Umpqua Rivers, which were made famous by Zane Grey and other notables, the Chetco, one of Oregon's wild and scenic rivers, is every bit a classic coastal stream. It rises in the Kalmiopsis Wilderness in the Siskiyou Mountains and courses some 40 miles over a rocky bottom and clean gravel beds that are ideal for spawning fish. It's a good river for both wading and floating, with the best access in the lower 20 miles. Coho and chinook fishing is from August through October, and steelheading from mid-December through January. The Chetco is known for big fish, each year giving up steelhead of twenty pounds and chinook weighing more than fifty pounds.

Charter boats are available at the Port of Brookings harbor. Those who tow boats to Brookings will find eight paved launch ramps in the harbor and slips for 610 pleasure craft. Although it is said to be the calmest harbor and safest bar crossing in Oregon, it's the same big ocean beyond; only the experienced and well-equipped boater should head for the offshore grounds.

Brookings Sports Unlimited, 625 Chetco Avenue; (541) 469–4012. Downtown Brookings on west side of U.S. 101. Full line of tackle, crabbing gear, rainwear, and boots. Fishing licenses, tags, and information.

Sporthaven Marina, 16374 Lower Harbor Road; P.O. Box 2215; (541) 469–3301. Port of Brookings harbor, south side of river, west of U.S. 101. Full-service fishing center, with tackle and bait for sale, crabbing gear for sale or rent. Fishing licenses, custom canning, and smoking. River guide service by day or half day. Ocean charter fishing for salmon and bottom fish. Information on local fishing and crabbing.

WEATHER AND TIDE INFORMATION

U.S. Coast Guard, Chetco River harbor; recorded message, (541) 469–4571

TRAVEL INFORMATION

Brookings-Harbor Chamber of Commerce, P.O. Box 940; (541) 469–3181 or (800) 535–9469; www.brookingsor.com

U.S. Forest Service, Chetco Ranger Station, 539 Chetco Avenue; (541) 469–2196

EVENTS

May	Azalea Festival, (541) 469–9741
July	Fourth of July Celebration and Fireworks, (541) 469–3181

GOLD BEACH

Population: 2,070

Location: *On U.S. 101, 37 miles north of the California–Oregon state line, 83 miles south of Coos Bay. Zip: 97444.*

Gold was once mined from the black-sand beaches of Curry County. In fact, in the mid-nineteenth century, hundreds of placer miners worked the beaches near the present site of Gold Beach, which lies smack on the ocean and along the south bank of the Rogue River. But now the broad, uncrowded beaches, stretching north and south from the mouth of the Rogue, attract whale watchers, beachcombers, clam diggers, kite fliers, hikers, surf fishermen, and windsurfers.

The area's main attraction is the Rogue, a designated wild and scenic river. The canyons and meadows of the Rogue River valley were home to American Indians for thousands of years. In the nineteenth century, trappers, miners, and homesteaders came to the Rogue, followed by loggers and ranchers. Although they ultimately settled the land, they never tamed the river.

The lower 52 miles of the river—the scenic section—are traversed mainly by jet sleds: shallow-draft boats powered by hydro-jet engines. Anglers use the sleds to reach favorite fishing spots. Jet-powered boats also deliver mail and take countless sightseers up the river and into the scenic Coast Range and Rogue canyons.

Waters above the scenic section are off-limits to powerboats. Here drift boats, kayaks, and inflatable rafts take anglers and adventurers along the wild Rogue. To control traffic in this section, access is limited and permits are required.

Many miles of trails serve hikers and backpackers, either along the ocean or along the Rogue. Upriver trails take hikers past pioneer ranches and a fishing cabin that belonged to author Zane Grey.

Those who prefer to explore by car will find several routes to their liking. On the north side of the U.S. 101 bridge, turn east and follow North Bank Rogue Road along the river to the bridge near Lobster Creek. Cross the bridge, and turn west on State Route 33, which returns to Gold Beach. The round-trip takes less than an hour, unless you decide to stop for fishing or a picnic.

Another loop trip starts just south of town, where you can turn east on Hunter Creek Road (County Route 635) and follow it to the end of the pavement. From there National Forest Secondary Route 3680 is a good gravel road maintained for auto travel. Take that to National Forest Secondary Route 3313, which goes to the Rogue River, where a turn left on State Route 33 leads back to Gold Beach. Before embarking on this loop, stop by the Gold Beach Ranger Station to check on the latest road conditions, and pick up a copy of the excellent Siskiyou National Forest map.

LODGING

Gold Beach Resort and Condominiums, 29232 Ellensburg; (541) 247–7066 or (800) 541–0947; www.gbresort.com. At the south end of town on the west side of U.S. 101. Twin, double, queen, and king beds in comfortably furnished rooms and condos with cable TV, Showtime, and refrigerators, some with whirlpool baths. Ocean view, indoor pool and spa, beach access, putting green, and tennis court. Complimentary continental breakfast. Moderate to expensive.

Inn of the Beachcomber, 29266 Ellensburg; (541) 247–6691 or (888) 690–2378; www.beachcomber-inn.com. Downtown, on west side of U.S. 101. Queen and king beds, cable TV, and HBO in large, well-appointed rooms, most fronting the ocean. Heated indoor pool and spa. Easy beach access. Moderate to expensive.

Ireland's Rustic Lodges, 29330 Ellensburg, P.O. Box 774; (541) 247–7718; www.irelandsrusticlodges.com. In town, south of Rogue River on west side of U.S. 101. Private cabins, vacation homes, and inn accommodations with queen beds, cable TV, fireplaces, ocean view, and beach access. Inexpensive to moderate.

Jot's Resort, P.O. Box 1200; (541) 247–6676 or (800) 367–5687; www.jotsresort.com. On north bank of the Rogue, west of U.S. 101 bridge. Full-service resort with 140 waterfront rooms and suites. Standard and deluxe units accommodate 2 to 4 persons in 1- and 2-bedroom condominiums. Cable TV, fireplaces, river and ocean views. Pool, restaurant and lounge, dancing and entertainment, sport shop and marina, boat launch and dock space, rental boats, fishing licenses. Books ocean-charter trips, jet-boat trips, and salmon and steelhead guides. Moderate.

UPRIVER LODGES

Along the wild section of the Rogue River are seven lodges that offer travelers a unique wilderness experience. They're spaced just far enough apart so hikers can pack light and enjoy a pleasant pace on the **Rogue River Trail** in the splendor of the **Wild Rogue Wilderness.** At day's end, hikers can slip off their day packs and enjoy showers, dinner, and comfortable beds. Breakfast and a sack lunch get hikers started in the morning toward the next lodge.

Plan a trip to fit any schedule—overnight, weekend, or week-long. For nonhikers, a jet boat goes to Paradise Lodge or any of the other lodges downstream.

Spring is the best time for hiking the Rogue River Trail, with fall the next best time. Summers are hot, and the traffic is heavy on both the river and the trail.

Drive and park near the trailhead at Foster Bar. From there, hike upstream to the lodges. Following are the lodges in the order they occur. Write or phone for more information.

Illahe Lodge, 37709 Agness-Illahe Road; Agness 97406; (541) 247–6111. On the Rogue River Trail, north bank, 1 mile upstream from trailhead at Foster Bar.

Paradise Bar Lodge, Box 456; Gold Beach 97444; (541) 247–6022 or (800) 525–2161. On the Rogue River Trail, north bank of the Rogue, 11.7 miles upstream from trailhead at Foster Bar. The upriver terminus for jet-boat tours.

The Lodge at Half Moon Bar, P.O. Box 10; Agness 97406; (541) 247–6968. On the south bank of the Rogue, across the river from Paradise Bar Lodge. Owner will ferry you across the river. Season is from March to November 1. Good place to spend a weekend or several days.

Marial Lodge, Box 1395; Grants Pass 97528; (541) 474–2057. On the Rogue River Trail, north bank of the Rogue, 4 miles above Paradise Bar Lodge, 15.7 miles from trailhead at Foster Bar. On the site of century-old homestead.

Black Bar Lodge, Box 510; Merlin 97532; (541) 479–6507. On the south bank of the Rogue and accessible only by prearrangement. The farthest lodge upstream from trailhead at Foster Bar, at

Rogue River Bridge at Gold Beach

30.4 miles, but only 9.6 miles downstream from the trailhead at Grave Creek Bridge.

Rogue River Reservations, Inc., P.O. Box 548; Gold Beach 97444; (541) 247–6022, (541) 247–6504, or (800) 525–2161. Books accommodations at all the upriver lodges, as well as fishing trips, float trips, and river access via jet boat or drift boat.

CAMPGROUNDS AND RV PARKS

Four Seasons RV Resort, 96526 North Bank Rogue Road; (541) 247–4503 or (800) 248–4503; www.fourseasonsrv.com. Located 6.5 miles east of U.S. 101, off North Bank Road—follow the signs. Angler's delight, offering full hookups, showers, laundry, boat launch, dock, tackle shop, licenses and tags, gas and oil, and guide service. Only 6 miles from Cedar Bend Golf Course. Putting green at the resort. Open all year. Moderate.

Indian Creek Recreation Park, 94680 Jerry's Flat Road; (541) 247–7704. A half mile east of U.S. 101 on the south bank of the Rogue. A full-service RV park and campground with 125 full-hookup and tent sites in a beautiful parklike setting. Showers, laundry, store, horseback trails, outdoor games, recreation room. Restaurant on premises. Moderate.

FOOD AND BEVERAGES

Grant's Pancake and Omelette House, Jerry's Flat Road; (541) 247–7208. A half mile east of U.S. 101, at Indian Creek Recreation Park, on south bank of the Rogue. Breakfast and lunch daily. Good selection of pancakes, waffles, eggs, omelettes, including egg substitutes for those on low-cholesterol diets, as well as traditional and specialty sandwiches. Large portions, so bring a big appetite. Moderate.

Nor'wester Seafood Dining and Lounge, Port of Gold Beach; (541) 247–2333. On the waterfront, west of U.S. 101, just south of the bridge. Dinner daily. Northwest seafood specialties include broiled halibut, salmon, and rockfish, as well as razor clams, Pacific oysters, steamed clams, scampi, and seafood combination platter. Menu also features steaks, lamb chops, chicken, and pasta. Full bar. Moderate.

Spada's, 29374 Ellensburg; (541) 247–7732. Downtown, on west side of U.S. 101. Breakfast, lunch, and dinner daily. Large menu includes omelettes, pancakes, steak and eggs, biscuits and gravy, eggs Benedict, deli-style sandwiches, burgers, pizza, charbroiled steaks, prime rib, seafood, and pasta dishes. Sunday champagne brunch, served from 9:00 A.M. to 2:00 P.M., is one of the best on the coast. Full bar. Moderate.

MUSEUM

Curry County Historical Museum, 920 South Ellensburg; (541) 247–6113. On the west side of U.S. 101, at the fairgrounds. Call for days and hours of operation. A small but interesting museum displaying photographs and artifacts of the county's towns and villages, the timber industry, sport and commercial fishing, Indian history and craft work, and more. Donations accepted.

WATER SPORTS AND ACTIVITIES

Sportfishing is one of the main attractions in the Gold Beach area, with offshore ocean fishing for salmon and bottom fish and angling in the lower river for salmon, bottom fish, perch, sea-run cutthroat, steelhead, sturgeon, and smelt. Upriver, the Rogue is famous for its superb salmon fishing and angling for summer and winter steelhead, as well as cutthroat trout. Many smaller streams attract fly and spin anglers, who test their skills on native cutthroat and rainbow trout.

Don Pedro's Guide Service, P.O. Box 155; (541) 247–7946 or (888) 638–0848; www.roguefishingguide.com. Guided salmon and steelhead trips on the Rogue River and estuary, as well as the Chetco and Coquille Rivers.

Rogue Outdoor Store, 29865 Ellensburg; (541) 247–7142. East side of U.S. 101, just south of the bridge. Full line of camping gear, fishing tackle, crabbing and clam-digging gear, maps, tide books, and rental gear. Licenses and tags. Good source of information about local outdoor sports.

TOURS AND TRIPS

No visit to the Gold Beach area would be complete without a trip up the Rogue River in a jet boat—an unforgettable experience for travelers of all ages, offered by several companies. The boats are safe, stable craft, piloted by experts with extensive experience on the Rogue. Special provisions allow the handicapped to enjoy the splendors of Rogue River jet-boat trips. Reservations are recommended.

Jerry's Rogue Jets, Box 1011; (541) 247–4571 or (800) 451–3645; www.roguejets.com. This company operates half-day or full-day whitewater adventures, as well as soft scenic river tours. Lunch or dinner is available with day trips for an extra fee. Awarded the Governor's Tourism Award in 1987, the company is committed to educational entertainment and the preservation of the unique wilderness area. The ticket office, a museum dedicated to the history of the Rogue River, and a gift shop are located at the south end of the Rogue River Bridge at the port. Reservations advised; tours are seasonal.

Rogue River Mail Boat Trips, P.O. Box 1165-G; (541) 247–7033 or (800) 458–3511; www.mailboat.com. On North Bank Rogue Road, east of U.S. 101. May through October, 64-mile trips depart daily at 8:30 A.M. and 2:30 P.M. Mid-June through mid-September, 80-mile trips depart daily at 8:00 A.M. and 2:45 P.M. Mid-May through mid-October, 104-mile trips depart daily at 8:00 A.M. Special, free transportation to and from boat for the handicapped. Latest fleet addition is the *Rogue Queen,* a glass-covered, 43-foot jet boat that carries seventy passengers and will skim over water only 10 inches deep.

Whitewater raft, kayak, and drift-boat trips are also popular and exciting ways to see and experience the Rogue. Several outfitters specialize in such trips and can provide everything needed. Advance planning and booking are essential. Write or phone the following outfitters for information.

Orange Torpedo Trips, P.O. Box 1111; Grants Pass 97526; (541) 479–5061. One- to six-day inflatable-kayak trips. Trips designed for novices and families. Camp or stay at river lodges.

Sundance Expeditions, 344 Thornridge Lane, Merlin 97532; (541) 479–8508 or (888) 777–7557. Raft and kayak trips. "The College of Kayaking" provides instruction, equipment, lodging, and river trips.

GOLF

Cedar Bend Golf Course, 34391 Squaw Valley Road; P.O. Box 1234; (541) 247–6911; www.cedar-bend-golf.com. Located 11 miles north of Gold Beach, 16 miles south of Port Orford, on Squaw Valley Road off U.S. 101. Nine-hole course in low, rolling hills, out of the wind and fog.

TRAVEL INFORMATION

Gold Beach Visitors Center and Chamber of Commerce, 29279 Ellensburg, #3; (541) 247–7526 or (800) 525–2334; www.goldbeach.org

U.S. Forest Service, Gold Beach Ranger District, 29279 Ellensburg; (541) 247–3600

EVENTS

June	Jet Boat Marathon, (800) 452–2334
	Wave Bash, (800) 452–2334
July	Curry County Fair, (800) 452–2334
September	Festival of Quilts, (800) 452–2334
December	Community Christmas Bazaar, (800) 452–2334

PORT ORFORD

Population: 1,025

☆

Location: *On U.S. 101, 54 miles north of the California–Oregon state line, 52 miles south of Coos Bay. Zip: 97465.*

Situated on a marine terrace above a protected natural harbor, Port Orford is the westernmost incorporated city in the contiguous United States. In recent years the town has suffered the same financial woes that have befallen many coastal communities whose economies have depended primarily upon timber and commercial fishing. Port Orford has been slower than most to recover. Nevertheless, the area offers some notable attractions worthy of the traveler's time.

Port Orford's harbor is a coastal cove, not an estuary, so vessels have no river bar to cross. In calm weather some commercial boats, sport craft, and sailing vessels anchor in the scenic cove. Most boats, however, rest in unusual berths at this unique waterfront; there are no customary docks, floats, or moorage slips. Instead, boats are cradled on rubber-tired dollies atop a large wharf and are launched and retrieved by a hoist capable of handling vessels up to 42 feet long and weighing up to 26,000 pounds.

Depending on the time of the year, commercial boats return to port with catches of salmon, blackcod (sablefish), bottom fish, shrimp, or crab. Port Orford is also the center of Oregon's sea urchin fishery.

In the timber world the Port Orford vicinity is well known for a beautiful tree bearing the same name. Port Orford cedar is an aromatic, straight-grained tree, native to a small local range. The durable wood has seen a number of uses over the years, from Indians' canoes and dwellings to battery separators, venetian-blind slats, house siding, and decking.

The tree's beauty, ironically, may lead to its eventual extinction. The attractive cedars have been cultured in nurseries

17

and used as ornamentals for more than seventy years. A root fungus, once confined to nurseries, has now spread to the forests and is attacking trees throughout their range. Only the discovery of a way to combat the spreading fungus will save the rest of these exquisite trees from extinction.

LODGING

The Castaway, P.O. Box 844, 97476; (541) 332–4502; www.castawaybythesea.com. Tucked away off the main road in the headland that protects Port Orford, this small motel has one of the most dramatic views of the Oregon coast. All suites and guest rooms have ocean views, cable TV, and phones; suites have kitchens and living-room areas. Pets allowed with deposit; nonsmoking rooms available. Inexpensive to moderate.

CAMPGROUNDS AND RV PARKS

Cape Blanco State Park, (541) 332–6774. About 5 miles west of U.S. 101, 5 miles north of Port Orford. Water and electricity at all 58 sites. Showers and tank dump. Good spot for flying kites and radio-controlled gliders. Plenty of hiking in an area rich in history. Great salmon and steelhead fishing, beachcombing, and photography opportunities. Nearby lighthouse and museum. Inexpensive.

Evergreen RV Park, 839 Coast Guard Road; P.O. Box 306; (541) 332–5942. Two blocks west of U.S. 101 on Ninth Street. Small park in a pleasant residential setting. Pull-through sites, showers, full hookups, laundry, and cable TV. Walking distance to restaurants, shops, parks, port, and lake. Inexpensive.

Humbug Mountain State Park, (541) 332–6774. About 7 miles south of Port Orford on U.S. 101. Has 30 full-hookup RV sites and 77 tent sites. Showers, tank dump, firewood, and laundry. Plenty of hiking opportunities, including a 3-mile trail to the top of 1,756-foot Humbug Mountain. Surf fishing on the beach at Brush Creek for surfperch. Trout fishing in Brush Creek. Moderate.

FOOD AND BEVERAGES

Bartlett's Cafe, 831 North Oregon Street; (541) 332–4175. On the west side of U.S. 101 at Ninth Street. Breakfast, lunch, and dinner daily. Has a complete menu of traditional offerings and is well known for freshly baked pies, pastries, and raised doughnuts.

Malts, shakes, sodas, floats, and sundaes available. Inexpensive to moderate.

SHOPPING AND BROWSING

The Wooden Nickel, 555 West 20th Street; (541) 332–5201; www.oregonmyrtlewood.com. West side of U.S. 101, south end of town. Summer: daily, 8:00 A.M. to 7:00 P.M. Winter: daily, 9:00 A.M. to 5:00 P.M. Myrtlewood factory and shop offering a large selection of myrtlewood cutting boards, artworks, dinnerware, and more. Also gifts, souvenirs, kites, and wind socks. Gift wrapping and shipping offered.

MUSEUM

Hughes House, Cape Blanco State Park; (541) 332–2975; www.hugheshouse.org. West off U.S. 101 at Cape Blanco Road, about 5 miles north of Port Orford. Open Thursday through Monday from 10:00 A.M to 3:30 P.M., April through October. Beautiful old house built in 1898 for Patrick and Jane Hughes, who settled the Cape Blanco area in 1860 and raised dairy cattle here. The house is furnished with many period antiques and displays historical photographs and artifacts.

BEACHES, PARKS, TRAILS, AND WAYSIDES

In Port Orford the beach is right downtown. Waves nearly lap at the edge of the Battle Rock Wayside parking lot at the south end of town. Another easy access is west off U.S. 101, where signs lead to the port.

Watch for state-park signs in town. Turn west and drive 1 mile to Port Orford Heads Wayside on the site of a former Coast Guard lifeboat station. Here are a small picnic spot and a paved trail to a headland that commands some of the most spectacular views on the coast. This is a great place for photography, watching whales, or just relaxing. Parking is limited, and there is no turnaround for trailers.

Just north of town, watch for the sign for Paradise Point Wayside. Garrison Lake Road leads 1 mile to the beach parking area. Here are miles of broad beach for combing, hunting agates, flying kites, or hiking.

Five miles north of town and 5 miles west of U.S. 101, Cape

Port Orford Heads Wayside

Blanco pokes into the Pacific farther than any other point of land in the contiguous states. Here stands the oldest lighthouse in Oregon, the **Cape Blanco Light,** operating since December 20, 1870. Towering 245 feet above the ocean, its million-candlepower light is visible 22 miles out.

WATER SPORTS AND ACTIVITIES

Beaches north and south of town—especially near Rocky Point, 3 miles south of town—offer fair to good clam digging. Surf fishing for perch and bottom fish is good from the beaches and the breakwaters near the port dock. In July smelt move into the port area.

Two tremendously popular rivers empty into the ocean near Port Orford: the Elk River (designated wild and scenic) just south of Cape Blanco, and the Sixes River just north of the cape. Both rivers are wadable most of the year, but best access is via drift boat.

Sea-run cutthroat trout move into both rivers in August and offer good angling well into September. The first salmon, usually jacks, begin showing up in September as well.

After the first fall rains in October, chinook salmon enter the Elk and Sixes and offer angling opportunities well into December, with November fishing usually best.

Anglers begin taking winter steelhead in December and continue catching them well into February. January is the peak month.

TRAVEL INFORMATION

Port Orford Chamber of Commerce, P.O. Box 637; (541) 332–8055; www.portorford.org

EVENTS

July   Port Orford Jubilee, (541) 332–8055

BANDON

Population: 2,940

Location: *On U.S. 101, 24 miles south of Coos Bay, at the mouth of the Coquille (koh-keel) River and along its south bank Zip: 97411.*

Named after a city in Ireland that is located on the Bandon River in County Cork, this Oregon community, sometimes called Bandon-By-The-Sea, could as fittingly be called Phoenix. Like the mythical bird, Bandon has twice risen from its own ashes after fire consumed it.

In 1914 a fire left a large part of downtown Bandon a smoldering heap. Then on September 26, 1936, fire again swept through the town. This time nearly 2,000 residents were evacuated, and Bandon was reduced to charred rubble.

On that "Black Saturday" the hope that Bandon would become the most prominent port between Portland and San Francisco was forever dashed. The long-term result, however, was the emergence of a seaside hamlet with a relaxed pace and innate charm neither Portland nor San Francisco could even remotely approximate.

Bandon's Old Town area lies a swerve off U.S. 101. Ease into it, find a parking spot, and enjoy its funky shops, fine galleries, and restaurants.

Adjacent to Old Town, just across First Street, is Bandon's refurbished waterfront and boat basin, where you can stroll the docks and piers, watch the commercial fleet, charter a fishing boat, or fish and crab right off the docks.

One of the most prominent Bandon landmarks—not to mention the most photographed, sketched, and painted—is the **Coquille River Light.** Built in 1896, the lighthouse operated until 1939, when it was replaced by an unmanned light on the south jetty. The squat but attractive lighthouse, with its 47-foot tower, has been restored and is kept in good repair as a historical site. View and photograph it from the south jetty area, just west of Old Town, or drive right to it via Bullards Beach State Park. In recent years the travel industry has gained importance in Bandon, and the town has grown and improved, attracting a lively lot of artists and artisans. More than three dozen artists live and work in the area. The city also has enough cowboy philosophers, yarn-spinning old salts, mystics, and iconoclasts to keep things interesting.

LODGING

Harbor View Motel, 355 Highway 101; P.O. Box 1409; (541) 347–4417 or (800) 526–0209. West side of U.S. 101, south side of Old Town district. Has 59 units with king and queen beds, refrigerators, cable TV, and Showtime. Stands atop a hill, commanding the best view in Bandon. From the northwest-facing balconies, view the river, ocean, Old Town, lighthouse, and waterfront. Walk to shops, restaurants, galleries, and boat basin. Continental breakfast. Moderate.

The Inn at Face Rock, 3225 Beach Loop Road; (541) 347–9441 or (800) 638–3092. On the east side of the road, south of town. Has 56 units with queen beds and cable TV. Spacious, recently remodeled suites have fireplaces, kitchens, 2 baths, and balconies and can accommodate up to 4 persons. Wheelchair access. Beautiful golf course adjacent. Top-rated restaurant and cocktail lounge on premises. Private access to beach. Moderate to expensive.

Lighthouse Bed & Breakfast, 650 Jetty Road Southwest; (541) 347–9316. South side of the river, west of Old Town, across from the lighthouse. Four guest rooms with king and queen beds and private baths, 1 with whirlpool. Excellent view of ocean, river bar, jetties, and lighthouse. Short walk to beach. Near Old Town. Cable TV and Showtime. Full breakfast. Moderate to expensive.

Sea Star Guest House, 370 First Street; (541) 347–9632. On the harbor, across the street from the small-boat basin. Four units, 2 with kitchens, 2 with community-kitchen privileges. Private entrances, private baths, cable TV, and Showtime. Near shops and restaurants. Excellent view. Inexpensive.

Sunset Oceanfront Lodging, 1865 Beach Loop Drive; P.O. Box 373; (541) 347–2453 or (800) 842–2407. On Beach Loop Road, next to Lord Bennett's (restaurant). Double and queen beds in a variety of rooms and suites. Cable TV, VCRs, sauna, fireplaces, ocean view. Beach access. Laundry facilities on premises. Inexpensive to moderate.

CAMPGROUNDS AND RV PARKS

Bullards Beach State Park, (541) 347–2209 (office); (541) 347–3501 (booth, mid-May through Labor Day). Situated along the north bank of the Coquille River, west of U.S. 101, about 2.5 miles north of Bandon. Has 100 electric hookups and 92 full hookups. Showers, tank dump, and firewood. A beautiful park for camping, picnicking, and day use. River and ocean surf fishing, crabbing, clam digging, kite flying, beachcombing, photography, biking, and horseback riding are main attractions. Excellent public boat ramp and parking area. Moderate.

FOOD AND BEVERAGES

Bandon Baking Company, 160 Second Street; (541) 347–9440; www.bandonbakingco.com. Nestled in Old Town Bandon, this informal bakery draws you in with sweet scents and cozy interiors. Customers line up to take out loaves of cranberry nut or pumpkin bread and decadent cookies; stay in for gourmet coffee and a baked goodie or a made-to-order deli sandwich. Open daily for breakfast and lunch. Inexpensive.

Bandon Boat Works, South Jetty Road; (541) 347–2111. On the south bank of the river, across from the lighthouse. Lunch and dinner Tuesday through Saturday. Brunch and dinner Sunday. One of Bandon's best restaurants, offering seafoods, pasta dishes, veal, beef, lamb, and, on Sundays, Mexican cuisine. Specialties include cioppino, seafood fettuccine, Mediterranean-style linguine, oysters flambé, rack of lamb, and three kinds of surf 'n' turf. Homemade desserts. Imported and domestic beers and wines. Moderate.

Harp's on the Bay, 480 First Street SE; (541) 347–9057. At the west end of First Street, just beyond Old Town. Dinner daily. At this award-winning restaurant and lounge, enjoy such appetizers as jumbo shrimp cocktail, sautéed mushrooms, razor clams, or smoked game hen. Try the house onion soup, clam chowder, or shrimp soup. Dinner selections include pasta, seafood, poultry, steaks, pork chops, and the house favorite: rack of lamb. Full bar. Moderate.

Lord Bennett's at the Sunset, 1695 Beach Loop Road; (541)

347–3663. West side of town, next to Sunset Motel. Lunch and dinner daily. Soups, salads, and sandwiches top the bill for luncheon fare, along with such entrees as Cajun chicken, shrimp omelette, and braised scallops. Start dinner with French onion soup, crab or shrimp cocktail, steamed clams, or spicy calamari. Then choose from an assortment of seafoods, steaks, or one of the house specialties: veal and lamb dishes, charbroiled chicken breasts, bouillabaisse, and fettuccine with shrimp and scallops. Full bar. Moderate.

Wheelhouse Restaurant & Crow's Nest Lounge, 125 Chicago Avenue, (Chicago and First); (541) 347–9331. Across the street from the boat basin. Breakfast, lunch, and dinner daily. Features fresh seafood, chicken, lamb, beef, salads, sandwiches, soups, and chowder. Specialties include seafood crepes, award-winning chicken Baja (with cheese and fresh Oregon shrimp), and rack of lamb. The lounge offers excellent atmosphere and a superb view of the harbor. Moderate.

SHOPPING AND BROWSING

Bandon Cheese Factory, 680 East Second Street; P.O. Box 1668; (541) 347–2456 or (800) 548–8961. East side of U.S. 101 at the north end of town. Daily, 9:00 A.M. to 6:00 P.M. Great aged cheeses, gourmet foods, fine wines, and more. Renowned for its excellent cheeses, for which gift packs are available and shipped anywhere.

Bandon Mercantile Company, P.O. Box 1076; (541) 347–4341. West side of U.S. 101 at Elmira, north end of town. Monday through Saturday, 9:30 A.M. to 5:30 P.M.; Sunday, 10:30 A.M. to 5:00 P.M. A general store of sorts that is stocked with assorted kitchen gadgets, cookware, cutlery, pottery, clothing, coffees, teas, wines, and gift items. This is a browsers' delight you won't want to miss.

Oregon Coast Jams, Misty Meadows Products, 48053 Highway 101; (541) 347–2575 or (888) 795–1719. About 5 miles south of Bandon, on the east side of the highway. What sprouted as a roadside stand and flourished as favorite stop for locals and visitors alike for more than 25 years has blossomed into a fine store, chock-full of jams, jellies, syrups, sauces, and condiments made from cranberries, blueberries, raspberries, boysenberries, strawberries, loganberries, and marionberries, as well as wild blackberries and huckleberries. Also on sale are wildflower honey, pepper jellies, barbecue sauces, a large selection of olives, and gift items. Variety packs, case lots, and shipping available.

Bandon Historical Society Museum

Second Street Gallery, 210 East Second Street; (541) 347-4133. In Old Town. Daily, 10:00 A.M. to 5:30 P.M. Great gallery for shoppers and browsers, where you can enjoy artworks free from sales pressure in a large, open, and well-lighted interior. Fine paintings, prints, sculptures, ceramics, bronzes, wall hangings, and handmade furnishings—most created by local and nearby artists and artisans.

MUSEUM

Bandon Historical Society Museum, 270 Filmore Avenue SE; P.O. Box 737; (541) 347-2164. At Filmore and U.S. 101, in the old city hall. Monday through Saturday, 10:00 A.M. to 4:00 P.M; Sunday, noon to 3:00 P.M. in summer. Many photographs of the area's maritime heritage and the great fire of 1936. Good displays of pioneer and Indian artifacts. Fine selection of publications. A small museum, but certainly worth a stop. Small admission fee for visitors over age 12.

BEACHES, PARKS, TRAILS, AND WAYSIDES

Extending northward from the north jetty at the mouth of the Coquille River, **Bullards Beach** offers miles of surf and sand for hiking, horseback riding, and beachcombing. Gravel beds, exposed by storm-tossed seas, offer good hunting for agates, jasper, and petrified wood. This is also an excellent beach for collecting driftwood. Stout winds, usually every afternoon during the summer, make for great kite flying, here and along the river.

To reach Bullards Beach, watch for the state-park sign about 2.5 miles north of Bandon, just beyond the bridge over the Coquille. Turn west off U.S. 101 and follow the road to the beach parking lot or park near the lighthouse.

The beach stretching southward from the south jetty is distinctly different. Here, great sea stacks punctuate beach and surf and serve as rookeries for many species of birds, including a colony of more than 10,000 murres. Other species include gulls, cormorants, tufted puffins, pigeon guillemots, black oystercatchers, auklets, and murrelets. Along the beaches, sandpipers, sanderlings, plovers, turnstones, and other shorebirds peck and dart and dodge the waves.

Famous Face Rock and **Table Rock** stand amid the sea stacks just off the beach. The best vantages for viewing and photography are off Beach Loop Road. The best beach access is via Jetty Road, where there is ample parking near the jetty. To reach either road, drive west on First Street in the Old Town district. Just after the road turns south, follow it up the hill to connect with Beach Loop Road or turn west onto Jetty Road.

WATER SPORTS AND ACTIVITIES

Surfperch are popular with Bandon anglers, who fish the beaches north and south of the Coquille, as well as from the jetties and the rocks near the lighthouse. Smelt move into the river in June and July, and many folks jig for them from the boat-basin docks.

Angling for salmon and bottom fish is good offshore through the summer months. In the early fall, salmon begin moving into the river and provide action until December, which heralds the start of the steelhead season.

The lower Coquille offers superb crabbing, from the bar upstream to the bridge. The best catches are made from boats, but many keepers are taken from the boat-basin docks and piers.

Bandon Bait Shop, 110 First Street; (541) 347–3905. On the waterfront in Old Town. Daily, 6:00 A.M. to 6:00 P.M. The place to buy bait and other fishing essentials. Crab rings for sale or rent.

GOLF

Bandon Dunes Resort, Round Lake Drive; (541) 347–4380 or (888) 345–6008. Two miles north of town on the west side of U.S. 101. A full-service golf resort with lodging available. Plans include a three-course, 54-hole golfer's paradise on 2,000 ocean-front acres. First 18-hole, 7,398-yard, par-72, walking-only course opened in May 1999 and shot to the top of *Golfweek*'s list of America's one hundred best modern golf courses built since 1959.

Bandon Face Rock Golf Course, 3235 Beach Loop Road; (541) 347–3818. South of town. Nine-hole, par-32 course in a scenic setting. Walking distance from the Inn at Face Rock. Open every day. Rental carts available.

TRAVEL INFORMATION

Bandon Chamber of Commerce, 300 SE Second Street; P.O. Box 1515; (541) 347–9616; www.bandon.com

EVENTS

May	Food & Wine Festival, (541) 347–9616
July	Fish Fry and Fireworks, (541) 347–9616
September	Bandon Cranberry Festival, (541) 347–9616
December	Festival of Lights, (541) 347–9616

CHARLESTON

Location: *West off U.S. 101, 6 miles west of Coos Bay on Cape Arago Highway, 20.6 miles north of Bandon via Seven Devils Road. Zip: 97420.*

Charleston and the nearby parks and beaches must rank among the most overlooked attractions on the Oregon coast, probably because they lie a few miles off U.S. 101. At Charleston are canneries, fish-processing plants, boatbuilding and repair facilities, and one of the largest commercial fishing fleets on the Oregon coast. The area is also popular with sport fishermen, crabbers, and clam diggers. For boaters Charleston has a large launch ramp, moorage, fuel, and repair services.

The busy harbor offers several shops worth a stop, and restaurants serving up everything from hearty fishermen's breakfasts to fine seafood dinners.

One of the best-kept sight-seeing and photography secrets in Oregon is the Coast Guard lookout at Charleston, which commands the best view of the bay, jetties, and Coos Bay bar—a place to watch fishing boats and freighters come and go. Take Boat Basin Drive off Cape Arago Highway almost a half mile to an unmarked road on the left and a small sign for Coast Guard Tower. That road, not recommended for trailers, leads to a small parking area atop a high bluff overlooking the bar.

One of the maritime treasures along this expanse of coast is the **Cape Arago Light Station,** which actually lies 2.5 miles north of the cape. The lighthouse can be seen and photographed from a number of vantages, including several spots along Cape Arago Highway, and from hiking trails along headlands south of the light. But Lighthouse Beach offers the best approach for frame-filling pictures.

Whether traveling north or south on U.S. 101, don't miss the Charleston Loop. After visiting the parks and beaches, northbound travelers should take the Cape Arago Highway into Coos Bay and North Bend. Those heading south should take Seven Devils Road, just south of town, which connects with U.S. 101 about 13 miles beyond.

LODGING

Capt. John's Motel, 8061 Kingfisher Drive; P.O. Box 5398; (541) 888–4041. On Kingfisher at Boat Basin Drive. Has 47 units with queen beds, cable TV, and some kitchens. Fish house for cleaning and cooking the catch. Nearby charter boats, fishing, crabbing, and clam digging. Across the street from the Portside Restaurant. The only motel in the boat-basin complex. Inexpensive.

CAMPGROUNDS AND RV PARKS

Bastendorff Beach County Park, 4250 Bastendorff Beach Road; (541) 888–5353. Just under a half mile west of Cape Arago Highway, 2 miles southwest of Charleston. Has 81 campsites: 56 with electricity and water to accommodate RVs up to 24 feet, and 25 tent sites. Showers, tank dump, firewood, fish-cleaning station, horseshoe pits, and hiking trails. Beautiful picnic area and great playground for the kids. Spectacular view of the beach, ocean, and jetties from the picnic area parking lot. Inexpensive.

Seaport RV Park, P.O. Box 5750; (541) 888–3122. On Boat Basin Drive, just off Cape Arago Highway. Full hookups at 26 sites. Showers, cable TV, and laundry. Close to charter boats, boat basin, and all water sports. Walk to shops and restaurants. Beaches nearby. Moderate.

Sunset Bay State Park, 13030 Cape Arago Highway; (541) 888–4902. West side of the highway, 3.6 miles south of Charleston. Has 29 full-hookup and 108 tent sites, showers, laundry, and firewood. Beautiful park setting, sheltered from the wind. Shallow bay is popular for swimming, scuba diving, and fishing. Broad beach and bathhouse. Boat launch for small boats. Hiking trails. Rock and surf fishing. Spectacular scenery. Naturalist on duty in summer. Moderate.

FOOD AND BEVERAGES

Chuck's Seafoods, P.O. Box 5502; (541) 888–5525. At Cape Arago Highway and Boat Basin Drive. Daily, 9:00 A.M. to 6:00 P.M.

Fresh, smoked, fresh-frozen, and locally canned seafoods, including shucked, shell, and smoked local oysters. Gift packs, shipped anywhere, feature coho and chinook salmon, albacore tuna, Oregon shrimp, Dungeness crab, smoked oysters, smoked salmon, and smoked sturgeon. Try the fresh smoked seafood on a beach picnic.

Fisherman's Grotto, Cape Arago Highway; (541) 888-3251. On the west side of the highway, near the north end of the bridge, across from England Marine Supply. Breakfast, lunch, and dinner daily. Hearty breakfasts, omelettes, steaks, sandwiches, fish and chips, cracked crab, and delicious clam chowder. Fish and shellfish specialties, fresh off the boat. Inexpensive to moderate.

Portside Restaurant, 8001 Kingfisher Drive; P.O. Box 5025; (541) 888-5544. In the Charleston marine complex, across the street from Capt. John's Motel. Lunch Monday through Friday, dinner every day. Award-winning restaurant and lounge with superb waterfront view. Fine steaks and prime rib available, but seafoods fresh off the boat are the specialty here. Features live Maine lobster and Dungeness crab, salmon, halibut, lingcod, shrimp, prawns, oysters, clams, scallops, calamari, and more. Excellent seafood combo dinner. Seafood buffet every Friday evening is highly recommended. Cocktails, imported and domestic beers, house wines, and wine list of imported, domestic, and Oregon wines. Moderate.

Qualman Oyster Farms, 5165 Troller Road; (541) 888-3145. In Charleston. The fresh oysters here can't get any fresher. The 145 acres of oyster beds on the South Slough produce 3,000 to 6,000 gallons of fresh oysters a year. Drive out at low tide to see the oysters growing on thousands of wooden stakes.

SHOPPING AND BROWSING

Kinnee's Gifts 'n' Shells, 91134 Cape Arago Highway; P.O. Box 5498; (541) 888-5924. Across the street from Chuck's Seafoods. Summer: daily, 9:00 A.M. to 6:30 P.M. Winter: daily, 10:30 A.M. to 5:30 P.M. A good selection of shells, souvenirs, cards, Oregon products, and nautical items in this snug shop.

BEACHES, PARKS, TRAILS, AND WAYSIDES

Just south of Charleston, along Cape Arago Highway, is one of Oregon's finest yet least-used playgrounds—a series of beaches and

Qualman Oyster Farms

parks to rival any on the West Coast.

About 2 miles south of Charleston, turn right off Cape Arago Highway to reach Bastendorff Beach and the south jetty. On the west side of the highway, 2.4 miles south of Charleston, begins a short trail leading to Lighthouse Beach. Although the trail is a good one, the slope to the beach is steep and requires caution. Also watch the tides here to avoid being stranded.

A mile farther south is **Sunset Bay State Park,** with its shallow bay protected by sandstone cliffs and an outer reef. Waters here warm faster than elsewhere; it's a popular place for wading and swimming. Currents can be treacherous, however, so swim only on an incoming tide. The splendid picnic area has a kitchen shelter. Hikers will enjoy trails through the forest and along oceanside cliffs from here to Cape Arago.

Shore Acres State Park is west of the highway, 4.5 miles south of Charleston. The parks along this stretch comprise 1,272 acres, all of which once belonged to Louis J. Simpson, a timber tycoon, shipbuilder, and prominent North Bend businessman. Shore Acres was the site of his oceanfront estate.

Simpson developed this property as a summer home and a Christmas gift for his wife in 1906. The house eventually outgrew those plans, however, with such amenities as a huge, heated indoor pool and a ballroom with more than 2,700 square feet of dance floor. Tennis courts and formal gardens enhanced the already spectacular setting.

The mansion burned to the ground in 1921, and although Simpson built another in its place, it was less elegant than the original and eventually fell into disrepair. The state purchased the property in 1942 and had to raze the house. A glass-enclosed observation building now stands on the site of the mansion.

The formal gardens are still cared for and delight visitors year-round. The caretaker's house is still intact in the garden area. A trail leads from the south end of the garden to a secluded beach, then beyond along the cliffs.

A parking area 1.1 miles south of Shore Acres overlooks Simpson Reef. Stop here to examine the rocky islet and reef where seals and sea lions bask and bark.

The highway ends 6 miles from Charleston at **Cape Arago State Park.** The picnic area, with kitchen shelter and rest rooms, is unmatched anywhere. There are trails and sites along the cliffs above the pounding surf. Trails also lead to some of the best tide pools on the coast.

WATER SPORTS AND ACTIVITIES

Opportunities for fishing, crabbing, clam digging, boating, and sailing abound in the Charleston area. A public fishing pier extends into South Slough on the waterfront. The pier and docks are popular for crabbing and fishing for a variety of species, including perch, flounder, sole, and smelt.

Minus tides expose many nearby clam-digging flats where diggers find large horseneck (locally called Empire clams) and hard-shell clams, cockles, and littlenecks.

Rock and surf fishing along the coastline south of Charleston produces various bottom species, such as greenling, cabezon, lingcod, and several kinds of rockfish. These same areas are good for gathering mussels at low tide.

The offshore salmon season usually begins in May and runs until Labor Day, unless early quotas call for early closures. Chinook fishing ranges from fair to outstanding throughout the season, with most fish running to about fifteen pounds and occasionally thirty pounds or more.

Offshore bottom fishing is good all year, but it is mainly dependent on weather and water conditions. Some of the best light-tackle fishing for greenling, black rockfish, and others is in August and September.

Betty Kay Charters, 7788 Albacore Lane; P.O. Box 5020; (541) 888–9021 or (800) 752–6303; www.bettykaycharters.com. At the small-boat basin. Modern, comfortable boat. Specializes in salmon and bottom-fish angling. Also features light-tackle bottom fishing for great sport. Everything furnished. Licenses sold on premises. Five-hour trips leave daily at 5:30 A.M. and 10:45 A.M. Bait and dry ice available.

Bob's Sport Fishing, 63486 Albacore Lane; (541) 888–4241 or (800) 628–9633. Charters and tours. Specializes in salmon, halibut, and bottom-fish trips.

Englund Marine Supply Company, 5080 Cape Arago Highway; (541) 888–6723. Near the north end of the bridge, across the highway from Fisherman's Grotto. Good selection of fishing tackle, foul-weather clothing, crabbing gear, tide tables, charts, boat supplies, and hardware.

GOLF

Sunset Bay Golf Course, 11001 Cape Arago Highway; (541) 888–9301. Just past the Sunset Bay campground entrance. A 9-hole course only about 3.5 miles from Charleston. Follow the signs for the state parks. Pro shop, refreshments, and power carts available.

OTHER ATTRACTIONS

South Slough National Estuarine Research Reserve, P.O. Box 5417; (541) 888–5558. Five miles southeast of Charleston on Seven Devils Road. Exit Cape Arago Highway just south of town. September through May: Monday through Friday, 8:30 A.M. to 4:30 P.M. June through August, daily. The nation's first estuarine sanctuary, comprising 4,800 acres of upland forest and 600 acres of tidal lands, including a variety of habitats, such as freshwater marsh, salt marsh, mudflats, and open water. Home to a great array of flora and fauna, including at least twenty-two species of commercially important fish and shellfish. Many songbirds, shorebirds, and waterfowl, as well as deer, elk, black bear, and bobcat use the area. Canoe launch and hiking and study trails. Workshops and canoe trips held during summer months. Pick up trail guides, bird checklist, and canoeing information at the interpretive center.

WEATHER AND TIDE INFORMATION

U.S. Coast Guard, Charleston; recorded message, (541) 888–3102

TRAVEL INFORMATION

Bay Area Chamber of Commerce Visitor Center, 50 Central Avenue, Coos Bay; (541) 269–0215 or (800) 824–8486; www.oregonsbayareachamber.com

EVENTS

August	Salmon Barbecue, (541) 756–4022
September	Shorebird Festival, (541) 267–7208

COOS BAY
Population: 15,520

✭
NORTH BEND
Population: 9,885

Location: *On U.S. 101, 120 miles north of the California–Oregon state line, 23 miles south of Reedsport. Zips: 97420/97459.*

C oos Bay and North Bend share a common boundary and, in places, are impossible to distinguish, creating one metropolitan area—the largest on the Oregon coast. Together with Charleston, they compose what has come to be known as "Oregon's Bay Area."

Ironically, though, the area's greatest asset and most obvious feature is often ignored by visitors and residents alike—the bay itself. Travelers bound north and south zoom through the twin cities on four lanes of U.S. 101, and, before they know it, they're in Reedsport or Bandon, with memories of the bay area already fading. Too many residents just take it all for granted.

Don't make the same mistake. Get off the highway and enjoy the restaurants, accommodations, parks, shops, museums, galleries, theaters, and, above all, the bay. This is the largest deepwater port between San Francisco and Puget Sound, but the adjacent lands aren't nearly so crowded and congested. It's also a sprawling estuary, rich in marine wildlife, and a great place to enjoy a variety of water sports and activities.

The bay area is also home to the Oregon coast's first casino, owned and operated by the Coquille Tribe. Even nongamblers will want to check out The Mill Casino, on U.S. 101 in North Bend, for its fine food at great prices, outstanding bay view, and big-name entertainment. (See under Food and Beverages and Casino.)

LODGING

Best Western Holiday Motel, 411 North Bayshore Drive; Coos Bay; (541) 269–5111 or (800) 228–8655; www.best western.com. Between northbound and southbound U.S. 101, downtown. Queen and king beds in 83 units, some with kitchens. Two-room suites and in-room whirlpools available. Cable TV, The Movie Channel, heated indoor pool, sauna, fitness center. Next to restaurant and near others, shops, and theaters. Moderate to expensive.

The Blackberry Inn Bed & Breakfast, 843 Central Avenue; Coos Bay; (541) 267–6951 or (800) 500–4567; www.my blackberryinn.com. Six blocks west of U.S. 101. Follow the signs for Charleston and the parks. Three guest rooms, two with private baths. Easy walk to town, restaurants, theaters, bay, tennis courts, and city park. Continental breakfast, but kitchen available to guests, with eggs and bread provided. Inexpensive to moderate.

Coos Bay Manor Bed & Breakfast Inn, 955 South Fifth Street; Coos Bay; (541) 269–1224 or (800) 269–1224. Three blocks west of southbound U.S. 101, between Johnson and Ingersoll Streets. Five guest rooms with twin, queen, and king beds, three with private baths. Colonial-style house built in 1911 on a street shaded with stately trees. Full breakfast. Moderate.

Edgewater Inn, 275 East Johnson Avenue; Coos Bay; (541) 267–0423 or (800) 233–0423; www.edgewater-inns.com. East of U.S. 101, south end of town. Queen and king beds in 82 units, 2 with kitchens. Cable TV, VCRs, heated indoor pool, fitness center, tanning bed, dock, in-room whirlpools, fishing and viewing deck, waterfront balconies, continental breakfast, and picnic area. View of ships. Coos Bay's newest motel. Moderate.

Pony Village Lodge, Virginia Avenue; North Bend; (541) 756–3191. A half mile west of U.S. 101, next to Pony Village Mall. Queen and king beds and cable TV in 119 rooms. Restaurant and lounge on premises. Entertainment and big-screen TV in lounge. Walk to mall. Moderate.

This Olde House Bed & Breakfast Inn, 202 Alder Street; Coos Bay; (541) 267–5224. At the corner of Second and Alder, 1 block west of northbound U.S. 101 and King's Table Buffet. Built in 1893. Queen and king beds in 5 rooms, all with private baths. Victorian furnishings. Full breakfast; free gourmet dinner for guests staying three nights or more. Moderate to expensive.

CAMPGROUNDS AND RV PARKS

Bluebill Campground, Oregon Dunes National Recreation Area; (877) 444–6777; www.reserveUSA.com. Located 2.8 miles west of U.S. 101, via Jordan Cove Road (causeway), just north of the McCullough and Haynes Inlet bridges. A pretty little Forest Service camp in a shore pine–forest setting on the edge of Bluebill Lake. Has 19 sites for RVs up to 22 feet long. Hiking trail around the lake. Rest rooms and water. Inexpensive.

Horsfall Staging Area and Campground, Oregon Dunes National Recreation Area; (877) 444–6777; www.reserve USA.com. Located 1.7 miles west of U.S. 101, via Jordan Cove Road (causeway), just north of the McCullough and Haynes Inlet bridges. Seventy paved, striped, and numbered sites for RV rigs with trailers, used mainly by ORV enthusiasts. Three ramps for unloading and loading ORVs. Ample dune access. Rest rooms. No water. Nearest water is at Bluebill Campground. Inexpensive.

Lucky Logger RV Park, 250 East Johnson; Coos Bay; (541) 267–6003 or (800) 267–6426. West on Johnson off U.S. 101 at the south end of Coos Bay, near Fred Meyer store. Top-quality facilities include 78 full-hookup sites for all sizes of RVs, showers, laundry, cable TV, minimart, wheelchair access. Near restaurants and shops. Expensive.

FOOD AND BEVERAGES

Benetti's Italian Restaurant & Lounge, 260 South Broadway; Coos Bay; (541) 267–6066. On the east side of northbound U.S. 101, downtown, across from the Egyptian Theater. Dinner daily. Fine Italian cuisine and a lounge with a view of the bay. Veal dishes—piccata, scaloppine, parmigiana. Scampi, New York steak, lasagna, cannelloni, ravioli, gnocchi, spaghetti, eggplant parmigiana—all served with soup, salad, and garlic bread. Cocktails, beer, and wine. Moderate.

Coney Station and Steak House Restaurant, 295 South Broadway; Coos Bay; (541) 269–6948. Northwest corner of Curtis and South Broadway (southbound U.S. 101), downtown. Monday through Thursday, 11:00 A.M. to 11:00 P.M.; Friday and Saturday, 11:00 A.M. to 1:00 A.M. Comfortable and popular restaurant and lounge. Appetizers include crab or shrimp quesadillas, crab or shrimp cocktail, oysters on the half shell, Buffalo wings, and nachos. Soups and salads. Charbroiled burgers, big deli-style sandwiches,

McCullough Bridge over Coos Bay

and nine different Coney Island dogs. Steak House dinners include filet mignon, steaks, prime rib, seafood combination platter, fillet of halibut or salmon (broiled, poached, grilled, or Cajun style), and pasta dishes. Tuesday special: prime rib, baked potato, and stir-fried vegetables, all you can eat, $6.95. Twenty beers and ales on tap. Microbrew sampler: five glasses for five bucks. Wine list and full bar. Dine in lounge or restaurant. Inexpensive to moderate.

The Hilltop House Restaurant & Lounge, 93405 Willsey Lane; North Bend; (541) 756–4160. Bay view overlooking the dunes. Lunch and dinner daily. One of the area's finest restaurants. Sandwiches, soups, and salads for lunch. Large list of shellfish appetizers. Superb steaks, prime rib, veal dishes, and seafoods. House specialties include bouillabaisse, stuffed English sole, lobster thermidor, and salmon Monte Carlo. Cocktails, beer, and wine. Great view of the bay, especially at sunset. Moderate.

Kum-Yon's Restaurant, 835 South Broadway; Coos Bay; (541) 269–2662. West side of southbound U.S. 101 at south end of downtown area. Lunch and dinner Tuesday through Sunday (closed Monday). American food available, but the best Oriental food in town is the attraction here, with a large selection of dinners, family dinners, and combination plates available. Excellent variety of appetizers (you could make a meal of them), soups, sweet and sour, chow mein, and boiled noodles. House specialties: Yakitori

(Japanese-style kebab), Pul-koki (charbroiled sirloin, thinly sliced and marinated in honey and spices). Carryout orders. Beer and wine. Inexpensive to moderate.

The Mill Casino, 3201 Tremont Avenue; North Bend; (541) 756–8800 or (800) 953–4800. East side of U.S. 101 at the south end of town. Breakfast, lunch, dinner, and snacks. Three great choices to fit any appetite any time—24 hours a day. Try the Snack Bar for salads, sandwiches, burgers, and pizza. Choose from a large selection of breakfast favorites, soups, salads, beef, poultry, seafood, and more while enjoying the sensational view at the Plank House Restaurant. Or eat your fill at the Cook Shack Buffet, with weeknight belt- and budget-stretchers: Monday through Saturday, midnight to 11:00 A.M., breakfast for $1.99; Sunday, 9:00 A.M. to 1:00 P.M., omelette bar, $4.95; Monday, 5:00 to 10:00 P.M., marinated-steak dinner, $4.95; Tuesday, 4:00 to 8:00 P.M., all the prime rib you can eat, $6.95; Wednesday, 5:00 to 10:00 P.M., all-you-can-eat seafood (fish or oysters), $4.95; and Thursday, 5:00 to 10:00 P.M., all the barbecued ribs you can eat, $4.95. Beer, wine, and cocktails available. (See also under Casino.)

Pancake Mill & Pie Shoppe, 2390 Tremont; North Bend; (541) 756–2751. West side of U.S. 101, south of downtown. Breakfast and lunch daily. Pancakes big and tasty, three-egg omelettes with fresh fillings, French toast, and waffles are breakfast favorites. Soups, salads, and deli-style sandwiches for lunch, homemade pies and cakes for dessert. Moderate.

SHOPPING AND BROWSING

Although shops and galleries are scattered throughout the bay area, most are concentrated in three places. In downtown Coos Bay, you'll find them along Broadway (southbound U.S. 101) between Commercial and Curtis Avenues, and in the Coos Bay Mall, across from the visitor center. In North Bend, several antique shops and galleries are on Sherman Avenue (southbound U.S. 101), between California and Washington Avenues. The biggest shopping center on the south coast is Pony Village Mall, less than a mile west of U.S. 101, on Virginia Avenue, in North Bend. There is plenty of free parking, on streets and in parking lots, and no meters anywhere in the bay area.

Beauty and the Beast Antiques, 615 Virginia Avenue; North Bend; (541) 756–3670. On northbound U.S. 101 at Virginia. Open Friday, Sunday, and Monday, noon to 4:00 P.M.; Saturday,

11:00 A.M. to 5:00 P.M. Antiques and collectibles, jewelry, glassware, furniture, and more in a large and pleasant shop.

The Oregon Connection (House of Myrtlewood), 1125 South First; P.O. Box 457; Coos Bay; (541) 267–7804 or (800) 255–5318. Just west of U.S. 101 at the south end of town, across from Fred Meyer store. Monday through Saturday, 9:00 A.M. to 5:30 P.M.; Sunday, 11:00 A.M. to 5:00 P.M. Gift shop with a large selection of myrtlewood kitchen items, cribbage boards, candleholders, jewelry boxes, plates and bowls, clocks and weather instruments, cutting boards, and carvings. Oregon wines, homemade fudge, and other taste treats. Tours of adjacent factory several times a day. Products packaged and shipped anywhere.

Wagon Wheel Antiques & Collectibles, 1964 Sherman Avenue; North Bend; (541) 756–7023. West side of southbound U.S. 101, downtown. Daily, 10:30 A.M. to 5:30 P.M. Antiques and small collectibles. Good selection of old and collectible toys and games.

CASINO

The Mill Casino, 3201 Tremont Avenue; North Bend; (541) 756–8800 or (800) 953–4800. On the east side of U.S. 101, at the south end of town. Open 24 hours a day. Slot machines, video poker, blackjack tables, poker tables, and bingo. Big-name entertainment at the Live Performance Hall. Full-service lounge features live music on weekends. Gift shop and restaurants on premises. Free valet parking. (See also under Food and Beverages.)

MUSEUMS

Coos Art Museum, 235 Anderson; Coos Bay; (541) 267–3901. One block west of southbound U.S. 101, in old post office building, downtown. Tuesday through Friday, 10:00 A.M. to 4:00 P.M.; Saturday, 1:00 to 4:00 P.M. (closed Sunday and Monday). Only art museum on the Oregon coast. Large display areas with various exhibits throughout the year—paintings, sculpture, and photography. Gift shop and sales gallery on premises. Free admission.

Coos County Historical Society Museum, 1220 Sherman Avenue, Simpson Park; North Bend; (541) 756–6320. West side of U.S. 101 at north end of town, next to the visitor center. Tuesday through Saturday, 10:00 A.M. to 4:00 P.M., year-round. Displays include pioneer kitchen, Indian artifacts, Horsfall family parlor, and Dr. Horsfall's desk and medical instruments. Old homestead tools, logging exhibit, and many old photographs. Logging locomotive and tender on premises. Nominal admission fee.

The *Marshfield Sun* Printing Museum, P.O. Box 783; Coos Bay; (541) 269-2775. Between Front Street and northbound U.S. 101, across from the Timber Lodge. Summer: Tuesday through Saturday, 1:00 to 4:00 P.M. Phone for tour in off-season. Historic newspaper and job-printing shop, displaying equipment used to publish *The Marshfield Sun* from 1891 to 1944. Museum has an old Washington hand press, a Chandler & Price platen press, and nearly 200 type cases and fonts, as well as other equipment.

WATER SPORTS AND ACTIVITIES

The Coos River system, Coos Bay, and the various inlets and tributaries offer abundant recreational opportunities from canoeing, kayaking, powerboating, sailing, and windsurfing to crabbing, clam digging, and fishing for a great variety of species.

Private property obstructs bay access along much of the south shore, but elsewhere access is ample and easy. Popular fishing, crab-bing, and clam-digging areas are along Jordan Cove Road (cause-way), west off U.S. 101, north of town. Take the same road to connect with the Trans-Pacific Parkway and reach the shoreline near Roseburg Forest Products, a BLM boat ramp, and the T-Dock area. The same causeway leads to the dunes and Horsfall Beach, popular with surf fishermen.

The area offers some kind of angling all year: steelheading, De-cember through February; surfperch and seaperch, February through summer; spring chinook, April to early summer; fall chi-nook, late September into December; and sturgeon, striped bass, and a variety of bottom fish most of the year.

Coos Bay has some of the best clam beds on the coast. Al-though razor clams are not so plentiful as they once were, diligent diggers find a few along the ocean beaches. Best digging, however, is for an assortment of succulent bay clams, including horsenecks or gapers (locally called Empire clams), hard-shells or quahogs, cock-les, and littlenecks, all of which are found on the flats near Charleston and on the South Slough, as well as along the north shore of the bay in the North Spit area. Minus tides are best for digging these species.

Soft-shell clams are found in upper bay areas and can be dug on any low tide. These are bonus clams, meaning that diggers can take thirty-six soft-shells in addition to the limit of bay clams.

Surplus Center, 310 South Broadway; Coos Bay; (541) 267–6711. Between northbound and southbound U.S. 101, downtown. Daily, 9:00 A.M. to 6:00 P.M. Large selection of fishing tackle and supplies, camping gear, rainwear, boots, waders, inflatable rafts, and canoes. Crabbing and clam-digging gear. Licenses and bait.

GOLF

Kentuck Golf Course, 94469 Golf Course Lane, Kentuck Inlet; North Bend; (541) 756–4464. Located 3 miles east of U.S. 101 on East Bay Drive at north end of McCullough Bridge. An 18-hole course with pro shop, club and cart rentals, refreshments. Set in a scenic valley in the foothills at the head of Kentuck Inlet on Coos Bay.

OTHER ATTRACTIONS

Little Theater on the Bay, 2100 Sherman Avenue; P.O. Box 404; North Bend; (541) 756–4336. On the west side of southbound U.S. 101, at Sherman and Washington. A full season of live theater each year, offering plays, musicals, and "Little Ole Opry On The Bay."

On Broadway Theater, 226 South Broadway; Coos Bay; (541) 756–8889. East side of southbound U.S. 101, downtown. Playwright's American Conservatory Theater presents live performances of plays and musicals each summer.

WEATHER AND TIDE INFORMATION

U.S. Coast Guard, Charleston; recorded message, (541) 888–3102

TRAVEL INFORMATION

Bay Area Chamber of Commerce, 50 Central Avenue; Coos Bay; (541) 269–0215 or (800) 824–8486; www.oregons bayareachamber.com

North Bend Visitor Center, 1380 Sherman Avenue; (541) 756–4613

EVENTS

March	Dune Mushers' Mail Run, (541) 269–1269
July	Fireworks Display, (541) 269–0215
	North Bend Jubilee, (541) 756–4613
	Oregon Music Festival, (541) 267–0938
	or (877) 897–9350
August	Blackberry Arts Festival, (541) 267–7232
September	Bay Area Fun Festival, (541) 267–5008
	or (800) 738–4849
	Prefontaine Memorial 10K Race,
	(541) 269–1103
	Oregon Shorebird Festival, Cape Arago,
	(541) 267–7208

LAKESIDE
Population: 1,453

Location: *About 1 mile east of U.S. 101, 12 miles north of North Bend, 9 miles south of Reedsport. Zip: 97449.*

The small community of Lakeside, situated on the northwest shore of Tenmile Lake and along Tenmile Creek, was once a thriving resort town. It still possesses a resort atmosphere, but the pace has slowed considerably. With the closing of its only remaining sawmill, however, outdoor recreation will likely become the area's economic mainstay.

Tenmile and North Tenmile Lakes are typical of lakes found in hill country. They are sprawling bodies of water with many arms, bays, and coves. The two, joined by a canal at their western ends, offer 42 miles of shoreline to explore by boat. The lakes are among the most popular on the coast for swimming, waterskiing, sailing, and fishing.

Just north of Lakeside and east of U.S. 101 lies Eel Lake. Though smaller than either of the other two, this is still among the largest lakes on the coast. Beautiful **William M. Tugman State Park** is on its west shore, offering excellent picnic and camping facilities, as well as a public boat ramp and beach.

In Lakeside are several restaurants, stores for stocking up on groceries and supplies, and a county park with picnic tables and good boat-launch facilities. To reach the park, turn east on North Lake Road, in downtown Lakeside, then south on Eleventh Street.

CAMPGROUNDS AND RV PARKS

Mid Eel Creek Campground, Oregon Dunes National Recreation Area; (541) 271–3611. Located 9.5 miles south of Reedsport, next to North Eel Creek Campground. Has 25 tent and trailer sites and turnarounds to accommodate RVs up to 16 feet long. Fire pit and picnic table at each site. Rest rooms, water, no hookups. Near dunes and lakes. Inexpensive.

North Eel Creek Campground, Oregon Dunes National Recreation Area; (541) 271-3611. West of U.S. 101 at Lakeside junction, 9 miles south of Reedsport. Has 53 tent and trailer sites and turnarounds to accommodate RVs to 22 feet long. Rest rooms, water, no hookups. Picnic table and fire pit at each site. Located in the dunes, 2 miles from the beach. Marked trails with scenic viewpoints. Inexpensive.

North Lake Resort & Marina, 2090 North Lake Road; (541) 759-3515. Just east of downtown Lakeside, on the northwest side of the canal bridge and southwest tip of North Lake. Has 105 sites with full hookups, water and electric, or no hookups. Fire pits at all sites. Showers, boat launch, moorage, fuel, boat rentals, groceries, bait, tackle, and propane. Moderate.

William M. Tugman State Park, 365 North Fourth Street (office); Coos Bay 97420; (541) 269-9410; booth, mid-May through Labor Day, (541) 759-3604; (800) 452-5682, reservations. Located about a mile north of Lakeside and 7 miles south of Reedsport, east off U.S. 101 on Eel Lake. Has 115 campsites with water and electric hookups. Showers, tank dump, beach, bathhouse, public boat launch. In a beautiful park setting with many trees and wild rhododendrons. Moderate.

SHOPPING AND BROWSING

Myrtlewood Factory, 3955 Coast Highway; P.O. Box 644; North Bend 97459; (541) 756-2220. West side of U.S. 101, 5 miles north of North Bend. Monday through Friday, 10:00 A.M. to 4:00 P.M. A pleasant and well-stocked shop that displays an assortment of myrtlewood furniture, bowls, cutting boards, jewelry boxes, lamps, candlesticks, carvings, cribbage boards, clocks, and more. Tours of adjacent 40,000-square-foot factory.

WATER SPORTS AND ACTIVITIES

Tenmile and North Tenmile Lakes are relatively shallow and support populations of warm-water, cold-water, and anadromous fishes. The angling ranges from good to outstanding, depending on the time of year and the species sought.

Warm-water species include bluegill, yellow perch, brown bullhead, largemouth bass, and whiterock or hybrid bass—a cross between white and striped bass. You can catch bluegill by the boatload much of the year. Bullhead fishing is best during the warmer months and at night. Largemouth bass are available all year, but spring and fall are peak times for fish of one to three pounds, with occasional lunkers of five to eight pounds. During the summer, night fishing produces the most and biggest bass. Hybrids are nearly dormant during the winter, but as the waters warm in spring, they become very active, cruising both lakes from near shore to well offshore. The lakes have given up hybrids exceeding ten pounds.

Eel Lake has a similar fishery, but it is deeper and colder, better suited to a cold-water fishery. There are largemouth bass in the lake, and the fishing for them can be good, but rainbow trout are the prime quarry here. Most anglers troll for the trout or still-fish with bait, but the fly fisherman will find great sport when conditions are right. Early mornings in sheltered coves or evenings after the wind has subsided are best for dry-fly action. Spring and early-summer mayfly hatches often spur feeding frenzies.

Lakeside Marina, south end of Eighth Street, in Lakeside; (541) 759-3312. Summer: daily, 6:00 A.M. to 9:00 P.M. Off-season: daily, 7:00 A.M. to 7:00 P.M. Bait, tackle, fuel, marine accessories, service, and repair. Boat and canoe rentals.

RENTALS

Far West Rentals, Hauser Depot Road; North Bend 97459; (541) 756-3491. About 5 miles north of North Bend, a half mile west of U.S. 101. Turn at Myrtlewood Chalet. Summer: daily, 8:00 A.M. to 8:00 P.M. Off-season: daily, 11:00 A.M. to 3:00 P.M. Four-wheel ATVs for rent by the hour or by the day. Helmets provided free. Dune and beach access. No deposit required.

Pacific Coast Recreation, 68512 Highway 101; North Bend 97459; (541) 756-7183. About 5.5 miles north of North Bend on the west side of U.S. 101, opposite the Hauser exit. Summer: 9:00 A.M. to 6:00 P.M. Winter: 9:00 A.M. to 3:00 P.M. Four-wheel ATVs for rent by the hour or day. Easy access to the dunes.

Spinreel Dune Buggy Rentals, 67045 Spinreel Road; North Bend 97459; (541) 759-3313. Two miles south of Lakeside, west off U.S. 101. Watch for signs. Summer: 9:00 A.M. to 6:00 P.M. Winter: 10:00 A.M. to 4:00 P.M. Four-wheel ATVs for rent by the

Tenmile Lakes, near Lakeside, on the Oregon coast

hour or the day. Small ATVs available for children. Largest selection on the Oregon coast. Deposit required. Free shuttle service to beach or dunes for nonriders in the party. Access to dunes and beach.

TRAVEL INFORMATION

Lakeside Chamber of Commerce, P.O. Box 333; (541) 759-3981; www.lksdchamber.presy.com

Oregon Dunes National Recreation Office; (541) 271-3611

REEDSPORT
Population: 5,030

*WINCHESTER BAY
Population: 1,000

Location: *At the junction of U.S. 101 and State Route 38, along U.S. 101 and the south bank of the Umpqua River, about 21 miles north of North Bend. Zip: 97467.*

A t the far eastern end of Douglas County in the Cascade Mountains, the North Umpqua River rises and flows westward, gathering the waters of two dozen other rivers and creeks before joining the South Umpqua near Roseburg. From there the mighty river courses north and west through the Coast Range, creating what might be called the Valley of the Green Giant, because that's exactly what the Umpqua is by the time its slate-green waters pass beneath the State Route 38 bridge at Scottsburg, the head of tidewater.

Flanked by emerald mountains, the great river parallels State Route 38 for another 16 miles and is joined by the Smith River before passing beneath the U.S. 101 bridge at Reedsport. Beyond, it rounds the big bend just past Gardiner, swings southward, and becomes Winchester Bay. Having traversed the breadth of Douglas County and wended its way through the canyons, gorges, and benchlands of two mountain ranges, the Umpqua has become the largest coastal river between the Columbia and San Francisco Bay.

Once an important transportation and commerce corridor, the Umpqua moved passengers and freight, via riverboat, between the coast and Scottsburg. The Willamette Valley was connected to Scottsburg by roads traveled by stagecoach and wagon. Sawmills in the area sent their lumber on schooners and steamers south to the burgeoning boomtown on the bay, San Francisco.

Today most people travel through this area in their own vehicles. Freight and lumber go by truck and train and, if destined for some distant port, eventually get loaded aboard freighters at the

Port of Portland or Coos Bay. The Umpqua and Smith Rivers and Winchester Bay are no longer merely modes of conveyance; they now provide a more important commodity to residents and visitors alike: fun.

This watery world has become a coastal playground, attracting campers, boaters, crabbers, clam diggers, anglers, beachcombers, wildlife watchers, photographers, artists, and folks who would just as soon sit back, relax, and let it all happen.

Great beaches, the longest in the state, sprawl northward and southward from the mouth of the estuary. And for 20 miles in the same directions, huge dunes provide yet more recreational opportunities and enjoyment.

To the east is some of the most scenic inland country on the coast, where you can follow the course of the Umpqua or Smith River along paved highways, or venture off into the Coast Range on graveled Forest Service roads.

In 1988, a contest sponsored by Harley-Davidson named State Route 38 one of "America's 10 Best Roads." It closely follows the course of the Umpqua through the Coast Range to Elkton and beyond. Smith River Road exits east off U.S. 101 just north of Reedsport and carries travelers along another beautiful river and into the forested mountains.

LODGING

Best Western Salbasgeon Inn of Reedsport, 1400 Highway Avenue; Reedsport; (541) 271–4831 or (800) 528–1234. On U.S. 101, town center. Queen beds in 42 rooms, some with kitchens. Cable TV, HBO, indoor pool, and spa. Spa and fireplace suites available. Moderate to expensive.

Winchester Bay Inn, 390 Broadway; P.O. Box 1037; Winchester Bay; (541) 271–4871 or (800) 246–1462; www.winbay inn.com. West of U.S. 101, 3 miles south of Reedsport. Has 52 units with queen beds, cable TV, and HBO. Spa units and kitchenettes. Continental breakfast. Near restaurants, shops, charter boats, beaches, and dunes. Moderate.

CAMPGROUNDS AND RV PARKS

The Marina RV Resort, 260 Marina Way; P.O. Box 1007; Winchester Bay; (541) 271–3407. At the Salmon Harbor Marina, west of U.S. 101. Full-service park with 56 full-hookup sites, cable

TV, picnic tables, and fireplaces, all with bay view. Showers, rest rooms, laundry facilities, and hiking/biking path. Excellent boat launch, moorage, and fuel nearby. Moderate.

Surfwood Campground, 75381 Highway 101; (541) 271-4020. East side of U.S. 101, a half mile north of Winchester Bay, 2.5 miles south of Reedsport. Has 163 sites: 141 full-hookup, 22 tent. Pull-throughs, showers, tank dump, firewood, cable TV, laundry, heated and covered pool and sauna, store, ice, car wash, shuffleboard, tennis court, horseshoes, and playground. Moderate.

Tahkenitch Campground, Oregon Dunes National Recreation Area; (541) 271-3611. On west side of U.S. 101, 7 miles north of Reedsport. Has 34 campsites with picnic tables and fire pits. Rest rooms, trailer sites for RVs to 22 feet, and turnaround. Water available May 15 to September 15. Hiker access to dunes and beach. No ORV access. Wooded setting, a half mile south of Tahkenitch landing and boat ramp. Inexpensive.

Tahkenitch Landing, Oregon Dunes National Recreation Area; (541) 271-3611. Seven miles north of Reedsport on east side of U.S. 101. Fire pits and picnic tables at 27 sites for RVs up to 22 feet. Graveled road and pads. Trailer turnaround, but sites are narrow and brushy. No hookups or water. Closed in winter. Boat ramp. Fishing dock with wheelchair access. Inexpensive.

Umpqua Lighthouse State Park; (541) 271-4118. West off U.S. 101, 6 miles south of Reedsport. Has 41 tent sites and 22 full-hookup sites for RVs to 44 feet. Showers, laundry, firewood. Beach and swimming at small lake. Hiking trails. Near ocean beaches and dunes. Moderate.

Windy Cove County Park, P.O. Box 265; Winchester Bay; (541) 271-4138 or (541) 271-5634. Three miles south of Reedsport, west off U.S. 101, across from Salmon Harbor boat basin. Has 75 full-hookup sites for RVs up to 30 feet long. Showers, picnic tables, and playground. An attractive park near beaches, dunes, charter boats, restaurants, and stores. Moderate.

FOOD AND BEVERAGES

Café Francais, 75318 Highway 101; Winchester Bay; (541) 271-9270. On the west side of U.S. 101. Dinner, Wednesday through Sunday. French country cooking is the specialty at this popular restaurant. The menu varies according to local market availability, but usually includes Umpqua oysters, baby rib lamb chops, chateaubriand, filet mignon, pork loin, scampi, scallops, baked salmon, and lingcod with capers. Meals include soup, salad, vegetables, potato, and homemade crusty French bread. Oregon, California, and French wines available. Moderate.

Don's Diner & Ice Cream Parlor, 2115 Winchester Avenue; Reedsport; (541) 271-2032. On U.S. 101, downtown. Lunch and dinner daily. Great diner food, including the best burgers in town. Also on the large menu are soups, salads, chili, and chowder, as well as hot and cold deli-style sandwiches. Dinner baskets include roasted chicken, fish, clam strips, shrimp, seafood combo, chicken breast fillets, and finger steaks. Good selection of ice cream, sodas, sundaes, shakes, and malts. Inexpensive to moderate.

Harbor Light Family Restaurant, U.S. 101 at State Route 38; (541) 271-3848. East side of U.S 101, north end of town. Breakfast, lunch, and dinner daily. Good food at reasonable prices. Breakfast includes clam fritters and eggs, smoked pork chop and eggs, oysters and eggs, omelettes, and traditional favorites. Among lunch offerings are soups, salads, sandwiches, and burgers. The dinner menu features appetizers, soups, salads, prime rib, steaks, pasta dishes, and fresh seafood: salmon, halibut, lingcod, and Winchester Bay oysters. Beer and wine. Moderate.

Sportsman's Cannery, P.O. Box 1011; Winchester Bay; (541) 271-3293 or (800) 457-8048. Between **B** and **C** docks, on the waterfront. West of U.S. 101, 3 miles south of Reedsport. Summer: daily, 7:00 A.M. to 7:00 P.M. Winter: daily, 9:00 A.M. to 6:00 P.M. Fresh, smoked, and canned seafoods. Gift packs shipped anywhere. Phone and mail orders. Salmon, albacore, sturgeon, halibut, and crab. Custom canning for anglers. "Catch what you can—we can what you catch." Daily cannery tours.

SHOPPING AND BROWSING

Reedsport's Old Town area has been refurbished and made much more inviting to visitors and residents. You'll find a number of gift shops, art galleries, and other stores worth a stop—most of them clustered along Fir Avenue (State Route 38).

In Winchester Bay, walk the side streets and Salmon Harbor waterfront to check out shops and galleries of interest.

MUSEUMS

Douglas County Coastal Historical and Information Center, Winchester Bay; (541) 271-4631 or (541) 440-4500. In the former Umpqua River U.S. Coast Guard Station, 1.5 miles south of Winchester Bay, near the lighthouse, or west off U.S. 101, 6 miles south of Reedsport. May through September: Wednesday through Saturday, 10:00 A.M. to 5:00 P.M.; Sunday, 1:00 to 5:00 P.M. Built in 1939 and occupied by the Coast Guard until 1971. Now houses historical displays, photographs, and information about early life on the Umpqua River—transportation, logging, shipping, and more. Nominal admission fee.

Umpqua Discovery Center, 409 Riverfront Way; Reedsport; (541) 271–4816; www.harborside.com/~discover. Located right on the Umpqua riverfront, this discovery center traces the area's heritage from the time before civilization through that of the Kuuich tribes and to the present. Museum-goers enjoy the surrounding scenery though a tower periscope, exhibits on coastal wildlife, and a boardwalk with amazing views of the river. Call for current hours; nominal admission fee.

BEACHES, PARKS, TRAILS, AND WAYSIDES

The **Oregon Dunes National Recreation Area** (N.R.A.) might be considered Oregon's largest park, because in many respects it certainly is a park, complete with trails, beaches, campgrounds, lakes, ponds, streams, and many recreational opportunities. It is managed by the U.S. Forest Service as part of the **Siuslaw National Forest** and has its headquarters in Reedsport, on the west side of U.S. 101 at the State Route 38 junction. N.R.A. headquarters are open weekdays from 8:00 A.M. to 4:30 P.M. all year and weekends during the summer.

The N.R.A. stretches some 42 miles from North Bend to Florence and comprises 32,000 acres. Here, dunes rise to heights of 700 feet and lengths of nearly a mile, making them the largest oceanside dunes in the world. Also within this vast area are 41 miles of broad beaches, thirty-two lakes and numerous ponds and marshes, 247 species of birds, fifty land mammals, four marine mammals (as well as twenty-five species of whales and dolphins offshore), twelve amphibians, three reptiles, and eighty-three fishes, not to mention coniferous and deciduous softwood and hardwood trees, shrubs, grasses, ferns, berries, and wildflowers. It's enough to boggle the mind of any nature lover.

An abbreviated glimpse of the dunes is offered to U.S. 101 travelers about 10 miles north of Reedsport at the **Oregon Dunes Overlook.** Boardwalks and ramps lead to two viewing platforms

ATV riders in Oregon Dunes

overlooking six typical wildlife habitats and ten dunes landforms. For those so inclined, trails lead to the dunes and beach.

About 6 miles south of Reedsport, a road leads west off U.S. 101 to **Umpqua Lighthouse State Park,** where there are hiking trails, picnic areas, a lake with a beach, abundant wildlife, superb views, unlimited photographic opportunities, and the Umpqua lighthouse, or **Umpqua River Light Station,** as it was commissioned.

The original Umpqua lighthouse, built in 1857 near the mouth of the river, was the first such structure erected in Oregon. But the flooding Umpqua undermined its foundation and toppled the building in February 1861.

The present light, which stands on a bluff high above the beach and dunes and has a focal plane 165 feet above the sea, has been operating since 1894. The red-and-white light beaming from its 65-foot tower is visible 19 miles out to sea.

About 3 miles east of U.S. 101 on State Route 38 is the **Dean Creek Elk Viewing Area,** which is a *must-see.* Magnificent Roosevelt elk have been using the bottomlands along the Umpqua River for many years. What was once a 923-acre ranch is now an elk refuge in public ownership. From 50 to 150 elk are often near enough for excellent viewing and photography, even without the aid of binoculars and telephoto lenses, although such optics are recommended.

WATER SPORTS AND ACTIVITIES

On Winchester Bay, at the small community by the same name, Salmon Harbor provides more than 900 boat slips with full hookups, showers, rest rooms, sewage pump-out station, fuel docks, bait docks, launch ramps, repair and service facilities, and more, making this the largest sport-boat basin on the Oregon coast. From here, powerboats and sailboats can steer west across the bar and into the Pacific, or up the bay and Umpqua River.

Despite all the sport-boat traffic here, this is no place for the inexperienced boater. Take heed: The Umpqua River bar is tricky and often treacherous. Winds, currents, and tide rips can churn the lower Umpqua River and Winchester Bay into dangerous waters for small boats. Exercise caution and use common sense.

The Umpqua is one of the coastal rivers that get runs of spring chinook. Anglers catch the big salmon from the bar all the way to the head of tidewater, but one of the most popular areas is just downstream from the Scottsburg bridge. Launch facilities are nearby, just off State Route 38.

Another spring visitor is the American shad, which arrives in May in great schools that move up the Umpqua and provide action from tidewater up. Shad are present in the river most of the summer, but the best fishing is in May and June.

Fall chinook enter the system in late September, and about the time their numbers dwindle, the first of the winter steelhead arrive and offer superb angling above tidewater through February.

Striped bass are present in both the Umpqua and Smith, and some consider the latter to be Oregon's best striper water. While these great fish are not present in the numbers they once were, most are big fish. Every year, anglers take stripers of twenty to forty pounds, with occasional fifty-pounders brought to gaff.

The lower Umpqua also offers some of the best sturgeon fishing in the state, with the first fish of the year taken by hardy anglers in January and February, even though this is a year-round fishery. The best sturgeon fishing is in the deep holes, particularly in the Big Bend area near Gardiner. This is a bait and big-tackle fishery for a quarry that might be as long as your boat.

A smallmouth-bass fishery has developed on the Umpqua in recent years, and anglers are making some fine catches of this worthy gamester. The bass are present in the system all year and as far downstream as Reedsport. The best angling, however, is from late April, when the rains begin to subside and the water drops and clears, through the summer and fall until the rainy season. Best catches are made above tidewater, particularly from Elkton upstream.

Surfperch and seaperch start moving into Winchester Bay in late winter and provide angling opportunities through spring from boats, shore, docks, or piers. Flounder, sole, rockfish, and lingcod round out the usual catch of bottom fish in the bay and lower river.

Crabbing is good throughout the bay, either from a boat or from docks and piers. Mudflats offer excellent clam digging on minus tides for horseneck, hard-shell, littleneck, and soft-shell clams and cockles. For razor clams, try the beaches north and south of the bay.

Todd Hannah, Guide & Outfitter, 171 Steelhead Drive; Elkton 97436; (800) 428-8585. Guided fishing for salmon, steelhead, sturgeon, shad, striped bass, and smallmouth bass. Trips booked for the Umpqua, Smith, Elk, Sixes, and Rogue Rivers; trips include meals and lodging.

Terry Jarmain, Umpqua River Guide; P.O. Box 213; (541) 271-5583 or (800) 635-5583; www.umpqua-river-guide.com. Tidewater guide for various species on the Umpqua and Smith Rivers—striped bass, sturgeon, perch, shad, and more. Also offers clam digging, crabbing, and scenic river trips.

Reedsport Outdoor Store, 2049 Winchester Avenue; (541) 271-2311. West side of U.S. 101, downtown Reedsport. Weekdays, 9:00 A.M. to 6:00 P.M.; Saturday, 10:00 A.M. to 3:00 P.M. Full-service outdoor store, offering outdoor clothing, rainwear, boots, bait, tackle, and crabbing gear, as well as outboard and boat sales and service. Fishing licenses and tags. Good source of fishing, crabbing, and clam-digging information.

GOLF

Forest Hills Country Club, 1 Country Club Drive; (541) 271-2626. West 0.7 mile off U.S. 101 at the southernmost traffic light in Reedsport. Nine-hole golf course. Pro shop, resident pro, club sales and repair, club and cart rental. Tennis courts, restaurant, and lounge on premises.

RENTALS

Tahkenitch Fishing Village, 80135 Highway 101; Gardiner 97441; (541) 271-5222. West end of Tahkenitch Lake, east side of

U.S. 101, 7.5 miles north of Reedsport. Rents 14-foot fiberglass boats with outboard motors by the hour, half-day, or day. Boat moorage and five RV sites available.

WEATHER AND TIDE INFORMATION

U.S. Coast Guard, Umpqua River; Winchester Bay; recorded message, (541) 271–4244

TRAVEL INFORMATION

Reedsport/Winchester Bay Chamber of Commerce, P.O. Box 11; (541) 271–3495 or (800) 247–2155; www.reedsportcc.org

Oregon Dunes National Recreation Area; Suislaw National Forest; 855 Highway Avenue; (541) 271–3611

EVENTS

March	Oregon Dune Mushers' Mail Run, (541) 271–3495
July	Fireworks Display, (541) 271–3495
	Ocean Festival, (541) 271–3495
August	Crab Bounty Hunt, (541) 271–3495
December	Holiday Bazaar and Gingerbread House Show, (541) 271–3495

FLORENCE
Population: 6,200

Location: *At the junction of U.S. 101 and State Route 126, 60 miles west of Eugene, 21 miles north of Reedsport, at the mouth of the Siuslaw (si-oos-law) River. Zip: 97439.*

One story says the city of Florence was named after State Senator A. B. Florence, who represented Lane County in the mid-nineteenth century. A more romantic and interesting version, and one more fitting the character of a charming seaport, is that the French ship *Florence* went aground near the mouth of the Siuslaw River in February 1875 and broke up in the surf. A plank bearing her name washed ashore, and several local Indians hung it above the entrance of the town's first hotel. Since then, the community has been known as Florence.

Like many river communities, Florence, in its early days, was dependent upon the Siuslaw (an Indian word meaning "faraway waters") for transportation and commerce. People traveled from home to town and back by boat. Mail, food, and supplies were delivered by boat. Children went to school by boat.

Highways have replaced waterways for such purposes, but Florence's river heritage is still evident. Even as the town grows and spreads northward, it seems to cling to its moorings along the river's north bank.

Florence was born of the river, and its first buildings were clustered along it. Several of them still stand in the riverfront area known as Old Town. After years of neglect and decay, much of Old Town has been renovated and is now the most interesting part of the city. With all its shops and waterfront restaurants, Bay Street is doing its best to bustle, but it can't quite resist the urge to amble.

LODGING

Driftwood Shores, 88416 First Avenue; (541) 997–8263; (800) 422–5091; www.driftwoodshores.com. Located 2.5 miles west of U.S. 101, via Heceta Beach Road, just north of Florence. Has 136 units with queen beds, cable TV, and ocean view. Studio and kitchen units available. Each 3-bedroom suite has full kitchen, fireplace, dining room, oceanfront balcony, master bedroom with private bath, and 2 smaller bedrooms with adjoining bath. Roll-aways and cribs available. Excellent restaurant on premises. Wheelchair access. Moderate to expensive.

Johnson House Bed & Breakfast, 216 Maple Street; P.O. Box 1892; (541) 997–8000 or (800) 768–9488; www.touroregon. com/johnsonhouse.com. On east side of Maple, 1 block north of Old Town waterfront. Double beds in 5 rooms with shared and private baths. Full breakfast. Moderate.

River House, 1202 Bay Street; (541) 997–3933 or (888) 824–2751; www.riverhousemotel.com. On the north shore of the river, near Old Town, west of the bridge. Has 40 units with queen and king beds, some with in-room whirlpools. Cable TV, whirlpool, bay view. Moderate.

Woahink Lake Suites, 83693 Highway 101 South; (541) 997–6516. On the east side of U.S. 101, 4 miles south of the Siuslaw River. Six remodeled, quiet, and roomy suites with queen and king beds, cable TV, and lakefront decks. Paddleboats and WaveRunners available for rent. Near Oregon Dunes National Recreation Area and Honeyman State Park. Moderate.

CAMPGROUNDS AND RV PARKS

Carter Lake Campground, Oregon Dunes National Recreation Area; (541) 271–3611. West off U.S. 101, 11 miles south of Florence. Has 23 sites with picnic tables, fireplace, and water. Hiking trails, fishing, boating, wildlife observation, and photography. Inexpensive.

Driftwood II ORV Campground, Oregon Dunes National Recreation Area; (541) 271–3611. Located 1.25 miles west of U.S. 101 on Siltcoos Dune and Beach Access Road, 10 miles south of Florence. Has 69 sites, some with picnic tables and fire pits. Trailer sites, turnaround, and rest rooms. Water in summer only. No hookups. Beach and dune access from campground. Hiking trails, fishing, wildlife watching, and photography. Inexpensive.

Jessie M. Honeyman Memorial State Park, 84505 Highway 101; (800) 452-5687. West side of U.S. 101, 3 miles south of Florence. A beautiful campground with 382 sites: 66 full-hookup, 75 electric, 241 tent. Showers, firewood, hiking trails, fishing and swimming at two lakes, dunes access, concession area. Well-maintained grounds. Reservations accepted. Moderate.

Lagoon Campground, Oregon Dunes National Recreation Area; (541) 271-3611. Located three quarters of a mile west of U.S. 101 on Siltcoos Dune and Beach Access Road, 10 miles south of Florence. Has 39 campsites with picnic tables and fire pits. Trailer sites, turnaround, rest rooms, water, no hookups. Beach and dune access. Hiking and nature trails, fishing, wildlife observation, and photography. Inexpensive.

Sutton Campground, Oregon Dunes National Recreation Area; (541) 271-3611. On Sutton Beach Road, 2.5 miles north of Florence, 0.8 mile west of U.S. 101. Has 92 campsites, no hookups. Trailer sites, turnaround, rest rooms, water, hiking trails, and trail access to dunes and beach. Fishing in estuary, creek, and lake. Wildlife observation and photography. Inexpensive.

Tyee Campground, Oregon Dunes National Recreation Area; (541) 271-3611. Located a tenth of a mile east of U.S. 101 on Westlake Road, 6 miles south of Florence. Has 14 campsites with picnic tables and fireplaces. Trailer sites, no hookups. Rest rooms, water, boat ramp. Fishing and boating with access to Siltcoos River and Siltcoos Lake. Inexpensive.

Waxmyrtle Campground, Oregon Dunes National Recreation Area; (541) 271-3611. Located three quarters of a mile west of U.S. 101 on Siltcoos Dune and Beach Access Road, 10 miles south of Florence. Has 56 sites with picnic tables, fire pits, no hookups. Trailer sites, turnaround, and water. Hiking, fishing, dune and beach access, wildlife observation, and photography. Inexpensive.

FOOD AND BEVERAGES

Blue Hen Cafe, 1675 Highway 101; (541) 997-3907. On west side of U.S. 101, downtown. Breakfast, lunch, and dinner Monday through Saturday. Breakfast and lunch Sunday. Ranks among the best breakfasts on the coast. Steak and eggs, biscuits and gravy, French toast, pancakes, omelettes. Chowder, soups, salads, sandwiches, and burgers. Features pasta dishes and chicken—

all home-style cooking. This is one of the most popular restaurants on the coast. Beer and wine. Moderate.

The Bridgewater Seafood Restaurant & Oyster Bar, 1297 Bay Street; (541) 997-9405. In Old Town, situated in a historic building erected in 1901. Lunch and dinner daily. Sandwiches, burgers, and such specialties as fettuccine with clam sauce, shrimp Creole, clam fritters, teriyaki chicken. Shrimp, crab, and calamari appetizers, as well as oysters on the half shell. Dinners include steak, chicken, and seafood. Oyster bar and garden patio. Cocktails, beer, and wine. Moderate.

Mo's Restaurant, 1436 Bay Street; (541) 997-2185. In Old Town. Lunch and dinner daily. Local chain chowder and fish house, serving burgers, salads, soups, chili, clam chowder, oyster stew, fish and chips, and seafood sandwiches. Large dinner menu with such seafood favorites as salmon, halibut, lingcod, clam fritters, oysters, prawns, scallops, calamari, and cioppino. Beer and wine. Moderate.

Surfside Inn, 88416 First Avenue; (541) 997-8263 or (800) 422-5091. At Driftwood Shores, 2.5 miles west of U.S. 101, via Heceta Beach Road, north of Florence. Breakfast, lunch, and dinner daily. Two-egg and three-egg omelettes, pancakes, waffles, and various egg dishes and specials, including the Fisherman—two eggs, hash browns, toast or English muffin, with fillet of salmon or halibut. For lunch, hot or cold sandwiches, including burgers and French dip, or bay shrimp or Dungeness crab on English muffin topped with melted cheddar. Louis-style salads topped with crab, shrimp, or both for lunch or dinner. Dinners include prime rib, chicken, leg of lamb, broiled steaks, salmon, oysters, scallops, shrimp scampi, halibut, and lobster. Cocktails, beer, and wine. Moderate.

Windward Inn, 3757 Highway 101 North; (541) 997-8243. West side of U.S. 101 at the north end of town. Breakfast, lunch, and dinner daily. Closed Mondays in winter. Breakfast menu includes homemade breads and pastries. Lunches and dinners include a variety of beef, veal, lamb, and seafood dishes. Full bar, including a wine list featuring Oregon wines. Moderate.

SHOPPING AND BROWSING

Florence's Old Town district is one of the most charming on the coast and is a shopper's delight. Many quaint shops and fine galleries stand on both sides of Bay Street, along the north bank of the river, east of the bridge. Others are situated on adjacent side streets: Laurel, Maple, and Nopal.

Before heading for Old Town, be sure to stop by the Florence Chamber of Commerce Visitor Center to pick up a copy of the *Old Town Walking Map and Directory.*

Blue Heron Gallery, 1385 Bay Street; P.O. Box 10000; (541) 997–7993. In Old Town. Daily, 10:00 A.M. to 6:00 P.M. Carvings, sculpture, glassworks, original paintings, limited-edition and open-edition prints. A fine gallery featuring marine art, seascapes, landscapes, and wildlife.

Catch the Wind Kite Shop, 1250 Bay Street; P.O. Box 1923; (541) 997–9500. At the old train depot, Old Town, near the bridge. Daily, 10:00 A.M. to 6:00 P.M. Part of the Oregon chain of great kite shops. All kinds of kites and accessories, wind socks, books, and magazines. If you're interested in learning about kites, this is the place to start.

Kitchen Klutter, 1250 Bay Street; P.O. Box 2025; (541) 997–6060. On south side of street in Old Town. Every kind of kitchen gadget imaginable and then some. A good place to browse and look for gifts.

Wind Drift Gallery, 1395 Bay Street; (541) 997–9182. In Old Town. Popular shop where marine art and nautical gift items are mainstays. Good selection of prints, sculpture, carvings, and castings.

MUSEUM

Siuslaw Pioneer Museum, 85294 Highway 101 South; (541) 997–7884. One mile south of the river, west side of U.S. 101. May 1 to Labor Day: Tuesday through Sunday, noon to 4:00 P.M. Winter: weekends, noon to 4:00 P.M. Displays of Indian artifacts, farm and homestead items, early logging equipment, and more. Nominal admission fee.

BEACHES, PARKS, TRAILS, AND WAYSIDES

Beaches extend north and south from the mouth of the Siuslaw. For access to the dunes and beach south of Florence, turn west on South Jetty Road, south of the U.S. 101 bridge. On the north side of the river, take Rhododendron Drive west of U.S. 101 to North Jetty Road, Harbor Vista, and Heceta (huh-*see*-tuh) Beach.

Carnivorous plants *Darlingtonia californica*

Or, approach Heceta Beach by turning west off U.S. 101 onto Heceta Beach Road, north of town.

Also north of town, about 6 miles and just east of U.S. 101, is the **Darlingtonia Botanical Wayside,** with interpretive signs and a short trail through a bog where the rare *Darlingtonia californica* grows. This unusual plant, also known as the cobra lily or pitcher plant, is native to southwestern Oregon and northwestern California and is carnivorous. Nectar lures insects into an opening under the plant's hood, where they become entrapped and are eventually consumed. These unusual plants bloom in May and June but are worth viewing any time.

If awards were given for most beautiful and best-kept parks, **Honeyman State Park** would certainly take top honors. Situated off both sides of U.S. 101, 3 miles south of Florence, this lovely park offers camping, picnicking, fishing and swimming in two lakes, and hiking on well-maintained trails.

WATER SPORTS AND ACTIVITIES

About 6 miles south of Florence, Westlake Road exits east off U.S. 101 and leads to a public boat ramp and fishing dock on **Siltcoos Lake.** This is the largest lake on the Oregon coast, and it offers some of the best freshwater fishing in the Florence area. Angling here is mainly for trout and warm-water species, namely good populations of rainbows and native cutthroat, largemouth bass, bluegill, crappie, yellow perch, and brown bullhead. The lake also gets a small run of coho salmon in late fall.

The Siuslaw River is important to local anglers. The river rises in the Coast Range and switchbacks some 100 miles through the mountains to empty into the Pacific near Florence. The lower 20 miles are navigable by sport boats and offer a good variety of angling that is sometimes outstanding.

The estuary is good for surfperch and seaperch from early spring through summer. Anglers take flounder and other bottom species here as well. Crabbing is good from boats or docks, and clam digging is good on minus tides for cockles and soft-shell clams.

Although the river gives up the occasional striped bass or sturgeon, the main effort is for the migrating salmonids. Action picks up in late summer when schools of sea-run cutthroat enter the river and provide sport for trollers and spin fishermen from the estuary upstream to the head of tidewater near Mapleton.

Both coho and chinook salmon use the Siuslaw system, and angling for them can be quite good from September through November. Jack salmon move in with the cutthroat and are present through the fall months. Steelhead follow in December and are present upriver through the winter.

There are good launching facilities, moorage, and campgrounds along the river from Florence to Mapleton, where State Route 126 parallels the river.

GOLF

Ocean Dunes Golf Course, 3345 Munsel Lake Road; (541) 997–3232 or (800) 917–GOLF. Located 1.6 miles east of U.S. 101, just north of Florence. Attractive 18-hole public course with driving range, snack bar, pro shop, and cart and club rental.

Sandpines Golf Links, 1201 35th Street; (541) 997–1940 or (800) 917–4653. About a half mile west of U.S. 101, at the north end of town. A highly acclaimed, award-winning 18-hole course. Designed by Rees Jones, the links lie amid rolling dunes and coastal forest. Pro shop, rental equipment, and carts.

OTHER ATTRACTIONS

C&M Stables, 90241 Highway 101 North; (541) 997–7540; www.touroregon.com/horses. East side of U.S. 101, 8 miles north of Florence. Half-hour and one-hour mountain horseback rides through stands of alder and mountain meadows. Beach rides up to three hours, and two-hour sunset rides. Daily, weekly, and monthly horse boarding. Call for hours.

Sandland Adventures, 85366 Highway 101 South; (541) 997–8087; www.sandland.com. South of the Siuslaw River 0.7 mile. Daily, 9:00 A.M. to 5:00 P.M. Dune buggy tours, ATV rentals, go-carts, bumper boats, and miniature golf.

Sea Lion Caves, 91560 Highway 101; (541) 547–3111; www.sealioncaves.com. West side of U.S. 101 (parking on east side), 11 miles north of Florence, 38 miles south of Newport. Daily, 9:00 A.M. to 6:30 P.M. One of the most popular attractions on the Oregon coast and billed as the world's largest sea cave. This natural sea cave is home to hundreds of sea lions, mostly visible in the spring and summer. Walkways and stairways to elevator that descends 208 feet into the caves. Spectacular views of ocean, Heceta Head, and lighthouse. Good spot for watching birds and whales. Gift shop on premises. Admission is $7.00 for adults and $4.50 for children ages 6–15.

TRAVEL INFORMATION

Florence Chamber of Commerce, 270 Highway 101; P.O. Box 26000; (541) 997–3128; www.florencechamber.com

EVENTS

May	Rhododendron Festival, (541) 997–3128
July	Independence Day Celebration, (541) 997–3128
September	Fall Festival, (541) 997–3128

YACHATS
Population: 620

WALDPORT
Population: 1,670

Location: *Yachats is on U.S. 101, 8 miles south of Waldport, 24 miles north of Florence. Zip: 97498. Waldport is at the junction of U.S. 101 and State Route 34, on the south shore of Alsea Bay, 15 miles south of Newport, 65 miles west of Corvallis. Zip: 97394.*

Yachats (*yah*-hots) is a corruption of the Chinook word *yahuts,* meaning "dark waters at the foot of the mountain," which is certainly descriptive of this area where the Coast Range abuts the ocean in an unyielding tumult of relentless surf against basalt bastions. On a calm day it can be an exciting contest to witness; in stormy weather it is awesome. Consequently, this is a favorite stretch of coastline for watching winter storms. It is equally popular for hiking, biking, and auto touring in the summer.

That more than fifteen motels serve such a small community should attest to the area's importance as a resort destination. Several motels are so near the sea that visitors not only can hear the pounding waves but also can feel them. The cocktail lounge at the Adobe has heavy plate-glass windowpanes to keep stormy seas from crashing right through.

South of town, **Cape Perpetua** offers one of the best views on the coast. Just south of the Devil's Churn, Klickitat Ridge Road (USFS Road No. 55) exits east off U.S. 101. About eight-tenths of a mile beyond, turn north on USFS Road No. 5553, which leads to the **Cape Perpetua Overlook,** where, on a clear day, the view is as far south as Cape Blanco and as far north as Cape Foulweather.

Klickitat Ridge Road is also the starting point for a self-guided auto tour that leads into the forested Coast Range then back to Yachats, via Yachats River Road. The 22-mile trip with sixteen planned stops takes at least one hour, but you could easily devote a half day or more.

Waldport, settled in the 1870s and 1880s, is said to have derived its name from the German *wald*, meaning "forest," and the English "port," making "forested port" a descriptive name. In the past, the wood-products industry was important here, but while logging remains a viable business, the sawmills are gone. Gone, too, are the canneries along the bay and river and all vestiges of once-thriving dairy farms.

Alsea (*al*-see) Bay and River were named after the Alsi tribe that lived here when the white settlers arrived. The word *alsi* means "peace." Peace has come to the Alsea River, which is now used primarily for recreation. And peaceful is an appropriate word to describe the tiny town of Waldport.

LODGING

Adobe Resort, 1555 Highway 101; P.O. Box 219; Yachats; (541) 547–3141 or (800) 522–3623; www.adoberesort.com. West side of U.S. 101. Queen beds, cable TV, and HBO in 97 units, most with an ocean view, some with fireplaces and balconies, some with small patios. Honeymoon suite and several apartment units available. Sauna and whirlpool. Comfortable cocktail lounge and superb restaurant and lounge on premises—both with ocean view. Moderate to expensive.

Cape Cod Cottages, 4150 Southwest Highway 101; Waldport; (541) 563–2106; www.dreamwater.com/thecottages. West side of U.S. 101, 2 miles south of Waldport. Cable TV in 10 1-bedroom and 2-bedroom cottages with kitchens, fireplaces, decks, and garages. Cottages accommodate 2 to 10 persons. Gift and lapidary shop on premises. Moderate.

The Oregon House, 94288 Highway 101; Yachats; (541) 547–3329; www.oregonhouse.com. Nine miles south of Yachats, on 3.5 acres with trees, creek, and ocean beach. Attractive lodging facilities offering 9 suites and studios accommodating up to 6 persons. All have kitchens, 4 have fireplaces, and 2 have in-room Jacuzzis. One bed-and-breakfast unit has private bath and in-room Jacuzzi. Great ocean view, privacy, trail to driftwood-strewn beach. Moderate.

Overleaf Lodge, 2055 Highway 101; (541) 547–4880 or (800) 338–0507; www.overleaflodge.com. West of U.S. 101 at the north end of town. All 39 rooms face the ocean, a stone's throw from the tumbling breakers. Each contains a refrigerator, microwave oven, hair dryer, coffeemaker, TV, and VCR. Some have ocean-view

Mouth of the Yachats River

whirlpool tubs, fireplaces, and balconies. Robes furnished for all guests. Exercise room and laundry facilities. Seaside trail extends 0.75 mile along rocky shore, then connects with a 5-mile stretch of sandy beach. Continental breakfast. Moderate to expensive.

Sea Quest Bed and Breakfast, 95354 Highway 101; Yachats; (541) 547–3782 or (800) 341–4878; www.seaq.com. On west side of U.S. 101, 6 miles south of Yachats, 19 miles north of Florence. Five guest rooms with private baths and private entrances, 4 with in-room Jacuzzi tubs. Full breakfast; nonsmoking. Short hike through a meadow to the beach. Moderate.

Shamrock Lodgettes, 105 Highway 101; P.O. Box 346; Yachats; (541) 547–3312 or (800) 845–5028; www.shamrock lodgettes.com. West side of U.S. 101 in Yachats, on the south bank of the river. Cable TV and HBO in 19 units. Rooms with king beds, fireplaces, and whirlpool tubs. Some kitchen units. Individual log cabins with fireplaces and kitchens. Coffee and tea in rooms. Nonsmoking. Beach and river access. Moderate.

CAMPGROUNDS AND RV PARKS

Beachside State Park, P.O. Box 1350; Newport 97365; (541) 563–3220; www.prd.state.or.us. West side of U.S. 101, 4 miles south of Waldport. Has 20 RV sites with electric and water hookups, picnic tables, and fireplaces; 61 tent sites with fireplaces, picnic tables, and nearby water. Showers, firewood, trails, and beach access. Reservations accepted. Moderate.

Cape Perpetua Campground, Siuslaw National Forest; (541) 547–3679. East of U.S. 101, 2.5 miles south of Yachats. Has 37 tent and trailer sites for RVs up to 22 feet long. Picnic tables, fireplaces, rest rooms, tank dump, water, handicapped access. Hiking trails and beaches nearby. Inexpensive.

Sea Perch Campground and RV, 95480 Highway 101; Yachats; (541) 547–3505. West side of U.S. 101, 5.8 miles south of Yachats. Has 20 RV sites with full hookups, picnic tables, and fire pits. Showers, laundry, cable TV, and beach access. Store with groceries, ice, deli foods, snacks, beer, and wine. Gift shop adjacent. Moderate.

Tillicum Beach Campground, Siuslaw National Forest; (541) 563–3211. West side of U.S. 101, 4.5 miles south of Waldport. Has 57 sites for tents and RVs up to 32 feet long. Picnic tables, fireplaces, rest rooms, and water. A beautiful campground set in the shore pines along the ocean. Summer naturalist programs. Inexpensive.

Carl W. Washburne Memorial State Park, (541) 547–3416; www.prd.state.or.us. West side of U.S. 101, 14 miles south of Yachats. Has 58 full-hookup RV sites and 8 tent sites. Showers and firewood. Fishing, hiking, beachcombing, kite flying, and clam digging. Good area for exploring tide pools. Moderate.

FOOD AND BEVERAGES

The Adobe, 1555 Highway 101; Yachats; (541) 547–3141. West side of U.S. 101, in Yachats. Breakfast, lunch, and dinner Monday through Saturday; brunch and dinner Sunday. Unusual pancake and French toast dishes, sumptuous rolled omelettes, Hangtown Fry, and French-style and Spanish-style egg dishes. Soups, chowder, and oyster stew. Large appetizer menu, steaks, and chicken, but seafood is a specialty, with salmon, halibut, tuna, mahimahi, shrimp, scallops, crab, razor clams, combo plates, and wonderful Yaquina Bay oysters. Moderate.

La Serre Restaurant and Bistro, Second and Beach Streets; Yachats; (541) 547–3420. West side of U.S. 101, downtown. Lunch and dinner daily, weekend breakfast. Poppy-seed griddle cakes, egg dishes, and omelettes, including smoked salmon, shrimp, and fresh spinach and mushroom. Large deli-style sandwiches, soups, and salads. Dinners include steaks, roasted chicken, chicken pot pie, and seafoods such as razor clams, Dover sole with shrimp, bouillabaisse, and cioppino. Moderate.

SHOPPING AND BROWSING

Earthworks Gallery, 2222 Highway 101 North; Yachats; (541) 547–4300; www.oregoncoast101.com/earth. On the east side of the highway, north of town. Open 10:00 A.M. to 5:00 P.M. daily. A large selection of fine works of pottery, glass, metal sculpture, and soapstone carvings. Also, original paintings and drawings, lithographs, photographs, mixed media, fiber art, and more. Traditional, contemporary, and whimsical works. Open, roomy, and well-lighted gallery, certainly worth a stop.

Sea Rose, 95478 Highway 101; Yachats; (541) 547–3005. West side of U.S. 101, 5.8 miles south of Yachats. Daily, 10:00 A.M. to 5:00 P.M. Large, well-stocked shell and gift shop. Large selection of collector's shells. Glass floats, carvings, wind chimes, and more. *Oregon Coast Shell Museum* on premises. A *must-see* for anyone interested in shells.

Touchstone Gallery, 2118 Highway 101 North; (541) 547–4121. East side of the highway at the north end of town. Open daily, 10:00 A.M. to 5:00 P.M. Jewelry, glass, ceramics, paintings, and bronzes by Northwest artists, all tastefully displayed in a bright, cheery setting.

Triad Gallery, 5667 Northwest Pacific Coast Highway; Seal Rock 97376; (541) 563–5442. About 2.5 miles north of the Alsea Bay Bridge, on the east side of U.S. 101. Open 10:00 A.M. to 5:00 P.M. Wednesday through Monday. An unusual, interesting, and airy gallery exhibiting abstract contemporary art, metalwork, jewelry, fiber art, paintings, fine-art photographs, and mixed media. New exhibits every month. A fine gallery, well worth seeing.

BEACHES, PARKS, TRAILS, AND WAYSIDES

The **Devil's Churn Wayside,** about 2 miles south of Yachats, is one of the most interesting diversions along the Oregon coast, especially on an incoming tide when the ocean is in a foul mood. Incoming waves rush landward up a narrow trench in the basalt rock. When they reach the end of the slit, they burst skyward with an explosive boom and shower of spray. Trails lead from the parking lot to the water's edge, where there are many tide pools to explore.

The **Cape Perpetua Visitor Center** is 2.5 miles south of Yachats, off the east side of Highway 101. Stop here for information on and maps of the cape and Siuslaw National Forest. The center is open daily in the summer from 9:00 A.M. to 6:00 P.M. and is closed Wednesday and Thursday in the off-season. The visitor center offers interpretive displays, films, slide shows, an information desk, rest rooms, and books and booklets for sale.

MUSEUM

The **Alsea Bay Bridge Historical Interpretive Center** is at the southwest end of the Alsea Bay Bridge. It's a fine little museum depicting the history of the Oregon coast, coast highway, and bridges. One display honors the famous bridge builder Conde B. McCullough. The center is open daily from 9:00 A.M. to 5:00 P.M. during the summer and 9:00 A.M. to 4:00 P.M. Wednesday through Sunday in winter.

WATER SPORTS AND ACTIVITIES

The main attraction in the Yachats area for fishermen is the silver smelt, which gather by the tens of thousands along the ocean beaches and rocky coves from mid-April to mid-October. Fishermen take them with long-handled, fine-mesh dip nets and seines. The fish are excellent fare, pan-fried or smoked. They're also good bait for a variety of game-fish species.

Lower Alsea Bay is a popular crabbing and clam-digging area. Crabbing requires a boat, but gathering cockles is easy with a shovel or rake and hip boots or waders. Farther upbay, along State Route 34, minus tides expose mudflats where you can dig soft-shell and horseneck clams.

Fall is prime time on the Alsea for chinook salmon. The river is known for its strain of big chinook, and every year fish of forty to fifty pounds or more are caught. The best fishing is upriver, above the delta area, where the river narrows and deepens. For about 10 miles east of Waldport, there are campgrounds, RV parks, and marinas along State Route 34.

GOLF

Crestview Hills Golf Course, 1680 Crestline Drive; (541) 563–3020. Located eight tenths of a mile east of U.S. 101 on

Range Drive, 1 mile south of Waldport (turn at the Burger Bar). Summer: daily, 7:00 A.M. to dusk. Off-season: daily, 8:00 A.M. to dusk. Nine-hole course, pro shop, club and cart rental. Restaurant on premises, open for breakfast and lunch.

TRAVEL INFORMATION

Siuslaw National Forest, Waldport Ranger Station; (541) 563–3211

Waldport Chamber of Commerce, P.O. Box 669; (541) 563–2133

Yachats Area Chamber of Commerce, P.O. Box 728; (541) 547–3530; www.yachats.org

EVENTS

March	Yachats Arts & Crafts Festival, (541) 547–3530
June	Beachcomber Days, Waldport, (541) 563–2133
July	Fireworks, Waldport, (541) 563–2133
	Community Smelt Fry, Yachats, (541) 547–3530
August	Celebrate Waldport Festival, (541) 563–2133
September	Salmon Derby and Bake, Waldport, (541) 563–2133
	Port of Alsea Crab Derby, Waldport, (541) 563–2133
October	Yachats Village Mushroom Fest, (541) 547–3530

NEWPORT

Location: *At the junction of U.S. 101 and U.S. 20, along the north shore of Yaquina Bay, 25 miles south of Lincoln City, 15 miles north of Waldport, and 57 miles west of Corvallis. Zip: 97365.*

No doubt, Newport is coastal Oregon's premier resort destination. It is centrally located and situated on beautiful Yaquina Bay, with broad beaches extending north and south. It's an easy and pleasant drive from the population centers of the Willamette Valley, and it is only three hours from Portland. Moreover, it offers visitors a wide assortment and diversity of activities and accommodations, from crabbing and clam digging to a spirited nightlife, from windsurfing and scuba diving to shopping and art-gallery hopping, from golf courses and tennis courts to museums and theaters, from burger joints and pizza parlors to fine restaurants, from RV parks and budget motels to plush condominiums and luxurious resort hotels.

Newport has grown considerably in recent years, and not without suffering the consequences. Escape the urban sprawl and congestion, however, by getting off U.S. 101 and visiting the more charming parts of the city.

East of U.S. 101, along the north shore of Yaquina Bay, is the Old Town bayfront, with restaurants, shops, and galleries galore, mingled with the working waterfront businesses. With trucks and vans being loaded with fresh seafood, and visitors and residents coming and going on narrow, crowded streets, gridlock is inevitable and parking impossible. But by planning the day and getting there early—say for breakfast—there should be no problem finding a parking spot.

Opposite Old Town, on the south shore of the bay, is the South Beach area, a *must-see,* if for no other reason than a visit to the **Oregon Coast Aquarium** and the famed **Mark O. Hatfield Marine Science Center.** Also in this area are a huge marina, an RV park, a public fishing pier, access to the south jetty area, and more to come as plans for the future are fulfilled.

Something Newport doesn't have much of these days is an off-season. With the increasing popularity of watching whales and winter storms and the various winter festivals and activities, Newport is becoming a year-round resort town.

LODGING

Best Western Agate Beach Hotel, 3019 North Coast Highway; (541) 265–9411 or (800) 528–1234. West off U.S. 101, just past Safeway, next to WalMart. Double and king beds and cable TV in 148 large, remodeled rooms and suites, half with ocean view, all with color remote TVs, videocassette players, refrigerators, and microwave ovens. Heated pool, spa, and room service. Restaurant and cocktail lounge on premises. Easy walk to Agate Beach. Moderate to expensive.

Embarcadero Resort Hotel & Marina, 1000 Southeast Bay Boulevard; (541) 265–8521 or (800) 547–4779; www.embarca dero-resort.com. East of U.S. 101 on the north shore of the bay. One- and two-bedroom condo units with kitchens, cable TV, fireplaces, queen beds, and decks overlooking the marina and bay. Restaurant and lounge on the premises. Moorage, bait-and-tackle shop, boat and moped rentals. Fishing and crabbing from private docks. Fish-cleaning station, crab cooker, and barbecue pit. Heated indoor pool, sauna, and whirlpool. Moderate to expensive.

Moolack Shores Motel, 8835 North Coast Highway; Box 420; (541) 265–2326; www.moolackshores.com. West side of U.S. 101, 3 miles north of Newport. A dozen thematically decorated rooms, plus a guest house, beach house, and condominium—all with cable TV. Antique, nautical, whaling, Western, and Hawaiian motifs, as well as Racer's Room, Camelot Room, Art Gallery Room, Hunting Lodge, and Oregon Room. Most rooms with ocean view, fireplaces, vaulted and beamed ceilings, and queen beds. Some have decks and kitchens. All have binoculars for whale and wildlife watching. Moderate to expensive.

Shilo Inn Oceanfront Resort, 536 Southwest Elizabeth; (541) 265–7701 or (800) 222–2244; www.shiloinns.com. West of U.S. 101, in the Nye Beach area. Watch for signs. Queen and king beds and cable TV in a variety of accommodations at this full-service resort. Main complex with 112 rooms, 2 family units, 1 master suite, heated indoor pool, and 4J's Restaurant. Also, 60 rooms, 3 parlor suites, 1 luxury suite, heated indoor pool, and Flagship Restaurant in the new addition. Suites and rooms available with in-room whirlpool tubs and kitchenettes. All rooms have remote-control TV and refrigerator. Ocean view. Moderate to expensive.

Sylvia Beach Hotel, 267 Northwest Cliff; (541) 265–5428 or (888) 795–8422; www.sylviabeachhotel.com. West of U.S. 101, on Nye Beach. Billed as an "oceanfront bed-and-breakfast for book lovers." Built between 1910 and 1913. Named after Sylvia Beach, a patron of literature and a Paris bookstore owner in the 1920s and 1930s. Has 20 rooms named after authors, each distinctly decorated: Agatha Christie, Mark Twain, E. B. White, Ernest Hemingway, Tennessee Williams, Willa Cather, Oscar Wilde. Rates include breakfast. Excellent restaurant on premises. Beer and wine list. Hot wine served in the library at 10:00 P.M. Moderate to expensive.

CAMPGROUNDS AND RV PARKS

Beverly Beach State Park, 198 North East 123rd Street; Box 684; (541) 265–9278 or (800) 452–5687. East side of U.S. 101, 6.3 miles north of Newport, 6.5 miles south of Depoe Bay. Has 279 campsites: 52 full-hookup, 75 electric-hookup, 152 tent. Showers, tank dump, and firewood. Hiking trails and easy access to several miles of broad beach. Situated along Spencer Creek in a beautiful park setting, with protected sites in wooded area. Reservations accepted. Moderate.

Newport Marine & RV Park, 600 Southeast Bay Boulevard; (541) 265–7758. East of U.S. 101, on south shore of bay, at South Beach. Has 38 RV sites near store and tackle shop, charter service, restaurant, public fishing pier, launch ramp, and full-service marina. Showers, full hookups, cable TV. Moderate.

Outdoor Resorts Pacific Shores Motorcoach Resort, 6225 North Coast Highway; (541) 265–3750 or (800) 333–1583; www.pacificshoresrv.com. About 3 miles north of Newport, on west side of U.S. 101. Has 287 sites, 100 pull-throughs, full hookups, cable TV, fire pits, picnic tables, showers, laundry, heated indoor pool, sauna, whirlpool, exercise room, and ocean view. Two adult lounges with TVs, fireplaces, and game tables. Billiard room, game room, children's lounge, and playground. Convenience store and gift shop on premises. Ice and propane available. Nature trails. Moderate to expensive.

Yaquina Bay and Newport's Old Town waterfront

South Beach State Park, P.O. Box 1350; (541) 867–7451. West off U.S. 101, 2 miles south of Newport. Has 265 sites, each with water, electricity, picnic table, and fireplace. Showers, tank dump, and firewood. Easy beach access. Reservations accepted. Moderate.

FOOD AND BEVERAGES

Mo's and **Mo's Annex,** 622 and 657 Southwest Bay Boulevard; (541) 265–7512. In Old Town bayfront district. Lunch and dinner daily. Famous local chain chowder and fish house, serving burgers, salads, soups, chili, clam chowder, oyster stew, fish and chips, and seafood sandwiches. Large dinner menu with such seafood favorites as salmon, halibut, lingcod, clam fritters, oysters, prawns, scallops, calamari, and cioppino. The first Mo's began here more than fifty years ago. The Annex was added in 1968. Although the original bistro may appear quite informal, that is its basic charm. The garage door, which is propped open to the sidewalk, is legendary. The story goes that a woman returned to her car in front of Mo's after dining and accidentally put her car in drive instead of reverse. Mo comforted the woman by saying, "We'll just put in a garage door so you can drive in anytime you want." Beer and wine. Moderate.

Rogue Ales Public House, 748 Southwest Bay Boulevard; (541) 265–3188. In Old Town. Lunch and dinner daily. Large selection of pizzas, appetizers, soups, chowder, salads, and pasta dishes. Features locally brewed Rogue ales. Moderate.

Shilo Restaurant, 358 Elizabeth Street; (541) 265–2449. At the Shilo Inn, on Nye Beach. Lunch and dinner daily. Great luncheon specialties, such as shrimp-stuffed tomatoes, Louisiana-style shrimp, grilled Pacific oysters, taco salad, lox and bagels, burgers, and other sandwiches, as well as soups, chowder, and oyster stew. For dinner, such tempting appetizers as bagel chips and lox mousse, stuffed mushrooms, and a half dozen others; special salads; and entrees of halibut, oysters, razor clams, stuffed sole, prawns, scallops, lobster, various steaks, chicken, and pasta. Full bar, including fifty-five imported beers. Moderate.

Tables of Content, 267 Northwest Cliff; (541) 265–5428. At Sylvia Beach Hotel, west of U.S. 101, on Nye Beach. Dinner daily, by reservation. Most meals are based around the freshest seafoods available in season. Menu changes each night, and dinners are served family style. Sample menu includes smoky currant soup, tossed salad, honey whole-wheat bread, lingcod Dijonaise, asparagus with walnut butter, oven-roasted potatoes, chocolate Grand Marnier cheesecake, and coffee or tea. Reasonable price includes everything from appetizer to dessert. Beer and wine available. Phone for day's menu and to make reservations. Moderate.

The Whale's Tale, 452 Southwest Bay Boulevard; (541) 265–8660. In Old Town bayfront district. Breakfast, lunch, and dinner daily. Delicious egg dishes include huevos rancheros, eggs Benedict, and eight great omelettes. Poppy-seed pancakes made with stone-ground wheat flour are a breakfast favorite. Burgers, deli-style sandwiches, soups, chowder, stews, and salads round out lunch menu. Popular dinners include a seafood sauté, grilled Yaquina oysters, mussels marinara, lasagna, cioppino, and German plate—a selection of sausage and meat, German potato salad, sauerkraut, and wonderful homemade black bread. Also, some excellent dinner specials. Beer and wine. Moderate.

SHOPPING AND BROWSING

Facets Gem & Mineral Gallery, 1125 Southwest Coast Highway; (541) 265–6330. East side of U.S. 101, just north of the bridge. Daily, 10:00 A.M. to 5:30 P.M. Large selection of shells, gemstones, mineral specimens, jewelry, and various gift items, tastefully displayed. Many rare and hard-to-find collector's items, including fine, museum-quality fossils. An interesting shop for nearly everyone. A *must-see* for those interested in minerals, gemstones, fossils, and the like.

Oceanic Arts, 444 Southwest Bay Boulevard; (541) 265–5963. In Old Town bayfront district. Daily, 10:00 A.M. to 6:00 P.M. Large gallery featuring a great variety of works in different media. Originals, prints, and contemporary crafts. Excellent custom-matting and framing services as well.

Rickert Gallery, 1107 South West Coast Highway; (541) 265–2466 or (800) 732–8831; www.rickert.com. In Old Town bayfront district. Daily, 10:00 A.M. to 5:30 P.M. A small but pleasing gallery featuring fine marine and wildlife art, limited-edition prints, oils, acrylics, and watercolors. More than thirty artists are represented at this gallery.

The Wood Gallery, 818 Southwest Bay Boulevard; (541) 265–6843 or (800) 359–1419. In Old Town bayfront district. Daily, 10:00 A.M. to 6:00 P.M. One of the finest and most interesting galleries on the coast. Many artworks and gift items. Best wood products and carvings to be found. Wildlife, marine art, whimsical objects—even an entire Porsche engine duplicated in wood at full scale. Mark this one a *must-see.*

MUSEUMS AND AQUARIUMS

Burrows House Museum, 545 Southwest Ninth; (541) 265–7509. One block east of U.S. 101, just beyond the visitor information center. June through September, 10:00 A.M. to 5:00 P.M.; October through May, 11:00 A.M. to 4:00 P.M. Closed Monday. Built in 1895. Displays depicting Lincoln County history, as well as period clothing and household antiques. Headquarters for Lincoln County Historical Society.

Mark O. Hatfield Marine Science Center, 2030 Marine Science Drive; (541) 867–0126. East of U.S. 101, on the south shore of the bay, at South Beach. Daily, 10:00 A.M. to 4:00 P.M. Outstanding museum and aquarium operated by Oregon State University. Many fine marine wildlife exhibits, ship models, aquariums, a hands-on tide pool, and book shop. Summer Seataqua program offers lectures, walks, tours, trips, workshops, and films. No admission fee. Classified a *must-see.*

Oregon Coast Aquarium, 2820 South East Ferry Slip Road; P.O. Box 2000; (541) 867–3474; www.aquarium.org. South of the bridge, east off U.S. 101, near Hatfield Marine Science Center. Daily, 9:00 A.M. to 6:00 P.M. in summer; 10:00 A.M. to 5:00 P.M. in winter. Since opening in 1992, this has become the premier man-made attraction on the Oregon coast. Aquariums, aviary, and outdoor tanks feature the fish, shellfish, seabirds, and sea mammals of the Pacific Northwest. Gift shop and restaurant on the premises. A *must-see*. Admission is $10.75 for adults, $9.50 for seniors, and $6.50 for children ages 4–13.

BEACHES, PARKS, TRAILS, AND WAYSIDES

The Newport area is blessed with an abundance of beaches with excellent access north and south off U.S. 101, in town off Elizabeth Street and Coast Street, and between Agate Beach and Newport off Ocean View Drive.

Agate Beach is in a small community by the same name, north of Newport and west of U.S. 101. The beach is a favorite of rock hounds who search the sands for agates, jasper, and petrified wood.

Farther north is **Beverly Beach,** with ample parking along the west side of U.S. 101. The beach is wide and windswept and is a favorite spot for flying kites. There's even a kite shop nearby. Also close by is a state park for picnics out of the wind.

Nye Beach is right in town, flanked on the west by the tumbling Pacific surf and on the east by one of Newport's older neighborhoods. This is also where most of the town's resort hotels stand.

South Beach State Park lies west of the highway about 2 miles south of town. Here are several miles of broad beach for hiking and beachcombing and two picnic areas—one near the beach and the other in a spot sheltered by trees and dunes.

Also in town, just north and west of the U.S. 101 bridge, is **Yaquina Bay State Park,** situated atop a bluff overlooking the north jetty and commanding a view of the bridge, bay, and ocean. In the park are many beautiful picnic sites and an old lighthouse.

The **Yaquina Bay Lighthouse,** which combines the keeper's quarters and light tower, is the oldest building in Newport. It was erected to serve as a harbor-entrance light, which first shone on November 3, 1871. Its life as a working lighthouse was short, because, as any Kansas landlubber could tell at first glance, the light was invisible to ships approaching from the north.

In 1974, the state restored the old lighthouse and furnished it with antiques on loan from the Oregon Historical Society. It is now on the National Register of Historic Places.

As any self-respecting deserted lighthouse ought to be, the Yaquina Bay Lighthouse has been haunted for most of its years, and yarns about its netherworld inhabitants abound. It is said to have guided ships through fog and unfriendly seas long after its lamp was snuffed.

Newport has another lighthouse that has been serving this stretch of coast since August of 1873, but even this stalwart sentinel, which seems to have been placed ideally on a westward promontory to serve as both a harbor and seacoast light, was built in the wrong place. It was originally planned for Otter Crest, several miles north, but the building materials were mistakenly landed on Yaquina Head, with no small amount of effort and danger to men and their vessels. When the mistake was discovered, nobody had any interest in reloading the materials, via the angry surf, and taking them north to their proper destination. Instead, the new structure became the **Yaquina Head Light,** rather than the Otter Crest Light.

The light is now the centerpiece of the one-hundred-acre **Yaquina Head Outstanding Natural Area,** managed by the Bureau of Land Management. To reach the area, turn west off U.S. 101 on Ocean Drive, just past the golf course.

WATER SPORTS AND ACTIVITIES

Yaquina Bay is an active center for waterborne recreation of every kind. Bay anglers catch perch, herring, and bottom fish from the jetties, shore, docks, and the public fishing pier. Crabbers, working from docks, piers, and boats, take tasty Dungeness crabs. Minus tides expose mudflats and bring out the clam diggers.

Offshore, salmon are popular but are often overshadowed by the plentiful and more reliable bottom species. Reefs and other offshore structures here are among the most productive fishing grounds along the coast. A charter fleet, headquartered at Yaquina Bay, plies these waters, with several trips a day when the weather is good.

Additionally, charter operations offer long trips to tuna grounds and halibut habitats well offshore, as well as shorter bay cruises and sight-seeing trips. Bay crabbing trips and whale-watching excursions are also popular.

Bayfront Charters, The Landing at Newport, 890 Southeast Bay Boulevard; (541) 265–7558 (twenty-four-hour phone) or (800) 828–8777. East of U.S. 101, on the north side of the bay. Four- and five-hour salmon trips, seven- and nine-hour combination trips, five-hour trips to inner reefs, eight-hour trips to "the rockpile," and twelve-hour trips to Heceta Banks for halibut. Bay crabbing and diving trips. Whale-watching and sight-seeing excursions. **Newport Marina,** 600 Southeast Bay Boulevard; (541) 867–3321. East of U.S. 101, on the south shore of the bay, at South Beach. Has 600 rental slips for vessels up to 58 feet long. RV spaces, cable TV, launch ramp, sling hoist, and boat-trailer parking. **Newport Marina Store & Charters,** 2122 Southeast Marine Science Drive; P.O. Box 716; South Beach 97366; (541) 867–4470 or (877) 867–4470. At the marina in South Beach. A well-stocked store offering bait, tackle, crabbing gear, boat rentals, groceries, lunches, and ice. Operates three boats for sportfishing and whale-watching trips. Bottom-fishing trips of five, six, eight, or ten hours—light tackle or conventional gear. Salmon trips of six or eight hours. Twelve-hour halibut or albacore trips. Custom trips. Two-hour whale-watching trips.

Newport Tradewinds, 653 Southwest Bay Boulevard; (541) 265–2101 or (800) 676–7819; www.newporttradewinds.com. In the Old Town bayfront district. Five-hour salmon and bottom-fishing trips, ten-hour combination trips. Eight-hour trips to "the rockpile," and twelve-hour trips to Heceta Banks for halibut and reef species. August to October, twelve-hour and thirty-three-hour trips for albacore tuna from 50 to 100 miles offshore. Bay crabbing. Whale-watching and scenic cruises.

Newport Water Sports, South Jetty Road; (541) 867–3742. West of U.S. 101, south side of the bay. Daily, 9:00 A.M. to 5:00 P.M. Complete scuba shop. Equipment sales and rental. Sailboards, surfboards, boogie boards. Fishing tackle and bait. Ice, beer, and pop.

GOLF

Agate Beach Golf Course, 4100 North Coast Highway; (541) 265–7331; www.agatebeachgolf.com. About 2.5 miles north of Newport city center, east side of U.S. 101. Nine-hole course with ocean view, pro shop, resident pro, driving range, and rental carts. Cafe on premises.

WEATHER AND TIDE INFORMATION

U.S. Coast Guard, Newport; recorded message, (541) 265–5511

TRAVEL INFORMATION

Greater Newport Chamber of Commerce, 555 Southwest Coast Highway; (541) 265–8801 or (800) COAST–44; www. discovernewport.com

EVENTS

February	Seafood & Wine Festival, (541) 265–8801
May	Loyalty Days & Seafair Festival, (541) 265–8801
June	Oregon Coast Gem & Mineral Show, (541) 265–8801
July	Lincoln County Fair & Rodeo, (541) 265–6237
December	Whale Watch Week, (541) 265–8801; www.whalespoken.org

DEPOE BAY
Population: 1,025

Location: *On U.S. 101, 12 miles north of Newport, 12 miles south of Lincoln City. Zip: 97341.*

Depoe Bay is a tiny town with a tiny harbor. A 50-foot-wide channel cuts 300 feet through rocky shoreline to connect the Pacific with a harbor that's only 750 feet long, 390 feet wide, and 8 feet deep at mean low tide. Nevertheless, more than one hundred commercial and sport boats are moored here all year, and another 150 crowd in during the summer. The attraction, of course, is the proximity of the ocean—from dock to sea in two minutes. Depoe Bay, often referred to as the "whale watching capitol of Oregon," offers some of the most inspiring ocean vistas along the coast.

Sharp-eyed film buffs will recognize the harbor, which was featured in the movie *One Flew Over the Cuckoo's Nest,* based on the novel by Oregon author Ken Kesey. This is where Randle McMurphy (Jack Nicholson) took his fellow escapees aboard a charter boat and headed out for a day of salmon fishing.

U.S. 101 is close to the ocean at Depoe Bay, where storm-tossed breakers wet the pavement and promenade and shoot misty geysers 60 feet into the air through spouting horns. Two such natural fountains exist in the volcanic rubble next to the seawall in downtown Depoe Bay.

LODGING

Channel House Bed & Breakfast Inn, 35 Ellingson Street; P.O. Box 56; (541) 765–2140 or (800) 447–2140; www.channel house.com. West side of U.S. 101, along the south bank of the harbor channel, next to the bridge. Double, queen, and king beds in 11 units, cable TV and Showtime. Kitchen units available. Spectacular ocean and channel view. Walk to harbor and shops. Rates include full breakfast for two. Moderate to expensive.

Surfrider Oceanfront Resort, 3115 Northwest Highway 101; P.O. Box 219; (541) 764–2311 or (800) 662–2378; www.surf riderresort.com. West side of U.S. 101, just north of Depoe Bay, at the mouth of Fogarty Creek. Queen and king beds in 40 units, cable TV, Showtime, and refrigerators. Kitchen units available. Some rooms have in-room whirlpools. Some have fireplaces. Also 3-bedroom house available, 1½ baths, sleeps 12. Beach access. Oceanfront balconies and patios. Excellent restaurant on premises is a local favorite. Moderate.

FOOD AND BEVERAGES

Sea Hag Food & Grog, 58 East Highway 101; P.O. Box 278; (541) 765–2734. East side of U.S. 101, north of the bridge, downtown. Breakfast, lunch, and dinner daily. Breakfast fare includes omelettes, egg dishes, and homemade biscuits and gravy. Sandwiches, chowder, and salad bar are luncheon specialties. Fresh seafood dominates the dinner menu. Friday seafood buffet includes salmon, halibut, lingcod, steamer clams, crab, shrimp—all you can eat. Cocktails, beer, and wine. Moderate.

Surfrider Restaurant, 3115 Northwest Highway 101; P.O. Box 219; (541) 764–2311 or (800) 662–2378. West side of U.S. 101, just north of Depoe Bay, at Surfrider Resort. Breakfast, lunch, and dinner daily. Excellent breakfast menu includes various egg dishes, omelettes, hotcakes, fruit waffles, and rollups. Large selection of traditional sandwiches, soups, seafoods, and salads fill out the lunch menu. Dinners include a variety of fish and shellfish, beef, chicken, ham, and liver. Wednesday buffet from 5:00 to 10:00 P.M. features prime rib or seafood plate at a bargain price. Cocktails, beer, and wine. Moderate.

SHOPPING AND BROWSING

Downtown Depoe Bay offers browsers, buyers, and sightseers a compact collection of shops, galleries, cafes, and restaurants set against a spectacular seascape—all lying along U.S. 101 for several blocks north and south of the town's historic bridge. Park next to the seawall or across the highway, and take a walking tour.

The Harbor Gallery, 211 Southwest Highway 101; P.O. Box 108; (541) 765–3113; www.harborgallery.com. Just south of the bridge, on the west side of the highway. Daily, 10:00 A.M. to 5:00 P.M.; summer till 6:00 P.M. Gifts, collectibles, historic photographs, prints, and fine art displayed on three floors. Good selection of works with coastal and nautical themes.

The Lookout Observatory and Gift Shop, P.O. Box 248; (541) 765–2270. West of U.S. 101, on Otter Crest Loop, between Depoe Bay and Newport. Daily, 9:00 A.M. to 5:00 P.M. Many products made of Oregon myrtlewood and cedar, nautical items, shells, coral, prints, and jewelry. Situated atop Cape Foulweather, 500 feet above the ocean. Ample parking provided by the state. Excellent lookout area.

Something Blue, 104 Northeast Highway 101; P.O. Box 158, (541) 765–4323. East side of the highway, next to Fuddy Duddy Fudge. Daily, 10:00 A.M. to 5:00 P.M. A country-style variety shop, featuring clothing, stuffed animals, cookware, baskets, wood products, art prints, candy, cookbooks, and more.

BEACHES, PARKS, TRAILS, AND WAYSIDES

Boiler Bay State Park (800–551–6949), 1 mile north of Depoe Bay, overlooks a picturesque cove where a small disabled freighter drifted ashore on May 18, 1910. The steam schooner *J. Marhoffer* caught fire while steaming northward above Yaquina Head. Officers and crew were forced to abandon ship, and the burning vessel eventually went aground. Her boiler and shaft broke loose, and the rest of the ship eventually succumbed to the fire and ravages of nature. But the boiler remains, even today, visible at low tide. Hence the name, Boiler Bay.

Two miles north of town is **Fogarty Creek State Park** (800–551–6949), which is the site of an annual Indian-style salmon bake. This is a beautiful picnic spot with a creek to wade and explore, hiking trails, and a small but attractive beach.

South of Depoe Bay, **Otter Crest Loop** (800–551–6949), takes travelers along a stretch of forested coastline with dizzying cliffs and promontories offering great ocean views. **Otter Crest State Park** (800–551–6949) is situated atop Cape Foulweather, 500 feet above the surf. Here, clear weather offers views north, south, and seaward for miles. This is a good spot for watching whales.

OREGON

Otter Crest, south of Depoe Bay

WATER SPORTS AND ACTIVITIES

Water recreation in the Depoe Bay area amounts mainly to ocean fishing and sight-seeing, both of which are year-round activities, weather permitting. Those who tow boats to the coast will find a launch ramp at the harbor, east of U.S. 101. For others, there's a fleet of charter boats specializing in salmon angling and fishing the nearby reefs for bottom species. They also offer whale-watching and sight-seeing excursions.

Dockside Charters, P.O. Box 1308; (541) 765–2545 or (800) 733–8915. East side of the bay, next to the Coast Guard station. Daily five-hour trips for salmon and bottom fish. Whale-watching and sight-seeing trips from less than an hour to four hours.

Tradewinds, P.O. Box 123; (541) 765–2345 or (800) 445–8730. Depoe Bay harbor, east side of U.S. 101, north end of the bridge. Charter service with twelve-vessel fleet. Five-hour salmon trips leave three times a day, bottom-fish trips twice daily. Long-distance trips and all-day tuna trips in season. One-hour and two-hour whale-watching trips. Sight-seeing trips of up to an hour leave every hour.

TRAVEL INFORMATION

Depoe Bay Chamber of Commerce, 70 Northeast Highway 101; P.O. Box 21; (541) 765–2889 or (877) 485–8348; www.depoebaychamber.org

EVENTS

April	Classic Wooden Boat Show, (541) 765–2889
May	Fleet of Flowers Memorial Service, (541) 765–2345
July	Boiler Bay Fireworks, (541) 765–2889
September	Indian-style Salmon Bake, (541) 765–2889

LINCOLN CITY
Population: 6,680

Location: *On U.S. 101, 42 miles south of Tillamook, 24 miles north of Newport, and 88 miles southwest of Portland. Zip: 97367.*

On December 8, 1964, the cities of Oceanlake, Delake, and Taft and the unincorporated communities of Cutler City and Nelscott combined to form Lincoln City. Evidence of the five districts still exists in the names of businesses, in listings on maps, and in the diversity of architectural and urban planning, or the lack of planning—business, industrial, and residential areas are strung together along U.S. 101, interspersed with wooded areas and vacant land. An art gallery might be neighbors with a construction company; a nice restaurant might be adjacent to a lumberyard. Overlook these minor shortcomings and enjoy a visit to Lincoln City.

The townspeople boast of having more oceanfront rooms available than any other city on the Oregon coast. The city also has many fine restaurants, a variety of interesting shops, and some top-notch galleries and antique shops, not to mention the beaches, parks, opportunities for indoor and outdoor recreation, and a couple of interesting oddities.

For example, the golf course just north of town straddles the forty-fifth parallel, the midway point between the equator and the North Pole.

One of the newest and most impressive additions to the Lincoln City landscape is the Chinook Winds Casino, located just west of U.S. 101, at the north end of town. (See under Food and Beverages and Casino.)

LODGING

'D' Sands Condominium Motel, 171 Southwest Highway 101; (541) 994–5244 or (800) 527–3925. West side of U.S. 101 in the Delake district, next to D River Wayside. Has 63 condominium units with full kitchens, balconies, and cable TV, some with fireplaces. Heated indoor pool and whirlpool. On the beach. Walk to galleries, shops, and restaurants. Moderate to expensive.

Ocean Terrace Condominium Motel, 4229 Southwest Beach; (541) 996–3623 or (800) 648–2119. West of U.S. 101 in the Taft district. Has 36 rentable units with kitchens, queen and king beds, cable TV, and Showtime. Some with electric fireplaces. Beach access—40 steps to the sand. Heated indoor pool, sauna, ocean view. Moderate to expensive.

Salishan Lodge, Gleneden Beach 97388; (541) 764–3600 or (800) 452–2300. East side of U.S. 101, 3 miles south of Lincoln City. Award-winning resort features 150 luxurious rooms with king beds, cable TV, balconies, fireplaces, and view of golf course, forest, or Siletz Bay. Heated indoor pool, sauna, whirlpool, golf course, indoor and outdoor tennis courts, miles of hiking trails, secluded beach, restaurants, gift shop, art gallery, library, beauty salon, fitness center, children's game room and playground, and covered bridges and walkways to main lodge. Expensive.

Sea Gypsy, 145 Northwest Inlet; (541) 994–5266; Oregon, (800) 452–6929; Washington, (800) 341–2142. West 1 block off U.S. 101, north bank of D River, Delake district. Queen and king beds in 159 studio, 1-bedroom, and 2-bedroom condo units with fully equipped kitchens, cable TV, and Showtime. Heated indoor pool and sauna. Ocean view. On the beach. Moderate.

Shilo Inn, 1501 Northwest 40th Street; (541) 994–3655 or (800) 222–2244. West off U.S. 101 at the north end of town, just before Lighthouse Square shopping center. Adjacent to and walking distance from Chinook Winds Casino. Queen and king beds in 248 rooms and suites with cable TV, refrigerators, microwave ovens, and room service—many with ocean view. A recent addition has 61 minisuites with fireplaces; all other rooms are newly remodeled. Heated indoor pool, sauna, whirlpool, gift shop, game room, and laundry. Ocean-view restaurant and cocktail lounge with evening entertainment. Easy beach access. Moderate to expensive.

Surftides Beach Resort, 2945 Northwest Jetty Avenue; P.O. Box 406A; (541) 994–2191; Oregon or Washington, (800) 452–2159. West of U.S. 101 in the Oceanlake district. Has

91 rooms and suites with queen and king beds, cable TV, and balconies, most with ocean view. Heated indoor pool, sauna, whirlpool, tennis courts, gift shop, and gallery. Moderate.

CAMPGROUNDS AND RV PARKS

KOA Kampground, 5298 Northeast Park Lane; Otis 97368; (541) 994–2961 or (800) 562–2791. On East Devils Lake Road, 1.3 miles east of U.S. 101, north of Devils Lake and Lincoln City. Full hookups, cable TV, showers, firewood, game and recreation room, horseshoes. Propane available. Near lake, ocean, and beaches. Moderate.

West Devils Lake State Park, 1452 Northeast Sixth Drive; (541) 994–2002 or (800) 452–5687. One mile east of U.S. 101. Has 32 full-hookup and 68 tent sites. Showers, tank dump, and firewood. On Devils Lake with boat-launch facilities. Short drive or walk to ocean beach, shops, and restaurants. Reservations accepted. Moderate.

FOOD AND BEVERAGES

Bay House Restaurant, 5911 Southwest Highway 101; P.O. Box 1010; (541) 996–3222. West side of U.S. 101, south end of town, in the Cutler City district. Dinner daily. Carefully prepared dinners include rack of lamb, Tuscan brochettes, steak and seafood combo, steamed shellfish, Australian rock lobster tail, and prawns. Cocktails, beer, and wine. Large wine list. Good view of Siletz Bay. Moderate.

Chinook Winds Casino, 1777 Northwest 44th Street; (541) 996–5825 or (888) 244–6665. West off U.S. 101 at the north end of town. Two superb restaurants. One offers abundant Las Vegas–style breakfast, lunch, and dinner buffets—all you can eat—with something to please every appetite. The Siletz Dining Room features Northwest seafood specialties—such as planked chinook salmon, charbroiled halibut, Dungeness crab, and Oregon oysters—as well as generous cuts of prime rib, pasta dishes, and more, all with a sweeping view of the Pacific Ocean. Wine list and full bar. Delicious food at modest prices. Inexpensive to moderate. (See also under Casino.)

The Dining Room, Salishan Lodge; Gleneden Beach 97388; (541) 764–3635. East side of U.S. 101, 3 miles south of Lincoln City. Dinner daily. Appetizers such as lobster bisque with cognac, scallops Normandy, Oregon shrimp cocktail, and French mushroom salad. Dinners include fresh local seafoods, beef, pork, and rack of Oregon lamb—a Salishan specialty. Largest wine list on the West Coast, with more than 1,500 offerings, including foreign, domestic, and Oregon wines. The cellar is stocked with more than 21,000 bottles. Expensive.

Dory Cove, 5819 Logan Road; (541) 994–5180. West 0.7 mile off U.S. 101 at the north end of town. Turn at Lighthouse Square. Lunch and dinner daily. Great fish and chips, chowder, burgers, grilled fillets, and steaks. Homemade pies. Beer and wine. Casual dining in a beautiful oceanfront setting. Moderate.

Kyllo's Seafood Grill, 1110 Northwest First Court; (541) 994–3179. West side of U.S. 101, on the north bank of the D River. Breakfast, lunch, and dinner daily. Large breakfast menu includes all traditional fare and many more adventuresome dishes, including blueberry pancakes, malted waffles with strawberries, huevos rancheros, crab eggs Benedict, and smoked salmon and red onion omelettes. Burgers and specialty sandwiches, chowder, and a great variety of salads. Salmon, halibut, calamari, crab cakes, Dungeness crab legs, Manilla clams, lobster, and scallops, among other seafood offerings. Chicken, barbecued ribs, steak, and prime rib. Seafood and chicken pasta dishes. Large dessert menu. Full bar. Moderate.

McMenamin's Lighthouse Brew Pub, 4157 North Highway 101; Suite 117; (541) 994–7238. At Lighthouse Square, west side of U.S. 101, north end of town. Daily, 11:00 A.M. to 11:00 P.M. Brewery and pub—a great spot for anyone who enjoys beers, ales, and stouts. Has twenty-five brews on tap, including a half dozen made on the premises. Hot deli-style sandwiches, pizza bread, burgers, soups, or salads. Food and brews to go. Moderate.

Shilo Restaurant & Lounge, 1501 Northwest 40th Street; (541) 994–5255. West off U.S. 101 at the north end of town. Breakfast, lunch, and dinner daily. Extensive menu includes hearty breakfasts of hotcakes, waffles, crepes, omelettes, croissant Benedict, New York steak and eggs, and various combinations. Lunch features deli-style and grilled sandwiches, large salads, pastas, seafood, and chicken. Appetizer and snack list includes smoked seafood platter, seafood sampler cocktail, oyster shooters, and more. Dinner features a large selection of salads and pasta dishes, beef, lamb, chicken, and fresh seafood: veal au lemon with pinenuts, scallops with chicken and tarragon, blackened sturgeon, Szechuan bay shrimp sauté, or orange roughy hazelnut. Full bar and wine list. Superb ocean view in lounge and dining restaurant. Moderate.

SHOPPING AND BROWSING

If you want to shop till you drop, Lincoln City is the place to go. Anchored at each end by one of the finest galleries on the coast—the long-established Ryan Gallery to the north and the newer Freed Gallery to the south—the rest of the city has more shops and galleries than any other community on the Oregon coast.

Each district has its own eclectic collection of gift, specialty, and antique shops, and here you'll also find a factory-outlet mall. Before you head out with your credit cards and comfortable walking shoes, you'll want to stop by the Chamber of Commerce Visitor Center to get brochures and maps that will lead you to the abundant shopping and browsing opportunities.

Factory Stores at Lincoln City, (541) 996–5000 or (888) 746–7333. On the west side of U.S. 101, in the heart of the city. Monday through Saturday, 9:30 A.M. to 8:00 P.M.; Sunday and daily in January and February, 9:30 A.M. to 6:00 P.M. Closed Thanksgiving and Christmas Day. Dozens of factory-outlet and specialty stores and plenty of free parking.

Freed Gallery, 6119 Southwest Highway 101; (541) 994–5600. On the west side of U.S. 101, at the south end of town. Daily, 10:00 A.M. to 6:00 P.M. A big, bright, and breezy gallery, displaying functional and decorative works of contemporary artists and artisans. Exquisite wood furniture and accessories, paintings, fine-art photography, fiber art, stoneware, porcelain, and raku.

Mossy Creek Pottery, 483 Immonen Road; P.O. Box 368; Gleneden Beach 97388; (541) 996–2415. A half mile east of U.S. 101 on Immonen Road, 3 miles south of Lincoln City, just north of the traffic light in Gleneden Beach. Monday through Saturday, 9:00 A.M. to 5:00 P.M.; Sunday, 10:00 A.M. to 5:00 P.M. Charming gallery and studio in an idyllic setting. The fine works of more than thirty Oregon potters tastefully displayed and available in all price ranges.

Ryan Gallery, 4270 North Highway 101; (541) 994–5391. East side of the highway, north end of town. Daily, 10:00 A.M. to 5:00 P.M. Spacious and pleasant gallery with 3,000 square feet of exhibit area on two levels. Carvings, metal sculptures, batiks, oils, and watercolors. Good selection of traditional and contemporary arts and crafts.

Winter storm near Roads End State Wayside

Snug Harbor Antiques, 5030 Southeast Highway 101; (541) 996–4021. East side of the highway, in the Taft district. Summer: Tuesday through Thursday, 10:00 A.M. to 4:00 P.M. Winter: Thursday through Sunday, 10:00 A.M. to 4:00 P.M. Top-quality antique furniture, appliances, cookware, and collectibles. An interesting shop.

CASINO

Chinook Winds Casino, 1777 Northwest 44th Street; (541) 996–5825 or (888) 244–6665. West off U.S. 101 at the north end of town. Open twenty-four hours a day. Large casino and convention center, operated by the Confederated Tribes of Siletz Indians. Slot machines, video poker, blackjack tables, poker tables, keno, bingo, and off-track betting. Two restaurants, snack bar, and full-service lounge. Concerts-by-the-Sea series brings big-name acts to Oregon's central coast. (See also under Food and Beverages.)

BEACHES, PARKS, TRAILS, AND WAYSIDES

More than 7 miles of beaches extend northward from Siletz (suh-*lets*) Bay to Roads End, north of Lincoln City. This great expanse of beach is popular for hiking, kite flying, and other oceanfront activities and is easily accessible for the entire length of the city. Improved public access areas are at the west end of Southwest 11th, 33rd, and 51st Streets and Northwest 15th, 21st, 26th, 35th, and 39th Streets.

The **D River State Wayside** is a popular spot in downtown Lincoln City. It's located on the west side of U.S. 101, on the south bank of the river. The wayside has ample parking, rest rooms, and easy beach access.

Roads End State Wayside is 1 mile north of Lincoln City and offers access to several miles of beach. Turn west off U.S. 101 on Northwest Logan Road at Lighthouse Square.

East Devils Lake State Park lies 2 miles east of U.S. 101 on East Devils Lake Road. It offers picnic sites, rest rooms, a boat ramp, fishing, and swimming.

WATER SPORTS AND ACTIVITIES

Water recreation in the Lincoln City area focuses on Siletz Bay and Siletz River in the south, Salmon River and its estuary in the north, and Devils Lake in and east of town.

Siletz Bay offers good crabbing from boats or docks at high tides and clam digging on the mudflats on minus tides. A variety of fishing opportunities exists all year on the 5-mile-long bay. Shore access is good in the Taft area, and boat fishermen work the entire bay. The bar is dangerous, however, so don't attempt to cross it.

For access to the river, drive south on U.S. 101 to Kernville, and turn east on State Route 229, which follows the river's course for some miles. The lower portion of the river is navigable by motorboats, the upper reaches by drift boat.

From early spring through summer, bay angling is fair to good for seaperch and surfperch and several species of bottom fish. A few early salmon venture into the bay in July and are taken near the Siletz Jaws, where Salishan Spit nearly touches the north shore at Taft.

In August, jack salmon move into the bay; they are taken well into September in the bay and river. September is also the month when the big chinook, sometimes reaching forty pounds or more, arrive and move upriver.

Salmon fishing holds up on the river well into the fall. As their numbers begin to dwindle, the first runs of winter steelhead begin showing.

North of Lincoln City, the diminutive Salmon River draws

crowds of anglers to its banks for what is sometimes outstanding salmon and steelhead fishing. The river, which heads in the Coast Range, is only about 24 miles long, and where U.S. 101 crosses it, it's only about a half-cast wide. Bank access on the river is good, and boat anglers use the lower river and estuary. Chinook salmon provide action from September well into October, and the steelhead follow in December and offer good sport until March.

The U.S. 101 bridge crosses the Salmon River north of Lincoln City just past the State Route 18 junction. About 0.6 mile beyond, Three Rocks Road exits to the west and leads about 3 miles to Knight Park on the north shore of the estuary, where there are picnic facilities and a public boat ramp.

Devils Lake is more than 2 miles long and covers about 640 acres. It's a shallow lake, providing habitat mainly for warm-water species, although stocked trout provide a fair fishery. Bullhead fishing is good during the summer, especially at night. Crappie and bluegill are also present in good numbers. Largemouth-bass fishing is sometimes good.

Boating, canoeing, waterskiing, and sailing are popular pastimes on the lake, and the shallow waters warm up enough in the summer for comfortable swimming.

Blue Heron Landing, 4006 West Devils Lake Road; (541) 994–4708; www.sweetwaterinn.biz. East just off U.S. 101, north of town. Full-service marina with moorage space for rent, fuel, ice, soft drinks, snacks, bait, tackle, fishing licenses, launch ramp, and rentals.

GOLF

Lakeside Golf and Fitness Club, 3245 Northeast 50th Street; (541) 994–8442. West of U.S. 101, north of town. An 18-hole golf course, racquet club, and fitness center. Open all year. Resident pro. Rental clubs and carts. Well-lighted indoor tennis courts, racquetball courts, exercise and weight room, whirlpool, sauna, and tanning beds.

Salishan Lodge Golf Links & Pro Shop, Gleneden Beach 97388; (541) 764–3632 or (800) 452–2300. West side of U.S. 101, just south of the traffic light, 3 miles south of Lincoln City. Par 72, 18-hole links, driving range, putting green, full-service pro shop, and resident pro.

RENTALS

Blue Heron Landing, 4006 West Devils Lake Road; (541) 994–4708; www.sweetwaterinn.biz. East just off U.S. 101, north of town. For fun on land or water, rent mountain bikes, canoes, kayaks, paddleboats, Sea-Doo and WaveRunner personal watercraft, and 12- to 15-foot aluminum boats with six- or eight-horsepower outboards. Also, pontoon boat available for parties on the water.

TRAVEL INFORMATION

Lincoln City Visitor and Convention Bureau, 801 Southwest Highway 101, Suite 1; (541) 994–8378 or (800) 452–2151; www.lcchamber.com; e-mail: lcchamber@netbridge.net

EVENTS

February	Antique Week, (541) 994–8378
May	Spring Kite Festival, (541) 994–8378
July	Lincoln County Fair & Rodeo, (541) 994–8378

NESKOWIN
Population: 180

Location: *On U.S. 101, 12 miles north of Lincoln City, 30 miles south of Tillamook. Zip: 97149.*

If it weren't for the modern highway leading to Neskowin (ness-*cow*-in), travelers might believe they had taken a trip in a time machine. In many ways, the tiny community exists in a time warp. It's a pastoral place, reminiscent of simpler days when folks weren't in such a rush.

There's not much to this little village: a state wayside, a grocery store, small galleries, a couple of restaurants, and adequate accommodations—even for conventions. A few creeks tumble down from nearby hills to keep things green in summer, wet in winter. Narrow streets, better suited to foot traffic and horses than to automobiles and recreational vehicles, wind through a tree-shaded residential area.

With two golf courses, Neskowin has more space given to fairways, roughs, and greens than to anything else. It's possible to play the first nine holes in the rolling hills east of the highway, then the next nine in the flat but deceptively challenging creek bottoms west of the highway. Golf makes Neskowin a good place to visit, and it's equally accommodating as a peaceful, quiet place to relax.

LODGING

Neskowin Resort, 48990 Highway 101 South; P.O. Box 447; (503) 392–3191; www.neskowinvacationrentals.com. West side of the highway, in Neskowin. Queen and king beds in 55 units with cable TV. Rooms, studios, and suites. Kitchens, private decks,

One of two golf courses in Neskowin

ocean view, recreation room, and play area. Cribs and rollaways available. Restaurant and lounge on premises. Short walk to the beach. Moderate.

Proposal Rock Inn, P.O. Box 790; (503) 392–3115. West side of U.S. 101, next to Neskowin Resort. Twin and queen beds, rollaways, and sleeper couches in 36 units with cable TV. Rooms and studios sleep 2 to 4. Suites sleep up to 8. Studios and suites have full kitchens and fireplaces. Some units with ocean view. Beach access. Inexpensive to moderate.

FOOD AND BEVERAGES

The Hawk Creek Cafe, 4505 Salem Avenue; (503) 392–3838. West of U.S. 101, near the head of the beach trail. Breakfast, lunch, and dinner daily. A little cafe with big appeal and great food. Among the breakfast offerings are three-egg omelettes, including a hot and spicy one stuffed with chili and cheese; biscuits and sausage gravy with poached eggs; imaginative hash brown dishes; and mystery hash "at the mercy of the kitchen." A large assortment of burgers, pizzas, subs, and deli-style sandwiches top the lunch menu. For dinner are burgers, shrimp, halibut steak, filet mignon, and New York steak. Wine and a good assortment of domestic and imported beers and Northwest microbrews. Moderate.

GOLF

Hawk Creek Golf Course, 48480 South Highway 101; (503) 392–4120. East side of the highway, in a beautiful valley with trees and a creek. Nine holes, 2,623 yards. Rental carts and clubs. Open all year.

Neskowin Beach Golf Course, One Hawk Avenue; P.O. Box 839; (503) 392–3377. West of U.S. 101. Nine holes, 3,012 yards. Flat, easy walking. Trees and two creeks. Excellent greens. Rental carts and clubs, full pro shop, resident pro, snacks, beer, and wine. Open April 15 to November 1.

PACIFIC CITY
Population: 1,500

Location: *2.5 miles west of U.S. 101 on Three Capes Loop, just south of Cape Kiwanda, 15 miles north of Lincoln City. Zip: 97135.*

A small retirement and vacation community at the south end of scenic Three Capes Loop, Pacific City is scattered about a coastal plain that lies beneath Cape Kiwanda along a photogenic bit of beach extending south to Nestucca (ness-*tuck*-uh) Bay. Just offshore stands the larger of two Oregon coast formations called Haystack Rock; this one is 327 feet tall.

This is an area popular with hang-glider and dune-buggy enthusiasts. The town's main claim to fame, however, is the Pacific dory fleet. Commercial fishermen and sport anglers launch their craft from the beach into the surf, as fishermen have for more than seventy years.

Dory fishing developed here as a response to the closing of the Nestucca River system to gillnetting in the 1920s. Good fishing grounds lie offshore, but because of the treacherous bar conditions on the bay, the only way to reach them is by flat-bottom dories that can be launched in the surf.

The fleet is said to be about one hundred strong, though far fewer boats are launched on any given day. Nevertheless, during the summer, dozens of four-wheel-drive boat-hauling rigs cross the soft sands to the firm beach each morning and are parked along the beach until the dories return. It's quite a show to watch and photograph. It is possible to find a charter operator willing to take individuals out for the ride and the fishing.

LODGING

The Inn at Cape Kiwanda, 33105 Cape Kiwanda Drive; (503) 965–7001 or (888) 965–7001; www.innatcapekiwanda.com. On the ocean, opposite Haystack Rock. Minibars, VCRs, cable TV, coffeemakers, and fireplaces in 35 rooms and suites, all of which have ocean-view balconies. Rooms with ocean-view Jacuzzis available. Laundry facilities and several small shops on premises. Across the street from Pelican Pub and Brewery. Short walk to beach and dory launch. Live piano music and wine tastings in lobby. Brewery tours, golf packages, and casino specials offered. Moderate to expensive.

The Inn at Pacific City, 35215 Brooten Road; (503) 965–6366 or (888) 722–2489; www.innatpacificcity.com. In town, 2 blocks south of the four-way stop, 5 blocks from the beach. Queen beds, remote cable TV, refrigerators, and microwave ovens in 16 rooms and kitchenettes—all in a courtyard setting. Ample parking for boats and recreational vehicles. Inexpensive to moderate.

Sandlake Country Inn, 8505 Galloway Road; Cloverdale 97112; (503) 965–6745 or (877) SANDLAKE; www.sand lakecountryinn.com. A half mile west of the Loop Highway at Sandlake Grocery, 8.5 miles north of Pacific City. Queen beds in 4 distinctly different units, each with TV, VCR, vintage movies, private bath, whirlpool tub, and fireplace. Full breakfast served *en suite*. The inn is situated on well-kept grounds in a quiet, rural area. Peace and quiet are top priorities here. The house was built in 1894 and has designer decor. Moderate to expensive.

CAMPGROUNDS AND RV PARKS

Cape Kiwanda RV Park, 33315 Cape Kiwanda Drive; P.O. Box 129; (503) 965–6230; www.capekiwandarvpark.com. On the east side of the highway, across from the dory-launch area. Has 130 sites with pull-throughs available. Full hookups, showers, laundry, and firewood. Moderate.

Sandlake Recreation Area, 7000 Galloway Road; Cloverdale 97112; (503) 965–6097. About 2.25 miles west of Three Capes Loop at Sandlake Grocery, 8.5 miles north of Pacific City. A U.S. Forest Service facility with more than 240 campsites in three campgrounds. Hiking trails, beach access, dunes access, rest rooms, and water. Popular with ATV and ORV enthusiasts. Inexpensive.

Dories in the surf near Haystack Rock

Whalen Island County Park. Located about 2.5 miles south of Sandlake Grocery and 6 miles north of Pacific City, just west of Three Capes Loop. Situated on a tiny island with 26 sites, picnic tables, fire rings, water, and rest rooms. Inexpensive.

FOOD AND BEVERAGES

Pelican Pub & Brewery, 33180 Cape Kiwanda Drive; (503) 965–7007; www.pelicanbrewery.com. At the dory-launch beach. Lunch and dinner daily. Snacks and appetizers include soft pretzels with pub mustard, bread sticks with butter and garlic, clam strips, and Cajun shrimp. Soups, chili, clam chowder, salads, fish and chips, deli-style sandwiches, burgers, and pizza. Kiawanda Cream Ale, Heiferweizan, MacPelican Scottish Ale, Doryman's Dark Ale, and Tsunami Stout on tap, among others. Great view of the ocean, Haystack Rock, and Cape Kiwanda. Moderate.

Riverhouse Restaurant, 34450 Brooten Road; (503) 965–6722; www.riverhousefoods.com. A quarter mile north of the stoplight on the west side of the road. Lunch and dinner daily; brunch Sunday; closed Monday and Tuesday in winter. On the Nestucca River. A local favorite. Small—only eleven tables—but an ambitious menu. Brunch: quiche, huevos rancheros, omelettes, pancakes, and crepes filled with ham and asparagus or shrimp and eggs and topped with creamy cheese sauce. Homemade soup and chowder daily; large open-face sandwiches served with choice of three salads. Also lunch-size salads and burgers. Dinners include coquilles St. Jacques, fillet of fish amandine, steamer clams, and salmon. Cocktails, beer, and wine. Live entertainment on Saturday nights. Moderate.

WATER SPORTS AND ACTIVITIES

This is one of the most productive fishing areas on the coast. In addition to the salmon and bottom-fish angling offshore, out to 7 miles and reached by surf dory, Nestucca Bay, the Nestucca River, and Little Nestucca River also are top producers.

On the bay, spring chinook angling begins in May and lasts into July. Fall chinook angling is in September and October, and summer steelhead from spring to early fall. Spring through summer is the time for surfperch, seaperch, flounder, and other saltwater species. Crabbing is good in the deeper parts of the bay. Clam digging on the flats and in the upper reaches of the bay is good on minus tides.

The Nestucca River is among the best spring-chinook streams on the coast, with good action from May through July. Fall chinook run from late August through September, and some big fish are caught each year in good numbers. Summer steelhead are in the river from midspring through the summer, and winter steelhead from mid-November to mid-February.

On the Little Nestucca fall chinook fishing starts in October, and there's excellent steelhead fishing through the winter. Bank access is good along the lower river.

Haystack Fishing Club, Inc., 34280 Brooten Road; P.O. Box 935; (503) 965–7555 or (888) 965–7555. On Cape Kiwanda Drive, at the Inn at Cape Kiwanda. Charter dory trips for fishing, crabbing, whale watching, and sight-seeing.

Nestucca Country, 34650 Brooten Road; P.O. Box 729; (503) 965–6410. Located 0.3 mile north of the stoplight, on the Nestucca River. A full-service tackle shop and marina. Bait, licenses, and tags. Good source of information on local fishing, crabbing, and clam digging. Check here for information on sport dory trips on the ocean. Weigh station for trophy catches. Rents 12-foot aluminum boats (no motors).

TRAVEL INFORMATION

Pacific City Chamber of Commerce, P.O. Box 331; (503) 965–6161 or (888) 549–2632; www.pacificcity.net

EVENTS

June	Blessing of the Dory Fleet, (503) 965–6352
July	Fireworks and Fish Fry at Cape Kiwanda, (503) 965–6161
	Dory Days Festival, (503) 965–6161

OCEANSIDE
Population: 250

NETARTS
Population: 200

Location: *Oceanside is about 10 miles west of Tillamook and U.S. 101 on the Three Capes Loop. Zip: 97134. Netarts is about 2 miles south of Oceanside and 18 miles north of Pacific City. Zip: 97143.*

Oceanside clings like lichen to the steep slope of a rocky headland overlooking a beach as broad as a boulevard. Three Arch Rocks National Wildlife Refuge stands offshore as a haven for sea lions, seals, and birds by the thousands.

South of Oceanside is the tiny community of Netarts and a bay by the same name. Netarts Bay is an elongated, shallow body of water, extending about 7 miles south to north. It is bounded on the east by Three Capes Loop and on the west by a long, club-shaped stretch of sand known as Netarts Spit.

LODGING

House on the Hill, 1816 Maxwell Mountain Road; Oceanside; (503) 842–6030 or (866) CLIFFTOP; www.houseon thehillmotel.com. On a promontory overlooking the Pacific and Three Arch Rocks. Queen beds in 16 units with cable TV. Some kitchen units available. Moderate.

Terimore Lodging by the Sea, 5105 Crab Avenue; P.O. Box 102; Netarts; (503) 842–4623 or (800) 635–1821. In town, on the bay. Queen beds in 25 units with cable TV, HBO, kitchens, and some fireplaces. Laundry facilities. Cottages also available—1 or 2 bedrooms with kitchens. Near all beach and bay activities. Inexpensive to moderate.

Oceanside and Three Arch Rocks National Wildlife Refuge

CAMPGROUNDS AND RV PARKS

Bay Shore RV Park and Marina, 2260 Bilyeu Avenue; P.O. Box 218; Netarts; (503) 842–7774. On the east side of Three Capes Loop, overlooking Netarts Bay. A clean, well-maintained park with 53 full-hookup sites. Showers, laundry, boat rentals, launch ramp. Moderate.

Cape Lookout State Park, 13000 Whiskey Creek Road West; Tillamook 97141; (503) 842–4981. West of Three Capes Loop, 12 miles southwest of Tillamook. Has 54 full-hookup RV sites, 185 tent sites, and 10 yurts. Showers, tank dump, firewood. Some facilities for handicapped. Reservations accepted. Moderate.

FOOD AND BEVERAGES

Roseanna's Oceanside Cafe, 1490 Pacific Northwest; Oceanside; (503) 842–7351. On the west side of the highway, in town. Lunch and dinner daily. Breakfast served only on weekends in winter. A small cafe with a large menu, good food, and a great view. Specialties are fresh seafoods, homemade chowder, and homemade desserts and pastries. Tillamook dairy products. Weekend entertainment. This is an area favorite. Moderate.

BEACHES, PARKS, TRAILS, AND WAYSIDES

Cape Meares State Park lies 3 miles north of Oceanside and has hiking trails, beaches, and superb viewpoints. Here, too, is the famous Octopus Tree, so named because of its unusual shape. Its splayed branches, creating a 10-foot-wide cradle at the base, are said to have been shaped by Indians when the tree was young, perhaps 2,000 years ago. The purpose, according to legend, was to create a burial tree for a tribal chief and his canoe.

Cape Meares Light, also in the park, was completed in 1890 and operated until 1963. Its tower stands 40 feet high and is built of iron. With a focal plane 217 feet above the sea, the fixed white light with red flashing beacon was visible 21 miles out to sea.

A mile north of Cape Meares is **Bayocean Spit,** where once stood a resort complex called Bayocean that was eventually swallowed by the encroaching seas. This is now a marsh, supporting abundant wildlife, especially seabirds, shorebirds, and waterfowl.

Netarts Spit and nearby beaches are popular beachcombing areas. The best beachcombing is in the winter and spring or any other time after storms. Winter storms often uncover rocky areas and gravel beds, exposing agates, jasper, and petrified wood. Strong westerlies blow glass floats and driftwood ashore.

There are good trails at both **Cape Meares** and **Cape Lookout State Parks.** Beaches there are also popular with beachcombers and hikers.

WATER SPORTS AND ACTIVITIES

Although anglers take a few bottom fish from Netarts Bay, the fishing here is only fair at best. Crabbing, however, can be outstanding, particularly from September to December. Rental equipment is available.

A boat will get you to the best clam-digging areas too. Most flats give up horseneck, hard-shell, and littleneck clams, as well as cockles. Upbay, there are softshell beds, downbay a few razor clams.

TRAVEL INFORMATION

Netarts, www.ohwy.com/or/n/netarts.htm
Oceanside, www.ohwy.com/or/o/oceanside.htm

TILLAMOOK
Population: 4,245

Location: *On U.S. 101, 42 miles north of Lincoln City, 66 miles south of Astoria, and 74 miles southwest of Portland. Zip: 97141.*

Situated on the rolling hills and tucked into the verdant valleys of Tillamook County's 1,115 square miles are 159 dairy farms that supply the raw material for Tillamook's booming cheese business. The county is home to approximately 23,300 persons and 22,000 cows.

Cheese is big business here. It takes five quarts (about ten pounds) of milk to make one pound of cheese, and at the Tillamook County Creamery Association (a.k.a. The Cheese Factory), cheesemakers produce fifty million pounds of cheese a year. One might expect the rivers here to be running white.

Approaching Tillamook from the east, on State Route 6, along the Wilson River and through the Tillamook State Forest, travelers might never know that the area was consumed by the worst forest fires of the twentieth century between 1932 and 1945.

The fiercest of those fires, started by a logging operation in the tinder-dry Coast Range during drought conditions, broke out on August 14, 1933. By the time the 3,000 firefighters brought the blaze under control, it had destroyed 270,000 acres of old-growth timber.

So great was the conflagration that it sent dense clouds of smoke and ash 40,000 feet in the air, blocking the sun's rays and sending chickens to roost in midday. The fire's ashes fell on ships 500 miles out to sea and accumulated along Tillamook County's beaches to a depth of 2 feet.

Two miles south of town and east of U.S. 101 stands one of two imposing buildings that dominated the landscape for fifty years since World War II. Built by the U.S. Navy as hangars for a fleet of eight K-type blimps, the buildings were, according to the *Guinness Book of World Records,* the largest all-wood buildings in the world, each measuring 1,000 feet long, 296 feet wide, and 170 feet tall. Ten million board feet of lumber went into their construction.

During World War II, U.S. Naval Air Station blimps at Tillamook patrolled the Pacific Coast from Eureka, California, to the San Juan Islands in Puget Sound. Although the blimps have been gone since 1945, one of the hangars remains intact and functions as a museum. The other burned to the ground in August 1992.

Northwest of Tillamook and north of Cape Meares, a narrow finger of sand—known variously as Tillamook Spit, Bayocean Spit, and Bayocean Peninsula—pokes between Tillamook Bay and the ocean. It's hard to believe that this was once a booming resort town, begun in 1906 by developer T. B. Potter. Among the one hundred buildings that once stood at Bayocean were a forty-room hotel and a huge natatorium containing a 50-by-160-foot heated saltwater pool with a wave-making machine and waterfall, as well as a gallery that seated 1,000 spectators.

When the north jetty was built at the entrance to Tillamook Bay in 1917, the sea began to erode the peninsula on which Bayocean stood. Enlargement and extension of the jetty in 1932 caused erosion to increase dramatically. Powerful currents and incessant breakers devoured the broad beach and eventually reduced beachfront buildings, including the natatorium, to rubble and driftwood.

In 1952 the spit was breached at its southern end by a mile-wide opening to the sea, turning the hapless community into an island. The following year the Bayocean post office was closed, and the last residents left.

After the south jetty was built in 1965, currents changed, and the spit began rebuilding itself. Today, it's a popular spot for beachcombing, picnicking, and observing abundant wildlife, with scarcely a clue that there was ever a dwelling there, let alone a busy resort town.

LODGING

Red Apple Inn, 815 Main Avenue; (503) 842–7511 or (800) 257–1185. On U.S. 101, in town. Queen beds in 22 units with cable TV, HBO, Showtime, Cinemax, and Disney Channel. Small but comfortable rooms. Adjacent to restaurant, open for breakfast, lunch, and dinner. Moderate.

Salmon anglers on Tillamook Bay

Shilo Inn, 2515 North Main; (503) 842–7971 or (800) 222–2244; www.shiloinns.com. East side of U.S. 101, north end of town. Queen and king beds in 68 comfortable and tastefully appointed units, each with remote-control cable TV, wet bar, microwave oven, refrigerator, and sofa bed. Heated indoor pool, sauna, whirlpool, steam room, and exercise room with weight machines. Minimart—open 24 hours—sells deli foods, groceries, magazines, beer, wine, bait, tackle, ice, gas, and oil. Superb restaurant and lounge on the premises. A full-service resort and Tillamook's finest accommodations. Moderate.

FOOD AND BEVERAGES

Bear Creek Artichokes, (503) 398–5411. East side of U.S. 101, 11 miles south of Tillamook in Hemlock. Summer: daily, 9:00 A.M. to 6:30 P.M. Off-season: daily, 10:00 A.M. to 5:00 P.M. Weekends only in November and December. Great fresh fruits and vegetables to complement the Oregon wines and Tillamook cheeses. Succulent artichokes in season. You-pick or they-pick veggies, fresh herbs, honey, and homemade jams and jellies.

Blue Heron French Cheese Company, 2001 Blue Heron Lane; (503) 842–8281 or (800) 275–0639; www.blueheron oregon.com. East off U.S. 101, north of downtown. Daily, 8:00 A.M. to 6:00 P.M. Shop late morning or early afternoon, and make it a lunch break. Chili, chowder, salads, and deli-style sandwiches, as well as all the cheese and wine you care to sample. Then shop for gifts, picnic specialties, or ice-chest items. All sorts of culinary delights, including Haus Barthyte mustards—the best in the West. Moderate.

La Mexicana Restaurant, 2203 Third Street; (503) 842–2101. Across the street from the courthouse. Lunch and dinner daily. Large lunch and dinner menu with all the Mexican favorites, including beef, chicken, pork, and seafood specialties. Try the Steak Ranchero or Mexican-style chicken, prawns, lobster, or oysters. Full bar, including domestic and imported beers, three kinds of margaritas, and homemade sangria. Moderate.

Shilo Inn, 2534 North Main; (503) 842–5510 or (800) 222–2244; www.shiloinns.com. East side of U.S. 101, north of downtown. Breakfast, lunch, and dinner daily; brunch Sunday. Outstanding omelettes and egg dishes, traditional breakfast fare with a flair. Super luncheon salads, including crab or chicken cobb, fresh spinach salad, and several house-specialty salads. Tillamook cheese and fruit board, seafood fettuccine, tortellini Alfredo, and great deli-style sandwiches, such as Tillamook cheese and crab or Old English prime rib—charbroiled and served on grilled sourdough bread. Dinner offerings include London broil, Cajun chicken sauté, halibut fish and chips, and excellent prime rib. Cocktails, beer, and wine. Moderate.

Tillamook County Creamery Association (The Cheese Factory), 4175 Highway 101 North; P.O. Box 313; (503) 815–1300; www.tillamookcheese.com. East side of U.S. 101, north end of town. Daily, 8:00 A.M. to 6:00 P.M., till 8:00 P.M. in summer. The finest of cheeses—cheddars, Swiss, Monterey Jack, low-fat, cheese curds, and special extra-sharp cheddars—available here. Daily factory tours. Retail sales and large gift-shop area, includes wine shop, deli, candies, and ice cream. A *must-see* for every traveler. Gift packs available.

MUSEUMS

Tillamook County Pioneer Museum, 2106 Second Street; (503) 842–4553; www.tcpm.org. Northbound U.S. 101 at Second. Open Monday through Saturday, 8:00 A.M. to 5:00 P.M.; Sunday, 11:00 A.M. to 5:00 P.M. Clearly the largest and best museum of its kind on the coast. It is located in the old county courthouse, built in 1905, and offers three full floors of topflight exhibits. In the basement are the last Tillamook-to-Yamhill stagecoach, a 1902 Holsman Horseless Carriage, a 1909 Buick, an old wagon, canoes, antique cameras and typewriters, washing machines and kitchen items, cheese-making equipment, and nautical and logging displays. On the main floor are displays of toys and musical instruments, Indian baskets and artifacts, china and glassware, and a fine gun collection. Second-floor displays include extensive collections of rocks, minerals, and fossils and a surprisingly large natural-history exhibit of more than 500 specimens. With more than 35,000 artifacts and antiques on display, this museum is classified a *must-see.* Admission is $3.00 for adults, $2.00 for seniors, 50 cents for children ages 12–17, and free for children under 12.

Tillamook Air Museum, 6030 Hangar Road; (503) 842–1130; www.tillamookair.com. Two miles south of town, east of U.S. 101—impossible to miss. Daily, 10:00 A.M. to 5:00 P.M. The blimp hangar alone is worth the trip, but it houses more than two dozen beautifully restored war birds and other historical aircraft, a theater, an exhibit room, gift shop, and forties-style diner. A *must-see.* Admission is $9.50 for adults, $8.50 for seniors, $5.50 for ages 13–17, and $2.00 for children ages 7–12.

Tillamook County Creamery Association (see Food & Beverages).

BEACHES, PARKS, TRAILS, AND WAYSIDES

Three Capes Loop will take you west-northwest along Tillamook Bay to the Bayocean area and **Cape Meares** and **Cape Lookout State Parks,** where there are hiking trails, picnicking, camping, and beach access. The scenic highway then continues south to Oceanside, Netarts, and Pacific City, all of which provide access to great beach areas.

South of Tillamook is a state park that's worth a visit. Take U.S. 101 south about 6.7 miles and turn east at the sign for **Munson Creek Falls.** Follow the road 1.5 miles to a small parking area and turnaround (not recommended for travel trailers). Two trails lead to the waterfall, which, at a height of 266 feet, is the highest waterfall in the Coast Range. The lower trail leads an easy quarter mile along the creek to the base of the falls. The upper three-eighths-mile trail gradually ascends 250 feet and is well maintained. But canyon walls drop away abruptly in places, so this is no place for small children. The view from the upper trail is spectacular and well worth the little extra effort the hike takes.

WATER SPORTS AND ACTIVITIES

It's said that *Tillamook* is an Indian word meaning "land of many waters," which is appropriate for an area with the second largest bay in the state, many rivers and creeks, and miles of beaches nearby. The most popular forms of recreation here are associated in some way with water.

Tillamook Bay provides year-round recreation for residents and visitors alike. Anglers take bottom fish all year. Perch fishing is good from late winter through the summer months. Spring chinook show up in April and are present into early summer. In August the first fall chinook and coho begin arriving in the bay.

Crabbing on the bay is good all year, particularly in the Crab Harbor area on the west side. The best crabbing is during the fall and winter.

Tillamook Bay is probably second only to Coos Bay as a clamdigging area. The bay is rimmed with beds that give up limits of horseneck, hard-shell, littleneck, and soft-shell clams, as well as cockles.

The Tillamook River, which enters the bay from the south, is a short stream of only 14 miles. Summer fishing is mainly for stocked rainbow and native cutthroat trout. Fall chinook move into the river in September and October and coho usually in November.

The 50-mile-long Trask River gets good runs of spring and fall chinook and both summer and winter steelhead. The Trask enters the south end of the bay just south of the Wilson River.

State Route 6 follows the Wilson River for much of its course through the **Tillamook State Forest.** The popular river gets runs of summer and winter steelhead, spring and fall chinook, and searun cutthroat. Each year the Wilson gives up some big steelhead and salmon. Best bank access is upriver, while the lower 10 miles is favored by drift-boat fishermen. The Wilson also has some excellent fly-fishing waters upstream.

OTHER ATTRACTIONS

Oregon Coast Explorer Train, Port of Tillamook Bay; (503) 842–8206 or (800) 685–1719; www.potb.org. Excursions by diesel train take you down the coast between Tillamook and Mohler, as well as on fall foliage trips over the Coastal Range and weekly sunset supper trips. Call for schedules, rates, and reservations.

TRAVEL INFORMATION

Tillamook County Chamber of Commerce, 3705 Highway 101 North; (503) 842–7525; www.tillamookchamber.org

EVENTS

June	Dairy Parade and Rodeo, (503) 842–7525
August	Tillamook County Fair, (503) 842–2272

✩ GARIBALDI
Population: 1,060

ROCKAWAY BEACH
Population: 1,000

Location: *Garibaldi is on U.S. 101, 9 miles north of Tillamook, at the north end of Tillamook Bay. Zip: 97118. Rockaway Beach is on U.S. 101, 5 miles north of Garibaldi, 10 miles south of Nehalem. Zip: 97136.*

If fishing and allied water sports are not the only attractions in Garibaldi, they are certainly the main ones. The town is home port to a large commercial fishing fleet, which makes fresh seafood readily available to local markets and restaurants. The harbor has boat-launching and mooring facilities and a fleet of modern charter boats. You can crab from boats or docks and piers and dig clams on minus tides at nearby flats.

Rockaway Beach is small—little more than a strip along Highway 101—yet it offers visitors more than 300 motel and inn rooms, many with commanding ocean views. Access to a 7-mile stretch of fine, broad beach is another of the town's assets.

LODGING

Silver Sands Motel, 201 South Pacific; P.O. Box 161; Rockaway Beach; (503) 355–2206 or (800) 457–8972. Queen beds in 64 units with cable TV and Showtime. Beachfront, ocean-view rooms and suites, some with kitchens, some with fireplaces. Covered and heated pool, sauna, whirlpool. Coffee and newspapers in rooms. Accommodations for up to six persons. Pets okay. Moderate.

CAMPGROUNDS AND RV PARKS

Barview Jetty County Park, (503) 322–3522. West of U.S. 101 at Barview, 2 miles north of Garibaldi. Has 253 sites: 40 full hookup, 20 electric hookup, 190 tent. Showers, tank dump, picnic

115

tables, fire rings, and jetty access. Inexpensive to moderate.

Jetty Fishery, 27550 Highway 101 North; Rockaway Beach; (503) 368–5746. West side of U.S. 101, 3 miles north of Rockaway Beach. Has 15 RV sites with electric and water hookups. Showers, store, boat rental, moorage, ice, propane, gas, and oil. Good spot for those who plan to fish, crab, and dig clams on Nehalem Bay and lower Nehalem River.

FOOD AND BEVERAGES

The Beach Pancake and Dinner House, 202 Highway 101 North; Rockaway Beach; (503) 355–2411. East Side of U.S. 101, downtown. Breakfast, lunch, and dinner daily. Breakfast includes pancakes, waffles, and egg dishes—served all day. Chicken, fresh seafood, and Mexican food. Chicken and dumplings a house specialty. Carryout. Moderate.

The Troller Restaurant & Lounge, Garibaldi; (503) 322–3666. On Mooring Basin Road, west of Highway 101. Open twenty-four hours a day from June 1 to October 1. Breakfast, lunch, and dinner daily. Traditional and unusual fare, including oysters and eggs, or trout and eggs. Burgers and other sandwiches, such as shrimp or crab and cheese, Bay City oysters, and albacore tuna. Fish and chips, clam strips, steamer clams, and more. Prime rib, steaks, chicken, surf 'n' turf, and fresh local seafood. Moderate.

WATER SPORTS AND ACTIVITIES

Garibaldi/D&D Charters, 607 Highway 101 North; Garibaldi; (503) 322–0007. Eight-hour bottom-fishing trips. Light-tackle rockfish angling and, weather permitting, trips to deep offshore reefs for big lingcod and rockfish. Salmon and halibut trips in season.

Jetty Fishery, 27550 Highway 101 North; Rockaway Beach; (503) 368–5746. West side of U.S. 101, 3 miles north of Rockaway Beach. Bait, tackle, fishing licenses and tags, boat and motor rental, gas and oil, moorage, dock crabbing, crab ring rental, fish-cleaning station, and clam-digging gear. Also fifteen RV spaces. On Nehalem Bay.

Siggi-G Ocean Charters, P.O. Box 536; Garibaldi; (503) 322–3285. At the Garibaldi boat basin, west of U.S. 101. Salmon, bottom fish, and combination trips include bait, tackle, cleaning, ice, and bags. Specializes in long-range, deep water fishing for big bottom fish when weather cooperates. Also offers crabbing, whale-watching, and bird-watching trips.

Troller Deep Sea Fishing, P.O. Box 605; Garibaldi; (503) 322–3666 or (800) 546–3666. West side of U.S. 101, at Fisherman's Wharf, in the boat basin. Large fleet of charter boats available for bottom fish, salmon, combination, and long-distance offshore trips as well as scuba-diving and whale-watching trips.

TRAVEL INFORMATION

Garibaldi Chamber of Commerce, 202 Highway 101; P.O. Box 915; (503) 322–0301 or (800) 556–0757

Rockaway Beach Chamber of Commerce, 103 South First Street; P.O. Box 198; (503) 355–8108; www.rockawaybeach.net

EVENTS

May	Blessing of the Fleet, Garibaldi, (503) 322–0301
	Kite Festival, Rockaway Beach, (503) 355–8108
July	Fun Day Parade and Fireworks, Rockaway Beach, (503) 355–8108
August	Arts & Crafts Fair, Rockaway Beach, (503) 355–8108

NEHALEM
Population: 230

MANZANITA
Population: 443

Location: *Nehalem is on U.S. 101 and the Nehalem River, 10 miles north of Rockaway Beach. Zip: 97131. Manzanita is just west of U.S. 101, 2 miles north of Nehalem, 11 miles south of Cannon Beach. Zip: 97130.*

Nehalem (nee-*hay*-luhm) is believed to be a Salish Indian word meaning "place where people live." While not all that many people live here, it is a gathering place for shoppers and browsers, as well as those interested in fishing and allied sports on Nehalem Bay and Nehalem River. In recent years Nehalem has blossomed into an attractive village, appealing to all who enjoy browsing through fine galleries and antique shops.

Named for a small shrub that grows wild along the coast, Manzanita is a quiet little village next to the ocean on the south slope of Neahkahnie (nee-uh-*kah*-nee) Mountain. The mountain stands 1,795 feet above sea level and is the most imposing headland on the north coast.

Indian legend has it that there's buried treasure on the mountain—booty from a Spanish galleon that went aground here, long before white men settled the land. Treasure seekers have made many futile hunts over the years, but nary a doubloon has been unearthed.

LODGING

The Inn at Manzanita, 67 Laneda Avenue; Manzanita; (503) 368-6754. A half mile west of U.S. 101, on the north side of the street, only 200 feet from the beach. Beautiful cedar two-story bed-and-breakfast inn. Four guest rooms, each with a whirlpool spa and fireplace or woodstove. Queen beds, wet bars, refrigerators, and cable TV. Separate house accommodates up to 8 persons. Continental breakfast brought to the room. Expensive.

118

Rockwork along U.S. 101, north of Manzanita

Nehalem Bay Floating Motel, Nehalem Bay; (503) 368–7047. Your opportunity to take a cruise without ever leaving the dock is this floating motel composed of a variety of vessels outfitted for overnight lodging. Choose from a 47-foot converted tug to a 35-foot barge house. Each unit is unique and all are equipped with cooking and refrigeration, gas barbecues, private outdoor lounging areas, and even life jackets! Your "neighbors" are likely to be elk, seals, blue heron, bald eagles, and jumping salmon. Moderate to expensive.

Sunset Surf Motel, 248 Ocean Road; P.O. Box 458; Manzanita; (503) 368–5224. On Manzanita Beach, just north of Laneda Avenue. Queen and king beds in 41 units with cable TV, HBO, and Showtime. Pool, beachfront units, most with ocean view, 30 with kitchens, some with fireplaces. Moderate to expensive.

CAMPGROUNDS AND RV PARKS

Nehalem Bay State Park, (503) 368–5154 (booth); (800) 452–5687 (reservations). Located 1.5 miles west of U.S. 101, 1 mile north of Nehalem, 1 mile south of Manzanita. Has 292 RV sites with electric and water hookups, picnic tables, and fireplaces. Showers, tank dump, and firewood. Hiker/biker camp. Horse camp with picnic tables, fire rings, rest rooms, and tie stalls for 18 horses. Hiking, biking, and horseback-riding trails. Access to miles of broad beach. The park is a 5-mile spit that separates Nehalem Bay from the ocean. Inexpensive.

Oswald West State Park, (503) 368-5943. West side of U.S. 101, 4 miles north of Manzanita, 10 miles south of Cannon Beach. Foot access only to 36 tent sites. Wheelbarrows for hauling gear to campsites. Ample parking on both sides of the highway. Camp on a beautiful headland amid the tall timber of a rain forest. Picnic tables, fireplaces, firewood, rest rooms, and water. Hiking trails. No advance reservations. Inexpensive.

FOOD AND BEVERAGES

Big Wave Cafe, Manzanita Junction at Highway 101; (503) 368-9283. West side of U.S. 101. Breakfast, lunch, and dinner daily. The menu here offers more than just traditional fare. Breakfast includes eggs with pork cutlets or German sausage, hobo eggs, huevos rancheros, Hangtown Fry, and buckwheat cakes. For lunch or dinner, try one of the big burgers, chicken sandwich, Philly steak sandwich, fish and chips, glazed salmon, or panfried oysters. Entrees include spicy spaghetti with clams and roasted bell peppers, charbroiled chicken with mango rum sauce, and pork loin with mushrooms and caramelized onions. Homemade pies and cheesecake. Daily specials. Beer and wine. Moderate.

Manzanita News and Espresso, 500 Laneda Avenue; (503) 368-7450. This cafe with adjoining gift shop and complete newsstand opens at 7:30 A.M. daily. Enjoy your paper of choice inside, surrounded by homey decor, or outside under the shade of a giant manzanita tree, while having an espresso or tea along with a pastry, bagel, quiche, or sandwich. Inexpensive to moderate.

Nehalem Bay Winery, 34965 Highway 53; Nehalem; (503) 368-5300. One mile east of U.S. 101, on State Route 53 at Mohler. Daily, 9:00 A.M. to 6:00 P.M. A charming old winery set in the pastoral beauty of the Nehalem Valley. Wine tasting, sales, gift packs, and winery tours.

SHOPPING AND BROWSING

Treasure Cave, 594 Laneda Avenue; Manzanita; (503) 368-7908. Just west of U.S. 101. Daily, 10:00 A.M. to 5:00 P.M.; sometimes closes Tuesday and Wednesday in winter. A large shop offering gifts, cards, clothing, glassware, antiques, and collectibles.

WATER SPORTS AND ACTIVITIES

Nehalem Bay is popular for crabbing and clam digging. Crabbing is good from boats much of the year, but it's best from fall through winter. Most abundant clams are softshell and littleneck.

Bay fishing is good for perch and flounder from early spring to the first rains of autumn. Chinook and coho salmon move into the bay in August and are caught into November. This is also a good area for sea-run cutthroat trout, which are present most of the year but most abundant in late summer. Winter months produce steelhead in the upper bay.

The Nehalem River is one of the longest coastal rivers, extending more than 100 miles through the Coast Range. It provides a fall chinook and coho fishery, winter steelhead angling, and year-round cutthroat fishing in the lower river.

GOLF

Manzanita Golf Course, Lakeview Drive; Manzanita; (503) 368–5744. South off Laneda Avenue on Lakeview Drive, 0.6 mile. A 2,192-yard, par-32, 9-hole course in a wooded residential area. Clubhouse, cart rental, putting green, and driving range.

RENTALS

Manzanita Fun Merchants, 186 Laneda Avenue; Manzanita; (503) 368–6606. A half mile west of U.S. 101 on the south side of the street. Sells and rents Funcycles—three-wheel recumbents.

TRAVEL INFORMATION

Manzanita Merchants Association, P.O. Box 164; Manzanita
Nehalem Bay Area Chamber of Commerce, P.O. Box 159; Nehalem; (503) 368–5100 or (877) 368–5100; www.doormat.com

EVENTS

| July | Nehalem Craft Fair, (503) 368–7577 |
| **August** | Nehalem Art Festival, (503) 368–6247 |

CANNON BEACH
Population: 1,260

Location: *West of U.S. 101, 14 miles north of Manzanita, 9 miles south of Seaside. Zip: 97110.*

A month after Lewis and Clark settled for the winter of 1805–6 near Astoria, Oregon, William Clark led a small party 20 miles south to a headland overlooking a "butifull Sand Shore." No doubt, his vantage point was Tillamook Head, and what he described, most believe, is the expanse of beach stretching southward to what is now the city of Cannon Beach.

The beach here is wide; the backdrop of craggy headlands is impressive. Adding to the area's visual appeal are the many sea stacks just offshore. Most prominent, and certainly the most photographed, is Haystack Rock, one of two on the coast and three in the state so named. The one here stands 235 feet high, 92 feet shorter than the one south of Cape Kiwanda, but nonetheless interesting for its surroundings.

The cannon after which Cannon Beach was named is from the U.S. Naval Survey schooner *Shark*, which broke up on Clatsop Spit at the mouth of the Columbia River on September 10, 1846. Part of the ship, including the cannon and capstan, washed ashore south of Tillamook Head. One of the area's early settlers hauled the cannon and capstan away and set them in concrete. They are now exhibited at the Columbia River Maritime Museum in Astoria. Cannons near the Cannon Beach exits on U.S. 101 are fair copies, made in 1953.

The architecture in Cannon Beach is an interesting mixture of the quaint and the contemporary, aptly earning the town its nickname—"Carmel of Oregon." Structures range from beachy little bungalows to hilltop manors, mostly glass and weathered wood,

122

and a lot of shingles, shakes, and shutters. The strict building codes are kind to the eye and the environment.

After a glimpse, it's not surprising to learn that Cannon Beach is an artsy little community and the cultural center of the north coast. A number of artists live and work in the area and sell their works at local galleries. A thriving repertory company keeps the theater arts alive and lively, and an annual arts program revitalizes residents and visitors every year.

LODGING

The Argonauta Inn, 188 West Second Street; P.O. Box 3; (503) 436–2205 or (800) 822–2468. On the beach, next to The Waves Motel. Not an inn per se but several cottages on the beach that accommodate 2 to 6 persons and feature queen beds, fireplaces, kitchens, antiques, fine-art prints, nautical items, ocean view, cable TV, whirlpool, hot tub, and more. Walk to shops and restaurants. Expensive.

Best Western Surfsand Resort Hotel, 100 East Gower; P.O. Box 219; (503) 436–2274; (800) 457–6100; www.surfsand.com. West side of Hemlock, south of downtown. Queen and king beds in 72 units, 30 with kitchens. Heated indoor pool, whirlpool spa, ocean view, fireplaces, cable TV, HBO, beach access. Walk to shops. Superb ocean-view restaurant and comfortable lounge on the premises. Moderate to very expensive.

The Ocean Lodge, 2864 South Pacific Street; (503) 436–2241 or (888) 777–4047; www.theoceanlodge.com. Designed with a 1940s beach resort in mind, The Ocean Lodge is the area's newest and one of its finest offerings. Located on the beach, the inn offers 45 1-bedroom suites with wet bars, refrigerators, microwaves, DVD players, fireplaces, and Jacuzzis. Morning brings a light breakfast and a newspaper. Moderate to expensive.

St. Bernards: A Bed and Breakfast, 3 East Ocean Road; P.O. Box 102; (503) 436–2800 or (800) 436–2848; www.st-bernards.com. East of U.S. 101, 4 miles south of Cannon Beach, 1 mile south of Cape Arch sign; 7 miles north of Manzanita, 0.6 mile north of U.S. 101 tunnel. Seven rooms and suites in an elegant château situated on 15 acres. Private baths, cable TV, VCR, refrigerators, and gas fireplaces in all rooms. Sauna, workout room, and conference room. Evening social hour in living room, full breakfast in conservatory, overlooking the gardens. Moderate to expensive.

Tolovana Inn, 3400 South Hemlock; P.O. Box 165; Tolovana

Park 97145; (503) 436–2211 or (800) 333–8890; www.v-v-a. com/tolovana. On South Hemlock, 2 miles south of downtown Cannon Beach. Queen beds in 96 1- and 2-bedroom and studio units with kitchens, fireplaces, and cable TV. Heated indoor pool, 2 saunas, whirlpool, and game room. Nonview rooms available. New conference center. On the beach. Moderate to expensive.

The Waves Motel, 188 West Second Street; P.O. Box 3; (503) 436–2205 or (800) 822–2468; www.thewavesmotel.com. On the beach, downtown, at Larch and Second. Twin, double, and queen beds in 37 units with cable TV. A variety of accommodations, including cottages and rooms with and without ocean views, kitchens, and fireplaces. Oceanfront spa. Easy beach access. Inexpensive to very expensive.

CAMPGROUNDS AND RV PARKS

RV Resort of Cannon Beach, 345 Elk Creek Road; P.O. Box 219; (503) 436–2231 or (800) 847–2231; www.cbrvresort.com. East of U.S. 101 at the third exit if traveling north, second exit if traveling south. Has 100 drive-through sites with full hookups and cable TV. Heated indoor pool, spa, showers, picnic area, hiking and biking trails, horse trails, recreation center, convenience store, laundry, propane, gas, and ice. Moderate.

FOOD AND BEVERAGES

Dooger's Seafood Grill, 1371 South Hemlock; (503) 436–2225; www.cannon-beach.net/doogers/. East side of the street, south of downtown. Breakfast, lunch, and dinner daily. Great breakfast menu includes hobo scramble, steak and eggs, Hangtown Fry, Belgian waffles, pancakes, biscuits and gravy, and wonderful three-egg omelettes. Lunch includes burgers, chowder, and seafood specials. Dinners are mostly great seafood—calamari, fish and chips, halibut, oysters, steamer and razor clams, crab legs, prawns, lobster, and more. Peanut butter pie, lemon cheese pie, deep-dish apple pie, chocolate fudge cake, and other desserts. Beer, wine, and nonalcoholic wine. Moderate.

Morris' Fireside Restaurant, 207 North Hemlock; (503) 436–2917. Downtown Cannon Beach. Daily, 8:00 A.M. to 10:00 P.M. Breakfast, lunch, and dinner are served in a hand-hewn log cabin–style restaurant featuring traditional Northwest cuisine, from steak to lobster. Moderate.

Downtown Cannon Beach

Wayfarer Restaurant & Lounge, 1190 Pacific; P.O. Box 219; (503) 436–1108; www.wayfarer-restaurant.com. At Oceanfront and Gower Streets, south end of Cannon Beach, adjacent to Surf-sand Resort. Breakfast, lunch, and dinner daily. Great breakfasts include Hangtown Fry, smoked salmon Benedict, cinnamon roll French toast, waffles, and omelettes. Seafood lunches, burgers, sandwiches, and salads. For dinner, start with one of a dozen appetizers, from crab cakes to stuffed Roma tomatoes. Entrees include halibut, salmon, lobster, oysters, chicken, steaks, and pasta dishes. Tempting desserts, such as Haystack Pie, chocolate ganache torte, white chocolate cheesecake, and marionberry pie. Full bar. Moderate.

The Wine Shack, 124 Hemlock; P.O. Box 652; (503) 436–1100; www.beachwine.com. West side of Hemlock. Closed Tuesday and Wednesday in winter. Well stocked with imported and domestic wines, Oregon wines, collector's wines, and items of interest to wine fanciers. Wine tasting each Saturday beginning at 1:00 P.M.

SHOPPING AND BROWSING

Cannon Beach's main shopping area is downtown, where many specialty shops, galleries, cafes, and bistros are situated along Hemlock and adjacent side streets, most in small shopping centers and minimalls. Find a parking spot and enjoy strolling through the compact shopping area.

Bronze Coast Gallery, 224 North Hemlock, Suite 2; (503) 436–1055 or (800) 430–1055; www.bronzecoastgallery.com. An impressive collection of bronze sculpture and painting by regional and nationally recognized artists.

BEACHES, PARKS, TRAILS, AND WAYSIDES

Beaches sweep north and south past the city of Cannon Beach, and most lodging facilities here are right on the beach or within a short walk of it. These are broad beaches with hard-packed sand near the surf line for easy hiking. Low tide exposes tide pools in rocky areas.

Hikers will find beautiful trails at **Oswald State Park** and **Neahkahnie Mountain** to the south. Just north of Cannon Beach is **Ecola State Park,** with picnic facilities, great views of Cannon Beach and the coastline, and trails for hiking and biking. The **Tillamook Head Recreation Trail** winds north from here to Seaside and affords the best view from land of **Tillamook Light.**

More than a mile off **Tillamook Head** is **Tillamook Rock,** atop which stands Oregon's northernmost lighthouse, completed in 1881. Although Tillamook Light ceased operating in 1957, its light and foghorn warned mariners of danger for seventy-six years. After being sold several times to private parties, the neglected light deteriorated badly. Its current owners, Eternity at Sea, made extensive repairs, and Terrible Tilly, as the old light was widely known, now functions as a columbarium—a repository for ashen remains of the cremated.

RENTALS

Mike's Bike Shop, 248 North Spruce; (503) 436–1266 or (800) 492–1266; www.mikesbike.com. One block east of Hemlock, downtown. Sells, services, and rents bicycles and Funcycles—three-wheel recumbents.

Sea Ranch Stables, 415 Fir Street; www.cannon-beach. net/searanch. Located behind the Sea Ranch RV Park. Open 9:00 A.M. to 4:30 P.M. Guests may only make reservations in person. Horseback rides to the beach, going north to the cove, and going south to Haystack Rock at very low tides. Night rides to Silver Point. No children under 7.

OTHER ATTRACTIONS

Coaster Theater, 108 North Hemlock Street; P.O. Box 643; (503) 436–1242; www.coastertheater.com. A busy theater and repertory company offering a summer stock program June through August. Other plays, concerts, and children's programs offered the rest of the year.

TRAVEL INFORMATION

Cannon Beach Chamber of Commerce, Second and Spruce Streets; P.O. Box 64; (503) 436–2623 or (800) 735–6177; www.cannonbeach.org

Haystack Program in the Arts, Portland State University; Division of Continuing Education; (800) 547–8887, ext. 3276

EVENTS	
April	Puffin Kite Festival, (503) 436–2274 or (800) 547–6100
June	Sandcastle Day, (503) 436–2623
October	Dog Show on the Beach, (503) 436–2274 or (800) 547–6100
November	Stormy Weather Arts Festival, (503) 436–2623, ext. 4

SEASIDE
Population: 5,580

GEARHART
Population: 1,090

Location: *On U.S. 101, 17 miles south of Astoria, 9 miles north of Cannon Beach, 79 miles northwest of Portland Zip: 97138.*

Unquestionably one of the premier resort destinations of the north coast, Seaside has become a year-round destination, especially on weekends. Since 1938, Portlanders have poured into town on weekends, via U.S. 26, also known as the Sunset Highway. When summer vacationers join the throngs, the city fairly bulges.

On U.S. 101 at Broadway is the visitor information center, which is classified a *must* for any visitor to Oregon's north coast. This is the biggest and best source of travel information on the Oregon coast and is staffed by friendly and knowledgeable people who are eager to answer your questions and make your coastal stay a pleasant one.

Broadway is Seaside's main east–west street, extending through town from U.S. 101 to the turnaround on the promenade, next to the Shilo Oceanfront. Park on Broadway or any nearby street to visit the many shops, restaurants, galleries, arcades, and attractions of the downtown area. Enjoy the unfettered pace and relaxed atmosphere, akin to the festive air of a carnival midway.

LODGING

Gearhart-By-The-Sea, 10th and Marion; P.O. Box 2700; (503) 738–8331 or (800) 547–0115; www.gearhartresort.com. Half mile west of U.S. 101 on North Marion, at the golf links. Queen beds and sofa beds in 80 condominium units with cable TV. One-bedroom, 2-bedroom, and 3-bedroom suites. Fireplaces, ocean view, heated indoor pool, spa, laundry, coffee shop, restaurant, and lounge. Walk to beach, pro shop, and golf course. Moderate to expensive.

Gilbert Inn Bed & Breakfast, 341 Beach Drive; (503) 738–9770 or (800) 410–9770; www.gilbertinn.com. West of U.S. 101, 1 block from the beach, downtown. Built in 1892. Three rooms and 2 suites with queen beds, down quilts, period furniture, private baths, and cable TV. Full breakfast. Moderate.

Riverside Inn Bed & Breakfast, 430 South Holladay; (503) 738–8254 or (800) 826–6151; www.riversideinn.com. One block west of U.S. 101, 2 blocks south of Broadway, on the east bank of the river. Has 11 rooms, each with separate entrance, private bath, cable TV. Kitchen units available. Continental breakfast. Moderate.

Shilo Oceanfront, 30 North Prom; (503) 738–9571 or (800) 222–2244; www.shiloinns.com. On the prom at the turnaround, west end of Broadway. Has 112 deluxe units with cable TV. Accommodations range from comfortable east rooms with queen beds to ocean-view rooms and suites with queen or king beds. Fireplaces and kitchens available. Heated indoor pool, sauna, steam room, whirlpool, and exercise room. Located at the center of Seaside's downtown area, near shops and galleries, on the beach. Superb restaurant and lounge on premises. Moderate to expensive.

10th Avenue Inn Bed & Breakfast, 125 10th Avenue; (503) 738–0643 or (800) 745–2378; www.10aveinn.com. West of U.S. 101, on the beach and promenade at the north end of town. Has 3 rooms, each with queen bed, cable TV, refrigerators, and private bath. No pets or children. Full breakfast. Moderate.

CAMPGROUNDS AND RV PARKS

Bud's Campground & Groceries, 4412 Highway 101 North; P.O. Box 2525; (503) 738–6855 or (800) 730–6855. West side of U.S. 101, about a mile north of Gearhart. Has 24 RV sites with full hookups and 6 tent sites. Cable TV, showers, laundry, picnic tables, horseshoe pits, store, beer and wine, bait and tackle, gifts, propane. Moderate.

Circle Creek Campground, HCR 63, Box 210, South Highway 101; (503) 738–6070. West side of U.S. 101, 1.5 miles south of Seaside. Large tent area with picnic tables and fire pits, as well as 47 full-hookup sites with cable TV, in a beautiful, grassy, creek-bottom area. Showers and laundry. Moderate.

FOOD AND BEVERAGES

Doogers Seafood Grill, 505 Broadway; (503) 738–3773. South side of the street, downtown. Lunch and dinner daily. Seafood sandwiches—crab, oyster, halibut. Daily lunch specials served until 4:00 P.M. Dinners served all day, including halibut fish and chips, calamari, oysters, petrale sole, razor clams, salmon, steaks, chicken, salads, and combo plate. Beer and wine. Moderate.

Pacific Way Cafe & Bakery, 601 Pacific Way, Gearhart; (503) 738–0245 Nestled in the center of town, 0.4 mile west of U.S.101. Open 8:00 A.M. to 9:00 P.M. Thursday through Monday. Charming cafe surrounded by boutiques; serves great soups, salads, and fresh bread from the bakery, as well as decadent desserts that go well with the espresso. Moderate.

Shilo Restaurant and Lounge, 30 North Prom; (503) 738–8481. On the prom at the turnaround, west end of Broadway. Breakfast, lunch, and dinner daily. Breakfast favorites include eggs Benedict, croissant Benedict, fresh fruits, hotcakes, Belgian waffles, crepes, seafood and vegetable omelettes. Lunches include fish and chips, broiled halibut or salmon, chicken stir-fry, quiche, lunch-size salads, and sandwiches. Dinner menu features seventeen appetizers; seafood specialties such as seafood mixed grill or coast cioppino; such broiler dinners as rack of lamb or teriyaki sirloin, as well as Shilo specials: prime rib, veal, and roast pork tenderloin. New York steak or prime rib served surf 'n' turf style with choice of lobster, shrimp, scallops, or king crab. Moderate.

Vista Sea Cafe, 150 Broadway; (503) 738–8108. At Broadway and Columbia, 1 block east of the turnaround. Lunch and dinner daily. Chowder, soups, and a good selection of super salads. Deli sandwiches, quiche, lasagna, and a dozen gourmet pizzas. Breads and pizza crusts are homemade daily. Moderate.

SHOPPING AND BROWSING

Downtown Seaside, west of U.S. 101, is full of shops and galleries of all kinds, as well as malls and minimalls. Other shops and galleries are scattered along both sides of U.S. 101 in both Seaside and Gearhart.

Seaside Antique Mall, 39 South Holladay, Seaside; (503) 717–9312; www.myantiquemall.com. Corner of Broadway and Holladay. Open Sunday through Friday, 10:00 A.M. to 5:00 P.M. (6:00 P.M. in the summer) and Saturday, 10:00 A.M. to 8:00 P.M.

Downtown Seaside

Huge selection of quality antiques and collectibles from more than eighty dealers.

Seaside Carousel Mall, 300 Broadway, Seaside; (503) 738–6728. Open daily. More than a dozen stores. A classic carousel in the center of the mall features accurate replicas of original vintage carousel horses from the early 1900s.

MUSEUM AND AQUARIUM

Seaside Aquarium, 200 North Prom, Seaside; (503) 738–6211. Opens Wednesday through Sunday from 9:00 A.M. to 5:00 P.M. Live exhibits featuring regional marine life include the Pacific octopus, wolf eel, and giant twenty-ray starfish. A big hit is feeding the seals. Also check out the hands-on Discovery Center and gift shop.

Seaside Museum and Historical Society, 570 Necanicum Drive; P.O. Box 1024; (503) 738–8320; www.seasurf.net/ ~smhs/. West of U.S. 101, 4 blocks north of the convention center on the west bank of the river. Call for hours of operation. Displays of Indian artifacts, fire equipment, printing equipment, early photographs, and other exhibits depicting the history of Seaside and vicinity. Admission is $2.00 for adults, $1.50 for seniors, $1.00 for youth ages 13 to 18, and free for children 12 and younger.

BEACHES, PARKS, TRAILS, AND WAYSIDES

Atlantic City has its boardwalk, Seaside its promenade, or prom, as it's known locally. This broad concrete walkway, with its decorative seawall and lampposts, was built in 1920. It parallels the beach for nearly 2 miles and is perfect for strolling or biking, day or night.

The west end of Broadway meets the promenade at the turn-around. There a plaque commemorates trail's end for the Lewis and Clark expedition. Several members of the expedition spent some weeks in the Seaside area during the winter of 1805–6.

December 28, 1805, only twenty days after Lewis and Clark established their winter headquarters at Fort Clatsop, the captains dispatched five men to the coast to find a suitable site for a salt-works. Five days later, the men, having traveled 15 miles, arrived near what is now Seaside.

The water was sufficiently high in salinity to make three or four quarts of salt a day. Between their arrival and their departure on February 20, 1806, they used five brass kettles to render 1,400 gallons of seawater into three and a half bushels of salt for the expedition's return trip. Visit the reconstructed salt cairn by turning west off U.S. 101 on Avenue G, then south on South Beach Drive to Lewis & Clark Way. Just follow the signs.

GOLF

Gearhart Golf Links, (503) 738–3538. On North Marian at 10th Street, a half mile west of U.S. 101. This public course is the oldest course in Oregon or Washington—established in 1892. Has 18 holes, pro shop, resident pro, cart and club rental. Sandtrap Restaurant and Lounge, open for breakfast, lunch, dinner, and drinks. Adjoining rental condos at Gearhart-By-The-Sea.

The Highlands Golf Course, (503) 738–5248. A half mile west of U.S. 101, 1.3 miles north of Gearhart. Watch for the signs. Public, 9-hole, 1880-yard, par-32 course. Clubhouse with snacks, coffee, soft drinks, beer, and wine. Pro shop. Equipment sales and rentals.

RENTALS

Wheel Fun Rentals, 151 Avenue A or 407 South Holladay Drive; (503) 738–8447. Several locations in north and south Seaside. Rents a variety of pedal-, electric-, and gasoline-powered vehicles: surreys, recumbent cycles, electric cars, mopeds, and more. Also rents skates and boogie boards.

TRAVEL INFORMATION

Seaside Visitors Bureau, 989 Broadway (Broadway at U.S. 101); (503) 738–3097 or (888) 306–2326; www.seasideor.com

EVENTS

February	Seaside Chocolate and Coffee Lovers Festival, (800) 444–6740
	Oregon Dixieland Jubilee, (503) 436–1212
July	Fireworks at the Beach, (800) 444–6740
August	Beach Volleyball Tournament, (800) 444–6740
September	Lewis & Clark Kite Festival, (503) 738–3097
	September in Seaside Hot Rod Happenin', (503) 717–1914
November	Christmas Gift Fair, (800) 444–6740

ASTORIA
Population: 10,100

Location: *At the junction of U.S. 101 and U.S. 30, on the Columbia River near its mouth, 17 miles north of Seaside, 95 miles northwest of Portland. Zip: 97103.*

Astoria is America's oldest West Coast city. In fact, it's the oldest continuously occupied settlement west of the Mississippi River, situated on a river that is second in size only to the Mississippi.

The Columbia River heads in British Columbia and flows south and west in a ragged route toward Oregon. The Snake River joins it near Pasco, Washington, just before the Columbia bends westerly. As it approaches Astoria, the great river broadens into an estuary more than 5 miles wide in places. At the mouth of the Columbia, 1,243 miles from its headwaters, the river's average discharge is 262,000 cubic feet of water per second.

Naturally, Astoria and the nearby environs are steeped in history. Here's where Captain Robert Gray discovered the Columbia River in 1792 and claimed it for the Americans. Here's where Lewis and Clark's Corps of Discovery spent the winter of 1805–6. Here's where John Jacob Astor founded a fur-trading post in 1811. Here's where the first pioneer families arrived in the 1840s and the first post office west of the Mississippi was established in 1847. Here's where coastal fortifications were built toward the end of the Civil War as protection against possible British invasion, via Canada, should the British side with the Confederacy.

Many of Astoria's fine old homes were built in the latter half of the nineteenth century. Some are still private residences; others, beautifully preserved or restored, are bed-and-breakfast inns. One of the most famous, the Flavel House, is a museum.

The Maritime Museum, located on the south bank of the Columbia River in downtown Astoria, stands as a monument to the area's maritime history. The maze of pleasingly displayed, beautifully restored or preserved, and expertly lighted treasures from the sea and river includes artifacts from shipwrecks, a great collection of ship models, whaling and commercial fishing exhibits, and much more—so much, in fact, that this is considered one of the finest museums of its kind.

Moored nearby is Lightship No. 604, *Columbia,* a 128-foot, 617-ton vessel built in East Boothbay, Maine, and launched in 1950. After serving for thirty years off the mouth of the Columbia, she was decommissioned, acquired by the Maritime Museum, and is now open for public tours.

The most prominent modern landmark in the area is the graceful Astoria Bridge, also known as the Astoria-Megler Bridge. Built by Oregon and Washington states in the early 1960s to span the Columbia and join the two states, it was opened to traffic in 1966. It's the world's largest continuous-truss bridge, with a main span of 1,232 feet, overall length of 4.1 miles, and main-span height of 198 feet above the low-water mark, sufficient to allow passage of the Navy's largest ships at high tide.

Astoria is a city for explorers, so get off the highways and get into the residential areas. Check out downtown sights. Walk the waterfront. Pick up a copy of a booklet entitled *Walking Tour of Astoria,* available at the museums and visitor center.

LODGING

Columbia River Inn Bed & Breakfast, 1681 Franklin Avenue; P.O. Box 804; (503) 325–5044 or (800) 953–5044; www.moriah.com/columbia. Franklin at 17th Street, 3 blocks south of eastbound U.S. 30. Queen beds in 4 rooms with private baths; the Bridal Suite features a fireplace and Jacuzzi. Gift shop on premises. Full breakfast, including homemade pastries, served in the main dining room. Near museums and shops. Moderate to expensive.

Grandview Bed & Breakfast, 1574 Grand Avenue; (503) 325–5555 or (800) 488–3250; www.pacifier.com/grndview. Three blocks south of Marine Drive, between 15th and 16th Streets. Double and queen beds in 7 attractively decorated rooms and 3 2-bedroom suites. Private and shared baths. Continental breakfast includes choice of five coffees, five teas, hot chocolate, milk, juices, and two or more kinds of fresh muffins. *Grand view* is no exaggeration, with most units granting views of the Columbia River. Inexpensive to moderate.

Rosebriar Inn Bed & Breakfast, 636 14th Street; (503) 325–7427 or (800) 487–0224. Franklin at 14th Street, 3 blocks south of eastbound U.S. 30. The 11 guest rooms include private baths, phones, and TV; larger units have fireplaces, spas, and views. Full breakfast. Moderate to expensive.

Shilo Inn, 1609 East Harbor Drive; Warrenton 97146; (503) 861–2181 or (800) 222–2244; www.shiloinns.com. West side of U.S. 101 at East Harbor Drive, south of Astoria. Queen and king beds in 62 rooms and minisuites with cable TV, microwave ovens, refrigerators, and wet bars. Indoor pool, sauna, spa, steam room, and fitness center. Restaurant and lounge on premises. Romance and fishing packages available. Moderate.

CAMPGROUNDS AND RV PARKS

Fort Stevens State Park, (503) 861–1671 or (800) 452–5687. Four miles west of U.S. 101, between Warrenton and Hammond. Oregon's largest state park with more than 600 campsites: 213 full hookup, 130 electric hookup, and 262 tent. Showers, tank dump, and many activities for visitors to the great coastal park, including hiking, biking, swimming, fishing, photography, and miles of beach-combing. A historical fort with interpretive displays to explore and study. Check out the wreck of the *Peter Iredale* on Clatsop Beach. Moderate.

FOOD AND BEVERAGES

Josephson's Smokehouse & Dock, 106 Marine Drive; P.O. Box 412; (503) 325–2190; Oregon, (800) 828–3474; elsewhere, (800) 772–3474; www.josephsons.com. Monday through Saturday, 8:00 A.M. to 5:30 P.M. One of the best seafood markets on the coast. Finest fresh-smoked salmon, halibut, tuna, scallops, and oysters, as well as cold-smoked Nova-style lox. Fresh seafoods of all sorts in season, including crawfish. Gift packs of canned, smoked, and pickled salmon, tuna, shark, and more. Mail-order catalog available.

Pier 11 Feed Store Restaurant & Lounge, (503) 325–0279. At Pier 11 mall, 1 block north of U.S. 30, between 10th and 11th Streets. Lunch and dinner daily. Lunch features deli-style sand-

Astoria Bridge

wiches, omelettes, crepes, salads, soups, and seafood luncheon plates. Dinners include steaks, chicken, and large seafood menu: oysters, prawns, crab, and razor clams. Daily specials. On the river with a great view. Full bar. Moderate.

Ship Inn, 1 Second Street; (503) 325–0033. Just north off U.S. 30 on Second Street, on the river. Lunch and dinner daily. Fish and chips and more, done to perfection. Halibut, cod, prawns, scallops, oysters, or a combination plate of all five, as well as squid, steamer clams, or sole Mornay available as a half order, full order, or dinner. Half and full orders include fries, coleslaw, and tartar sauce. Dinners come with soup, salad, fries, tartar sauce, beverage, and ice cream. Appetizers and sandwiches available, as well as pork sausages and Cornish pasties. Cocktails, wine, and a large selection of domestic and imported beers. Watney's Red Barrel and Guinness Stout on tap. Great view. Moderate.

SHOPPING AND BROWSING

Although shops and galleries are scattered about greater Astoria, the main shopping area is downtown Astoria and along the riverfront, north of U.S. 30. Ample on-street parking invites shoppers and browsers to park and stroll eastbound and westbound U.S. 30 and adjacent side streets.

MUSEUMS

Columbia River Maritime Museum, 1792 Marine Drive; (503) 325–2323. North side of U.S. 30, on the river. Daily, 9:30 A.M. to 5:00 P.M.; closed Monday, October through April. A truly superb museum with an extensive maritime collection: entire boats, a steamboat pilothouse, the bridge of a World War II destroyer, operating submarine periscopes for viewing river traffic, ship models, numerous historical displays, photographs, and a shop with maritime gifts and books. A *must-see.*

Flavel House, 441 Eighth Street; (503) 325–2203; www.clatsophistoricalsociety.org. Just south of U.S. 30, downtown. Follow the signs. Daily, 10:00 A.M. to 5:00 P.M. Situated in a beautiful Queen Anne mansion, once the home of Captain George Flavel. Exquisite architecture and ornamental interior complement the historical exhibits.

Heritage Museum, 1618 Exchange; (503) 325–2203. Exchange at 16th. Daily, 10:00 A.M. to 5:00 P.M. Astoria's old city hall houses the Clatsop County Historical Society's permanent and rotating exhibits, including artifacts from the *Peter Iredale* shipwreck and from other historical sites.

BEACHES, PARKS, TRAILS, AND WAYSIDES

Miles of beach extend southward from the south jetty at the mouth of the Columbia River. To reach the beach, head for **Fort Stevens State Park,** which lies 4 miles west of U.S. 101, between Warrenton and Hammond. In addition to the fine beach areas, there are 8 miles of bike trails, 5 miles of hiking trails, picnic areas, and old fortifications and gun emplacements with interpretive displays.

Fort Stevens was built in 1865. In 1897 it underwent extensive refortification to improve harbor and coastal defenses. It had eight concrete batteries and armaments, including 10-inch rifled cannons capable of lobbing 617-pound projectiles 9 miles.

The greatest activity at the fort was during World War II when 2,500 men were stationed there. New 6-inch guns were installed, which had a range of 15 miles.

On June 21, 1942, the fort had the distinction of being the first American fort to be fired on by a foreign enemy since the War of 1812. The Japanese submarine making all the noise did no damage, and, because the sub was out of range, the fort did not return fire. In fact, in the fort's history, the guns were never fired in battle.

Fort Stevens was deactivated after World War II and used by the Corps of Engineers for some time. The state leased the land in 1976 and has since operated it as Oregon's largest state park.

On October 25, 1906, the *Peter Iredale*—home port Liverpool, England—was twenty-eight days outbound from Salina Cruz. An iron-and-steel, four-masted bark under full sail, she was standing off the mouth of the Columbia when fierce winds and treacherous currents drove her aground on Clatsop Beach. Despite a furious surf, tangles of rigging and debris, and steel masts that, according to the ship's captain, "snapped like pipe stems," all hands escaped safely to shore. Time and tide have taken their toll, but the mighty ship's rusting skeleton remains visible on the beach for visitors to examine and photograph.

The Corps of Volunteers for Northwest Discovery, led by Captains Meriwether Lewis and William Clark, came within sight of the Pacific Ocean in November 1805. Within a month, the party established its winter headquarters in northwest Oregon and built a small fort they named after the friendly local Clatsop tribe.

A reconstructed fort, built by local citizens in 1955, now occupies the same spot. It's managed by the National Park Service and is open all year. During the summer months, park rangers dressed in period costume portray life as it was here for Lewis and Clark and their party of explorers. They demonstrate the use of flintlock rifles, candle-making techniques, buckskin sewing, woodworking, and canoe building. The **Fort Clatsop National Monument** lies 3 miles east of U.S. 101, just south of Astoria.

In town the expertly restored **Astoria Column** provides the best vantage for panoramic views and photography. It stands atop **Coxcomb Hill,** which rises 635 feet above the Columbia River. To reach it, turn south off U.S. 30 at 12th Street downtown and follow the signs up the hill, through a lovely residential area. Climb the 166 steps to the observation platform, and you will be able to see and photograph great expanses of Oregon and Washington, Astoria, the Columbia River estuary, bridges, jetties, ships, Youngs River and Youngs Bay, the ocean, and mountains. This is a great place to enjoy a sunrise breakfast or to watch a Pacific sunset.

WATER SPORTS AND ACTIVITIES

Fishing is the main water sport in this area, and the fishing centers on the lower Columbia and nearby offshore areas, although surf fishing is seasonally good and the jetties can be productive.

Salmon angling is predominantly an offshore summer fishery. Charter boats are available in Astoria, Warrenton, and Hammond. Anglers who tow their own craft will find launching and mooring facilities in the same areas, but a note of caution is in order. The Columbia bar is dangerous. It did not earn the nickname "Graveyard of the Pacific" for its gentle waters and ease of navigation. Only experienced boaters with craft built for heavy seas should navigate these waters. Even experienced boaters with adequate boats should check on conditions with local boaters, marina owners, and the Coast Guard before venturing out.

Fishing for salmon and steelhead in the lower river can be quite good, but it is affected by the usual fisheries-management concerns, as well as various Indian treaties and the governments of two states. Regulations are abundant and abundantly abstruse. Read them carefully; then check with locals for translation.

One of the top angling attractions of the lower Columbia is the sturgeon fishery. Although these prehistoric fish are available all year, the best fishing here is in the summer, when great runs of forage fish move into the river. Some charter operators offer sturgeon trips. If you try it on your own, check with tackle-shop proprietors for the latest information.

The ocean beaches in this area are the best in Oregon for digging razor clams. There's a midsummer closure along the beaches north of Tillamook, so check the regulations before going.

Charlton Deep Sea Charters, P.O. Box 637; Warrenton; (503) 338–0569 or (503) 861–2429; www.ifish.net. Deep-sea fishing charters on the 50-foot *Ruby Sea* by Captain Mark Charlton. Halibut, sturgeon, salmon, bottom fishing, tuna, and crabbing trips.

WEATHER AND TIDE INFORMATION

National Weather Service; www.noaa.gov

TRAVEL INFORMATION

Astoria-Warrenton Area Chamber of Commerce, 111 West Marine Drive; P.O. Box 176; (503) 325–6311 or (800) 875–6807; www.oldoregon.com

April	Astoria-Warrenton Crab and Seafood Festival, (503) 325–6311
June	Scandinavian Festival, (503) 325–4600
July	Fourth of July Celebration, Astoria, (503) 325–6311
	Warrenton's Fourth of July, (503) 325–6311
August	Clatsop County Fair, (503) 325–4600
	Regatta Festival, (503) 325–6311
October	Great Columbia Bridge Run, (503) 325–6311
November	Santa Lucia Festival of Lights, (503) 325–4600

ASTORIA

WASHINGTON

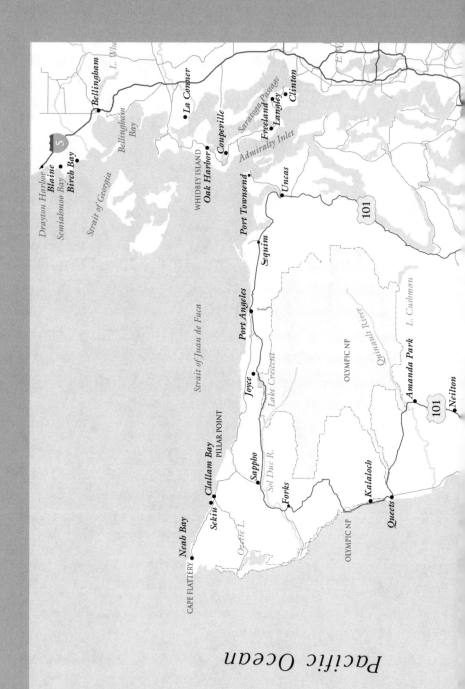

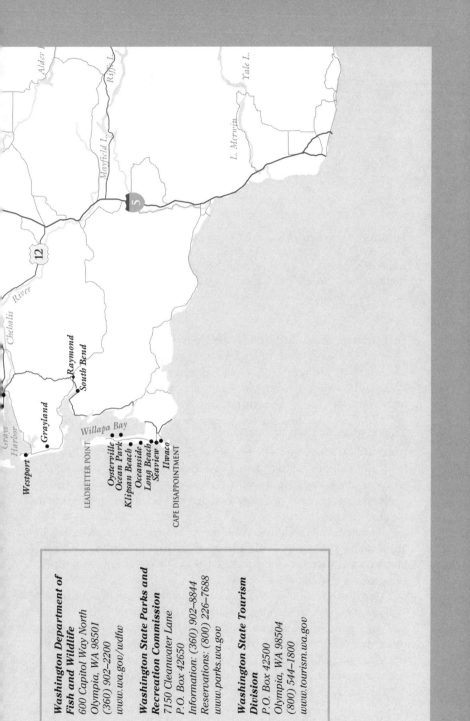

Washington Department of Fish and Wildlife
600 Capitol Way North
Olympia, WA 98501
(360) 902–2200
www.wa.gov/wdfw

Washington State Parks and Recreation Commission
7150 Cleanwater Lane
P.O. Box 42650
Information: (360) 902–8844
Reservations: (800) 226–7688
www.parks.wa.gov

Washington State Tourism Division
P.O. Box 42500
Olympia, WA 98504
(800) 544–1800
www.tourism.wa.gov

LONG BEACH
Population: 1,365

ILWACO
Population: 875

Location: *Long Beach is 1 mile north of the U.S. 101 junction at Seaview on State Route 103. Zip: 98631. Ilwaco is on U.S. 101, 2 miles south of Seaview, 11 miles northwest of the Astoria Bridge over the Columbia River. Zip: 98624.*

Pointing northward from Cape Disappointment and the mouth of the Columbia River is a long finger of surf-lined sand, shrubs, and scrub forest that separates the Pacific Ocean from Willapa Bay. Strung along the peninsula are seven tiny towns that offer visitors a wide range of attractions.

Chief among these in the south are Long Beach and Ilwaco, with Seaview in between. Ilwaco is a waterfront community where commercial, sport, and charter boats are moored a short distance from the Columbia River bar. Long Beach is a resort community with an abundance of travel accommodations and access to its namesake beach, which city fathers have proclaimed the "world's longest beach."

The peninsula's climate is ideal for growing cranberries, which are a major cash crop, with 465 acres in production. The Ocean Spray cooperative here has produced as much as 3.7 million pounds of berries in a single year.

On the bay side of the peninsula, oysters are big business. Willapa Bay oysters, shipped throughout the country and to many foreign destinations, add an estimated $18 million to the region's economy. All the oyster beds on the bay are privately owned, so there is no public harvest. Fresh oysters are available at local seafood markets, and most area restaurants serve them.

About 13.5 miles north of Long Beach is a community that was established because of the area's abundant oyster beds. Oysterville was founded in 1854 by I. A. Clark and R. H. Espy, grandfather of poet, author, and language maven Willard R. Espy. The town, once the county seat, now dozes on the bay shore, home to fewer than fifty year-round residents.

Oysterville was placed on the National Register of Historic Places in 1976. A number of its buildings, standing since the 1860s and 1870s, have been restored, making the idyllic town a worthwhile spot to visit. Stop by the church to pick up a walking-tour guide and map.

LODGING

Chautauqua Lodge Motel, 304 14th Northwest; P.O. Box 757; Long Beach; (360) 642–4401 or (800) 869–8401; www.chautaqualodge.com. Located 14 blocks north of Long Beach city center. Twin, double, and queen beds in 180 units with cable TV. Fireplaces and ocean-view rooms available. Indoor pool, whirlpool, sauna, and recreation room. Near the golf course. Potlatch Restaurant & Lounge on premises, open daily for breakfast, lunch, and dinner. Inexpensive to expensive.

The Lion's Paw Inn, 3310 Pacific Highway South; Box 425; Seaview; (360) 642–2481 or (800) 972–1046. Located just 1.5 miles from downtown Long Beach, this charming bed-and-breakfast is a cheery yellow 1911 Craftsman house surrounded by old-fashioned gardens. The inn has 4 guest rooms, and the interior features original fir and cedar walls and a grand stone fireplace in the great room. Loaner kites, fleece bathrobes, and bicycles are provided. Strolling distance from the beach. A homemade breakfast is prepared each morning. Moderate.

The Shelburne Country Inn & Shoalwater Restaurant, 4415 Pacific Way; P.O. Box 250; Seaview 98644; (360) 642–2442 or (800) 466–1896; www.theshelburneinn.com. In Seaview, 2 miles north of Ilwaco, on State Route 103 at North 45th. Has 17 guest rooms, furnished with antiques, with private and shared baths. Established in 1896. Listed on the National Register of Historic Places. Room rates include an excellent country-style breakfast. Facilities for handicapped. Widely acclaimed Shoalwater Restaurant on premises. Moderate to expensive.

CAMPGROUNDS AND RV PARKS

Andersen's on the Creek RV Park, Route 1; Box 480; Long Beach; (360) 642–2231 or (800) 645–6795; www.andersensrv.com.

Located 3.5 miles north of the northernmost traffic light. Has 15 tent sites and 60 full-hookup RV sites with cable TV. Showers, laundry, playground, beach access. Propane available. Moderate.

Fort Canby State Park, P.O. Box 488; Ilwaco; (360) 642–3078; Interpretive Center: (360) 642–3029. Has 250 campsites, 60 with full hookups. Each site has picnic table and stove. Rest rooms accommodate the handicapped. Showers, tank dump, 2 boat ramps at Baker Bay, 4 hiking trails, 2 lighthouses, and interpretive center. Ocean view, beach access, summer interpretive programs. Store sells groceries, supplies, and fishing tackle. Reservations accepted. Moderate.

Ocean Park Resort, P.O. Box 339; Ocean Park 98640; (360) 665–4585 or (800) 645–4634; www.opresort.com. At 259th and R Streets, 2 blocks east of Pacific Highway on nine-and-a-half acres. Has 140 RV sites with full hookups and cable TV. Showers, laundry, heated pool, spa, recreation room, horseshoe pits, volleyball court, wheelchair access. Moderate.

FOOD AND BEVERAGES

The Ark Restaurant, P.O. Box 95; Nahcotta 98637; (360) 665–4133; www.arkrestaurant.com. About 10 miles north of Long Beach, via State Route 103. Dinner daily and Sunday brunch. Hours and days vary seasonally. Recognized by many as one of Washington's most outstanding restaurants and acclaimed by the *Washington Post, Newsweek, Town and Country,* and *Food and Wine,* among others. The cuisine is varied, but depends mainly on fresh local ingredients. Tempting entrees include panfried salmon with chanterelles, lime, cilantro, sherry, and cream; scallops sautéed with sun-dried tomatoes in balsamic cream sauce; grilled lamb chops with polenta and curry Madeira sauce; Greek-style prawns; Gorgonzola-stuffed filet mignon; sautéed chicken and scallops; and the famous Ark Oyster Feed—all the fresh, grilled Willapa Bay oysters you can eat. The menu also includes Boston clam chowder, an assortment of appetizers, and light entrees. Homemade breads, pastries, and desserts. Espresso and special coffee blends. Full bar featuring Northwest brews and wines. Moderate to expensive.

Chuck's Restaurant & Lounge, P.O. Box 503; Long Beach; (360) 642–2721. In north Long Beach, North 19th Street at Pacific. Breakfast, lunch, and dinner daily. Specializes in old-fashioned family dining. Chicken-fried steak with cream gravy, steaks, and seafood are specialties. Friday night prime rib. Cocktails, beer, and wine. Moderate.

The Crab Pot Restaurant, 1917 Pacific Highway South; Long Beach; (360) 642–8870. On State Route 103 in south Long Beach. Lunch and dinner daily. Specializes in fresh local seafood. Whole-crab dinners, steamer clams, fish and chips, chowder, and crab Louis. Fresh seafood market included. Gift packs available. Beer and wine. Moderate.

Dooger's Seafood & Grill, 900 South Pacific; Long Beach; (360) 642–4224. Located just a few blocks from the strolling district of downtown, this pleasant but casual seafood cafe offers country decor, ocean art, and fresh seafood simply served. Dinner is served all day; luncheon menu is offered until 4:00 P.M. Specialties include fish and chips, seafood fettucini, and ⅓-pound Dooger burgers. Beer and wine. Moderate.

Shoalwater Restaurant, P.O. Box 250; Seaview 98644; (360) 642–4142; www.shoalwater.com. At the Shelburne Inn, on State Route 103 at 45th Street, 2 miles north of Ilwaco. Open daily for lunch and dinner. Truly one of the Northwest Coast's finest restaurants, offering great soups and salads, including mussel chowder and seafood Caesar salad. Tempting appetizers include smoked seafood mousse with local smoked oysters, or pâté Shoalwater—Oregon duck-liver pâté with homemade cranberry chutney. Homemade pasta dishes. Entrees, served with homemade bread and seasonally fresh accompaniments, include baked chinook salmon, grilled sturgeon, roasted stuffed quail, bacon-wrapped sirloin—most served with interesting and delicious sauces. Cocktails, beer, and wine. Moderate to expensive.

SHOPPING AND BROWSING

Cranberry Museum and Self-Guided Farm Tours, 2907 Pioneer Road; Long Beach; (360) 642–5553. This 1,200-square-foot museum houses interesting exhibits on the cranberry industry. The ten-acre demonstration cranberry farm offers self-guided tours of the bogs, which are beautiful year-round but especially during the peak growing and harvest season from mid-September to mid-October. Call for seasonal hours of operation; donations accepted.

Marsh's Free Museum, 409 South Pacific Avenue; Long Beach; (360) 642–2188; www.marshsfreemuseum.com. On State Route 103, between South Fourth and South Fifth. Open daily, except Christmas. A Long Beach landmark, the museum is home to Jake the Alligator Man and other oddities. Marsh's also houses a collection of music machines and Victorian games. Antiques, shells, gifts, souvenirs, glass floats, and a variety of oddities.

MUSEUMS

Ilwaco Heritage Museum, 115 Southeast Lake Street; Ilwaco; (360) 642–3446. At the convention center downtown, east off First Street, 1 block south of the traffic light. Daily, 9:00 A.M. to 5:00 P.M.; Sunday, noon to 4:00 P.M.; winter, till 4:00 P.M. Displays of western and Indian art, peninsula history, the Old West, and a 50-foot-long miniature landscape and model railroad. Gift shop.

World Kite Museum, Third Street Northwest; Long Beach, (360) 642–4020. Hours are 11:00 A.M. to 5:00 P.M. Open daily, June through August; Friday through Monday, September through October; and Saturday and Sunday, November through May. Admission is $1.50. This unique museum pays homage to the kite, an object of fascination in Long Beach. Exhibits show the 2,500-year-old history of kites around the world and include displays of rare kites.

BEACHES, PARKS, TRAILS, AND WAYSIDES

The Long Beach Peninsula *is* beaches, parks, trails, and waysides. Along its ocean side is a broad beach of fine basaltic sands packed hard enough to drive automobiles on. It stretches north to south for 28 uninterrupted miles. On the bay side are salt marshes and a wildlife refuge that is home to hundreds of thousands of birds and mammals.

Two miles west of the Astoria Bridge, on the south side of U.S. 101, is **Fort Columbia State Park.** Built a century ago, during an era of intensive coastal fortification, Fort Columbia was first occupied by a regular garrison of troops in 1904 and continued to operate through both world wars, though its guns were never fired at an enemy.

The fort is now one of the state's Heritage Sites. Its guns have been removed, but its batteries are open for tours. The enlisted men's barracks have been restored and now function as an interpretive center. The commandant's quarters are now a museum, and the Coast Artillery Hospital is a youth hostel.

Fort Canby, which lies about 3 miles west of Ilwaco, via North Head/Fort Canby Road off U.S. 101, was established in

Fort Columbia State Park

1875. With its huge bunkers and gun emplacements, it functioned with Forts Columbia and Stevens to guard the mouth of the Columbia. It became a state park in 1957.

The park's 1,700 acres—with campgrounds, picnic areas, hiking trails, and miles of beach—are situated between North Head and Cape Disappointment, with a lighthouse at each end. The **Lewis and Clark Interpretive Center** is also in the park proper, with exhibits that depict the adventures and hardships of the famous Corps of Volunteers for Northwest Discovery.

Construction of the **Cape Disappointment Light** was completed in 1856, after many delays. Although its tower is only 53 feet tall, its light is 220 feet above the water, making it the highest on the Washington coast, as well as the oldest.

The **North Head Light,** built in 1898, has a tower that stands 65 feet tall, with its light 194 feet above the water, visible 20 miles out.

To view and photograph the lighthouse, follow the signs to Fort Canby and to each specific light. Easy hiking trails lead short distances from the parking areas.

At the extreme north end of the Long Beach Peninsula is **Leadbetter Point State Park,** 3 miles north of Oysterville on Stackpole Road. Small dunes, shrubs, grasslands, sparse forests, ponds, and marshes characterize the area. On the west side are beach and ocean; to the east is Willapa Bay.

Much of the south end of the bay, including a 6-mile-long island, is a wildlife refuge. At Leadbetter Point and throughout the wildlife refuge, abundant birdlife resides all year with seasonal increases when migratory waterfowl use the area. Other residents include beaver, otter, raccoon, deer, elk, and black bear.

WATER SPORTS AND ACTIVITIES

The great ocean beach that attracts so many beachcombers, hikers, and kite flyers to this area also provides some of the best razor-clam digging in the state. Clam diggers need a license to harvest these strictly regulated bivalves and should check regulations carefully before digging. The beaches are closed to digging much of the year, and spring and fall openings depend on how well the clam populations are faring.

Fishing along the ocean beaches is mainly for surfperch and seaperch, which are also taken from the bay shore as well as from the north-jetty area and Baker Bay, near Ilwaco. Jetty fishermen also take bottom fish and the occasional lingcod. Along the lower Columbia, shore anglers also take flounder and sole.

The fishery for Columbia River salmon and steelhead is heavily regulated, so be sure to check the regulations carefully before keeping any salmonids caught here. The main salmon fishery is offshore, and at times it can be excellent. Those who tow their own boats will find adequate launching facilities at Ilwaco, but keep in mind that the mouth of the Columbia is often treacherous and never a place for the novice boater.

The lower Columbia also offers some fine sturgeon fishing all year, but particularly during the late spring and early summer. Farther upriver, anglers take largemouth bass in the many sloughs and creeks.

The charter fleet at Ilwaco is ready to serve anglers. These experienced skippers know the Columbia bar and where to find fish offshore. They fish the runs of salmon and work the reefs for bottom fish. Some also offer river fishing for sturgeon.

Beacon Charters & RV Park, P.O. Box 74; Ilwaco; (360) 642–2138 or (877) 642–6414. At the east end of the Ilwaco water front. Salmon, bottom fish, tuna, and sturgeon trips, as well as narrated historic river tours on the lower Columbia. Bait and tackle provided. A 60-site, full-service RV park on the grounds.

Pacific Salmon Charters, P.O. Box 519; Ilwaco; (360) 642–3466 or (800) 831–2695. At the Ilwaco waterfront. Modern fleet of charter boats. Salmon, bottom fish, and combination trips offshore. Sturgeon fishing trips on the lower Columbia. Trips are six to eight hours. All gear furnished. Will arrange to have your catch canned, smoked, stored, or shipped.

TOURS AND TRIPS

Shoalwater Bay Navigation Company, P.O. Box 29; Nahcotta 98637; (360) 665–6246. At the Nahcotta Boat Basin, across from the Ark Restaurant. Narrated cruises of about two hours on beautiful Willapa Bay, aboard a 17-foot Boston Whaler that accommodates two to six passengers. Leaves once a day, weather permitting, before high tide. Circumnavigates Long Island, explores historic and commercial sites, and covers area's wildlife. Phone for departure times.

GOLF

Peninsula Golf, (360) 642–2828. On State Route 103 at 97th Street, just north of Long Beach. Both an 18-hole course and a 9-hole course with putting green, clubhouse, snack bar, fountain, club and cart rental, and pro merchandise.

WEATHER AND TIDE INFORMATION

U.S. Coast Guard, Ilwaco; recorded message, (360) 642–3565

TRAVEL INFORMATION

Long Beach Peninsula Visitors' Bureau, P.O. Box 562; Long Beach; (360) 642–2400 or (800) 451–2542; www.funbeach.com

Refuge Manager, Willapa National Wildlife Refuge; Ilwaco; (360) 484–3482

EVENTS

April	Ragtime Rhodie Festival, Long Beach, (360) 665–6652 or (800) 451–2542
May	Loyalty Day Parade, Long Beach, (360) 642–2400
	Loyalty Day Celebration, Ilwaco, (360) 642–2520 or (800) 451–2542
June	Annual World's Longest Beach Run, Long Beach, (800) 451–2542
	Garlic Festival, Ocean Park, (360) 665–4448
July	Fourth of July Fireworks, Long Beach, (800) 451–2542
	Annual SandSations, Long Beach, (800) 451–2542
September	Labor Day Festival, Ocean Park, (360) 642–2400
October	Cranberrian Fair, Ilwaco, (360) 642–3446
	Water Music Festival, (360) 642–4829
	Kite Festival, Long Beach, (360) 642–4020
November	Wild Mushroom Festival, Long Beach, (800) 451–2542

WESTPORT

Population: 1,900

Location: *West of U.S. 101, via State Route 105, 23 miles southwest of Aberdeen, 32 miles northwest of Raymond. Zip: 98595.*

Since its earliest days, Westport has been a sea town, dependent on the ocean for its livelihood and for its connection with the rest of the world. It is situated on a small peninsula called Point Chehalis (chuh-*hay*-lis) that juts northward to within 2 miles of Point Brown on the opposite shore. The two points form the jaws of Grays Harbor, a large bay more than 12 miles wide in places and reaching inland more than 15 miles to the cities of Aberdeen and Hoquiam.

Grays Harbor was named after explorer and fur trader Captain Robert Gray. He crossed the bar and passed Chehalis Point in 1792 aboard his ship *Columbia Rediviva,* looking for Indians who would trade pelts for trinkets.

By the early 1900s, Westport had become an important whaling port. Ironically, vessels still depart the harbor and cross the bar in pursuit of whales that now get hurrahs instead of harpoons, as observers thrill to the sight and nearness of the huge mammals.

It's the smaller but more numerous denizens of the sea, however, that attract the great majority of visitors to Westport each year: salmon, rockfish, lingcod, flounder, halibut, tuna, and shark. Anglers by the thousands converge on Westport each season. And there to serve them is not only the largest fleet of charter boats on the Washington coast, but also an entire city, with its motels and inns, campgrounds and RV parks, restaurants and taverns, delis and markets, tackle shops and cold-storage facilities poised for the purpose of making anglers happy.

155

LODGING

Albatross Motel, 200 East Dock Street; P.O. Box 1546; (360) 268–9233. Downtown, 3 blocks from the waterfront. Twin, double, queen, and king beds in 13 units with cable TV, some with ocean view. Near shops, restaurants, and charter operators. Inexpensive to moderate.

Chateau Westport Motel, 710 West Hancock Avenue; P.O. Box 349; (360) 268–9101 or (800) 255–9101; www.chateau westport.com. At West Hancock and South Surf Streets, west of southbound State Route 105. Queen and king beds in 110 rooms, suites, and studios with cable TV. Heated indoor pool, sundeck, hot tub, ocean view, and fireplaces. Continental breakfast. Moderate to very expensive.

Coho Motel & RV Park, 2501 North Nyhus; (360) 268–0111 or (800) 572–0177. One block from Float 12 in the boat basin. Has 28 rooms and 80 full-hookup RV sites with cable TV. Showers, laundry, fish-cleaning facilities. Moderate.

Glenacres Inn of Westport, 222 North Montesano; P.O. Box 1246; (360) 268–9391. On State Route 105. Situated on eight wooded acres. Has 8 rooms with private baths and antique furnishings. Deck, gazebo-covered hot tub, barbecue and picnic area, badminton and volleyball, horseshoe pit, horse-trailer space, and corral. Continental breakfast. Also 4 guest cottages with full kitchens. Moderate.

CAMPGROUNDS AND RV PARKS

Grayland Beach State Park, (360) 267–4301. Off State Route 105 in Grayland, 6 miles south of Westport. Has 60 full-hookup sites for RVs up to 40 feet long. Showers, picnic areas, self-guided interpretive trail. On 210 acres with beach access, beachcombing, kite flying, surf fishing. Moderate.

Ocean Gate Resort, 1939 State Route 105; P.O. Box 67; Grayland 98547; (360) 267–1965 or (800) 473–1956. On State Route 105 in Grayland, 6 miles south of Westport. Has 20 tent and 22 RV sites with full hookups, showers, laundry, firewood, picnic tables, playground. Also 6 cabins with kitchens. Inexpensive to moderate.

Pacific Motel and Trailer Park, 330 South Forrest; (360) 268–9325. On southbound State Route 105. Has 80 RV sites with full hookups, cable TV, showers, pool, recreation room, and barbecue. Also 11 motel rooms and an apartment. Moderate.

Westport and the waterfront

Twin Harbors State Park, (360) 268–9565 or (360) 753–4055. West of State Route 105, 2 miles south of Westport. Has 332 campsites: 49 with full hookups, picnic table and stove at each site. Kitchen shelter, showers, tank dump. Park is on 317 acres with 17,710 feet of ocean frontage. Moderate.

FOOD AND BEVERAGES

Coley's Seafood and Sub Shop, 2309 Westhaven Drive; (360) 268–9000. On the waterfront. Breakfast, lunch, and dinner daily, 4:00 A.M. to 10:00 P.M. Fishermen's breakfasts and lunches to go—stuffed croissants, sandwiches, salads, fruits, cold cuts, and bread. Deli and hors d'oeuvre trays, smoked salmon, cracked crab. Moderate.

Sourdough Lil's, 301 East Dock Street; P.O. Box 1599; (360) 268–9700. In town, a half block from the waterfront. Lunch and dinner daily. Burgers and other sandwiches, salads, soups, clam strips, fish and chips, chicken, and pasta dishes. Dinners include oysters, salmon, shrimp, and steaks. Beer, wine, espresso, cappuccino, and other coffees available. Inexpensive to moderate.

MUSEUM

Westport Maritime Museum, 2201 Westhaven Drive; P.O. Box 1074; (360) 268–0078. At the old Coast Guard Station, on the waterfront. Summer: Wednesday through Sunday, noon to 4:00 P.M. Weekends in April and May. Winter: Saturday, Sunday, and holidays, noon to 4:00 P.M. Displays of cranberry-industry and logging equipment. Indian artifacts, agates and other gemstones, shipwreck relics, Coast Guard memorabilia, and many historical photographs, all housed in a beautiful old Nantucket-style Coast Guard building. Also on the premises are reassembled skeletons of a sea lion, a porpoise, and a gray whale. Tours of Grays Harbor Lighthouse daily during summer; weekends only after Labor Day.

WATER SPORTS AND ACTIVITIES

Westport is built for all kinds of saltwater angling. In the boat basin are docks, floats, ramps, and an arched bridge leading to a 1,000-foot-long fishing pier, from which sportsmen take crabs, perch, cod, rockfish, flounder, sole, lingcod, and even salmon.

Westport's huge charter fleet serves anglers, whale watchers, bird-watchers, and sightseers. Bottom fishing is good most of the year, weather and water conditions permitting. Salmon angling is a summer fishery offshore, with limit catches the rule rather than the exception. Albacore tuna show well offshore in July and through early fall. Several charter operators are now running shark trips and combination shark/tuna trips. Peak season for watching and photographing whales is from March to mid-May.

Many of the charter operators and other businesses have toll-free phone numbers. Some of these are seasonal phones, however, usually in service from late spring to early fall.

Cachalot Charters, 2511 Westhaven Drive; (360) 268–0323 or (800) 356–0323. On the waterfront, across from Float 12. Fast, comfortable boats offering salmon, bottom fish, and tuna trips. Rental tackle available. Bait furnished. Free coffee and fish bags. Whale watching on weekends, March through May.

Deep Sea Charters, P.O. Box 1115; (360) 268–9300 or (800) 562–0151. On the waterfront, across from Float 6. Half-day and full-day salmon trips. Bottom fishing trips every day for rockfish, lingcod, and others. Tuna trips 50 to 100 miles offshore. Whale-watching and estuary tours. Get on the "tuna call list" to be called when the albacore show.

Islander Charters, Motel, and RV Park, 421 East Neddie Rose Drive; (360) 268–9166 or (800) 322–1740. On the waterfront, next to the South Jetty. Charters fishing trips aboard the 65-foot *Neddie Rose,* 50-foot *Jackie Dee,* 50-foot *Lucky Pierre,* and 50-foot *Exodus.* Motel has queen beds in 31 rooms with cable TV. RV park has 65 full-hookup sites with cable TV. Pool, showers, laundry facilities, ocean view, beach access. Restaurant on premises serves breakfast, lunch, and dinner daily. Moderate.

Ocean Charters, 2315 Westhaven Drive; (360) 268–9144; Washington, (800) 562–0105. On the waterfront. Offers six-person boats for small parties or larger boats to accommodate up to twenty-five. Salmon, bottom fish, tuna, and shark trips. Overnight tuna/shark trips include food, bunk, bait, and tackle. Just bring a sleeping bag.

TOURS AND TRIPS

Westport/Ocean Shores Passenger Ferry, 321 Dock Street, Float 6; (360) 268–0047. Operates between Westport and Ocean Shores on weekends in May, daily June 1 to Labor Day. Departs Westport dock every one and a half hours from 8:45 A.M. to 7:15 P.M.

OTHER ATTRACTIONS AND SERVICES

Coley's Seafood, 2309 Westhaven Drive; (360) 268–9000. Will smoke, can, freeze, and store the fish you catch.

Westport Aquarium, 321 Harbor Street; (360) 268–0471. A half block from the waterfront. Open Saturday and Sunday, 10:00 A.M. to 4:00 P.M. (Call to confirm hours.) Displays local fish and shellfish.

WEATHER AND TIDE INFORMATION

U.S. Coast Guard, Westport; recorded message, (360) 268–0622

TRAVEL INFORMATION

Westport/Grayland Chamber of Commerce, 2895 Montesano South; (360) 268–9422 or (800) 345–6223; www.westportwa.com or www.westportcam.com

Westport Marina, P.O. Box 1601; (360) 268–9665; www.port grays.org

EVENTS

March	Grayland Driftwood Show, (800) 473–6018
April	Crab Races and Crab Feed, (800) 345–6223
May	Blessing of the Fleet, (800) 345–6223
July	Annual Fireworks and Dock Crunch, (800) 345–6223
	Beach Party and Kite Festival, (800) 473–6018
August	Brady's Annual Oyster Feed, Westport, (800) 473–6018
	International Longboard Classic, Westport, (800) 473–6018
	Westport Seafood Festival, (800) 473–6018
October	Cranberry Harvest Festival, Grayland, (800) 473–6018
December	Harbor Lights, Westport, (800) 473–6018
	Santa by the Sea, Westport, (800) 473–6018

ABERDEEN
Population: 16,565

HOQUIAM
Population: 8,972

Location: *On U.S. 101, 104 miles south of Forks, 83 miles north of Astoria Bridge, 48 miles west-southwest of Olympia. Zips: 98520/98550.*

Aberdeen was named after a city in Scotland. The Gaelic word means "the meeting of two rivers," which is appropriate for this Washington town established at the confluence of the Chehalis (chuh-*hay*-lis) and Wishkah (*wish*-kah) rivers. The name Hoquiam (*hoh*-kwee-uhm) derives from the Indian term ho-qui-umpts, meaning "hungry for wood," which referred to the abundance of driftwood at the mouth of the Hoquiam River. The term would also aptly describe the side-by-side cities today, with their sawmills, wood-products factories, and lumber-laden ships bound for Asia.

This is an area mainly dependent on logging and the manufacture and shipping of lumber and wood products. Aberdeen's first sawmill was built in 1884. The shipbuilding industry flourished until the 1920s, followed by the establishment of plywood, shake, and pulp mills as well as furniture and other wood-product factories. The area, like so many of its kind, shows some wear from years of industrial use and scars from recent recessions and slumps in the wood-products industry.

Nevertheless, the Aberdeen/Hoquiam area is of interest to travelers and may offer even more in the near future. It has long been a convenient stopover for travelers heading north to the Olympic Peninsula and Olympic National Park or south to the beaches and parks of Washington and Oregon. The communities offer adequate eateries and overnight accommodations. For those with time to linger, there are museums, some handsomely restored homes, and a number of annual events worth investigating.

This is also an important stopover area for nonhuman travelers.

161

When in port at Aberdeen, the brig *Lady Washington* is open for tours.

(Photo courtesy Grays Harbor Historical Seaport)

In April and May, the 98 square miles of Grays Harbor estuary, tidelands, and marshes attract shorebirds by the hundreds of thousands. They congregate here each spring to rest, feed, and store fat for their long journey north to arctic and subarctic nesting areas.

To reach the south shore areas and marshes on the estuary, take State Route 105 west off U.S. 101 in south Aberdeen, which leads to Westport. State Route 109, west off U.S. 101 in Hoquiam, follows the north shore all the way to the ocean.

No doubt, the greatest allure this area holds for travelers is the ambitious project launched in 1988 after many months of planning and fund-raising. Called the Grays Harbor Historical Seaport, this major undertaking could be one of the most important and enjoyable maritime attractions on the Pacific coast when completed. The project includes a maritime museum, boardwalks, specialty shops, and the *Lady Washington,* a replica of a ship that plied the Pacific in the 1700s. (See Museums.)

LODGING

Hoquiam's Castle, 515 Chenault Avenue; Hoquiam; (360) 533–2005; www.hoquiamscastle.com. This twenty-room Victorian house, built in 1897 by lumber baron Robert Lytle, has been transformed from a museum to a premiere bed-and-breakfast featuring cut crystal chandeliers, stained and leaded glass windows, and the original woodwork. Declared a state and national historic site, the inn offers only 5 suites within its 10,000-square-foot quarters. Gourmet breakfasts and afternoon and evening snacks and beverages. Moderate.

Lytle House Bed & Breakfast, 509 Chenault Avenue; Hoquiam; (360) 533–2320 or (800) 677–2320. West of U.S. 101, next to Hoquiam's Castle. Eight guest rooms in a fine old Victorian home furnished with antiques. Full breakfast. Moderate.

Olympic Inn, 616 West Heron Street; Aberdeen; (800) 562–8618. On southbound U.S. 101, downtown. A modern motel with queen beds in 55 rooms, cable TV, in-room coffee, and in-room refrigerators. Laundry facilities. Kitchen units available. Inexpensive to moderate.

FOOD AND BEVERAGES

Billy's Restaurant, 322 East Heron Street; Aberdeen; (360) 533–7144. On southbound U.S. 101, downtown. Lunch and dinner daily. A restored saloon that serves tasty and hearty burgers and other sandwiches as well as salads, steaks, and seafood dinners. Full bar. Moderate.

MUSEUMS

Aberdeen Museum of History, 111 East Third Street; Aberdeen; (360) 533–1845. Four blocks east of northbound U.S. 101, between Broadway and North I Street. Summer: Wednesday through Sunday, 11:00 A.M. to 4:00 P.M. Winter: weekends, noon to 4:00 P.M. Situated in the old National Guard Armory. Pioneer, farm, logging, and other exhibits. Model of downtown Aberdeen before the destructive 1903 fire. Antique fire trucks, canoe collection, blacksmith shop, mercantile store, and more.

Grays Harbor Historical Seaport, 813 East Heron Street; P.O. Box 2019; Aberdeen; (360) 532–8611. On the waterfront. Monday through Friday, 9:00 A.M. to 5:00 P.M.; daily in summer. Historic maritime displays and tours of the *Lady Washington*, a replica of one of Captain Robert Gray's sailing ships, used in the eighteenth-century exploration of the Pacific Coast. Sailing cruises of Grays Harbor daily during the summer.

Polson Museum, 1611 Riverside Avenue; P.O. Box 432; Hoquiam; (360) 533–5862; www.polsonmuseum.com. On U.S. 101. June through Labor Day: Wednesday through Sunday, 11:00 A.M. to 4:00 P.M. September through May: weekends, noon to 4:00 P.M. A beautiful twenty-six-room mansion that's now a national historic site, set amid trees and rosebushes. Sawmill and logging exhibits, kitchen appliances and utensils, sports equipment and photographs, early fashions and furnishings, all pleasingly displayed.

WEATHER AND TIDE INFORMATION

U.S. Coast Guard, Westport; recorded message, (360) 268–0622

TRAVEL INFORMATION

Grays Harbor Chamber of Commerce, 506 Duffy Street; Aberdeen; (360) 532–1924; www.graysharbortourism.com

EVENTS

July	Bite of Grays Harbor and Splash Festival; Aberdeen, (360) 532–1924
	Hoquiam River Festival, (360) 533–3447
September	Loggers' Playday, Hoquiam, (360) 532–0905
December	Holly Days in Hoquiam, (360) 532–1924

OCEAN SHORES
Population: 3,032

PACIFIC BEACH
Population: 1,200

Location: *Ocean Shores is west of U.S. 101, via State Route 109 and State Route 115, and about 20 miles west of Hoquiam. Zip: 98569. Pacific Beach is on State Route 109, west of U.S. 101, 16 miles north of Ocean Shores. Zip: 98571.*

Several small communities lie along the Pacific, from Ocean Shores north. Ocean City (population: 500) is 8 miles to the north. Copalis Beach (population: 900) is 3.5 miles farther. Two miles above Pacific Beach is Moclips (population: 700). The village of Taholah is 9 miles north in the Quinault Indian Reservation, but there are no tourist facilities there, and the beaches are closed to the public.

At the southern end of this stretch is a peninsula that separates Grays Harbor from the ocean. The flatland here is characterized by broad sweeps of sandy beach and prairies of beach grass, laced with narrow lakes and freshwater canals. Northward, lowlands give way to rocky bluffs, grasses succumb to shrubs, and highlands belong to timber.

Before 1960 the Ocean Shores area was a ranch owned by the Minard family. It was purchased for $1 million and subsequently developed. Today it is a residential and resort area of about 6,000 acres, with 6 miles of ocean beach where residents and visitors enjoy flying kites, riding horses, fishing, clam digging, hiking, and searching the surf and drift lines for seaborne treasures.

LODGING

The Canterbury Inn, P.O. Box 310; Ocean Shores; (360) 289–3317 or (800) 562–6678. Has 44 oceanfront condominiums, now all nonsmoking, with cable TV, HBO, Disney Channel, private balconies, and kitchens with microwave ovens and dishwashers. Heated indoor pool and spa. Moderate to expensive.

Iron Springs Resort, 3707 State Route 109, P.O. Box 207; Copalis Beach 98535; (360) 276–4230. A longtime Washington coast favorite with 23 cottages (some duplexes) and 2 apartments with kitchens and fireplaces, accommodating 2 to 10 persons. All linens and bedding furnished. Rental TVs available or bring your own. Heated, covered pool. On 100 beautiful wooded acres. Moderate to expensive.

Ocean Crest Resort, Sunset Beach; Moclips 98652; (360) 276–4465 or (800) 684–8439. One mile north of Pacific Beach, on State Route 109. Has 45 units with cable TV. Studios and 1- and 2-bedroom apartments accommodate 2 to 6 persons. Fireplaces and balconies. Kitchens available. Recreation center with exercise equipment, spa, sauna, heated indoor pool, tanning bed, and sundecks. Nightlighted beach and surf. Wooded setting. Children's play area. Beauty salon, gift shop, and gallery, as well as a fine restaurant on premises. Cocktail lounge with ocean view and entertainment. Inexpensive to moderate.

The Sandpiper Beach Resort, 4159 State Route 109, P.O. Box A; Pacific Beach; (360) 276–4580 or (888) 702–3224. Located 1.5 miles south of Pacific Beach. Twin and queen beds in 29 units with fireplaces and ocean view. Studios and units with 1 to 3 bedrooms. On the beach. Kite and gift shop on premises. No in-room phones or TV. Moderate.

The Sands Resort, P.O. Box 57; Ocean Shores; (360) 289–2444 or (800) 841–4001. On Ocean Boulevard. Cable TV and HBO in 105 units, some with kitchens. Heated indoor pool, sauna, whirlpool, hot tubs, game room, wheelchair access. Inexpensive to moderate.

Shilo Inn, 707 Ocean Shores Boulevard Northwest; Ocean Shores; (360) 289–4600 or (800) 222–2244. Satellite TV with premium channels and VCRs in 113 deluxe suites with computer data ports, microwave ovens, refrigerators, coffeemakers, hair dryers, irons, and ironing boards. Indoor pool, spa, sauna, steam room, and fitness center. Restaurant on premises. Moderate to expensive.

CAMPGROUNDS AND RV PARKS

Ocean City State Park, (360) 289–3553. Two miles north of Ocean Shores on State Route 115, on the ocean. Has 150 tent sites and 29 full-hookup RV sites for vehicles of any size. Picnic tables, fireplaces, showers, firewood in summer, kitchen shelter, tank dump. Wheelchair access. Inexpensive.

Pacific Beach State Park, (360) 276–4297. Just off State Route 109 in Pacific Beach. Has 32 basic and 32 RV sites with water and electric hookups for vehicles to 45 feet. Picnic tables, showers, tank dump. On the beach. Inexpensive.

FOOD AND BEVERAGES

Mariah's at the Polynesian, 291 Ocean Shores Boulevard; Ocean Shores; (360) 289–3315. Breakfast, lunch, and dinner daily. Traditional and unusual breakfast fare. Large selection of seafoods, pasta dishes, and Polynesian cuisine. Full bar. Moderate.

Ocean Crest Resort Restaurant & Lounge, Sunset Beach; Moclips 98562; (360) 276–4465. One mile north of Pacific Beach on State Route 109. Breakfast, lunch, and dinner daily. Traditional and special breakfast offerings include shrimp Benedict, frittata, and petite filet and eggs. Lunch selections include burgers and other sandwiches, soups, salads, and such entrees as butter clams, crab-and-shrimp soufflé, teriyaki stir-fry, and shrimp-stuffed chicken breast. The dinner menu lists more than a half dozen appetizers. Good selection of charbroiled steaks and chops, chicken, pasta, and quail. Superb seafood dishes include broiled Quinault River salmon, grilled or sautéed Willapa Bay oysters, steamed Hood Canal clams or mussels, and baked Dungeness crab casserole. Full bar. Moderate to expensive.

SHOPPING AND BROWSING

Cutting Edge Kite Shop, 676 Ocean Shores Boulevard Northwest; Ocean Shores; (360) 289–5682 or (800) 379–3109. Monday through Friday, 10:00 A.M. to 6:00 P.M.; Saturday, 9:00 A.M. to 6:00 P.M.; Sunday, 10:00 A.M. to 5:00 P.M. Carries a large selection of kites, wind socks, wind toys, flags, and more. Kite repair.

Gallery Marjuli, Homeport Plaza; Point Brown Avenue; Ocean Shores; (360) 289–2858. Daily, 10:30 A.M. to 5:00 P.M. Gifts and artwork. Limited-edition prints. Marine art. Mount St. Helens glass, vases, pottery, stationery, and more.

WATER SPORTS AND ACTIVITIES

Surf fishing is best along the ocean beach in the Ocean Shores vicinity and from the north jetty when water conditions permit. Surfperch and seaperch are the main species taken from the surf. The jetty gives up perch, rockfish, cabezon, lingcod, and salmon.

The beach from the jetty north to Moclips and beyond is good for digging razor clams in season. In fact, the motels and resorts along this stretch of coast fill up fast not only on weekends during the summer but also during minus-tide periods.

Duck Lake and Lake Minard and the 23 miles of interconnecting freshwater canals provide plenty of opportunities for canoeing, waterskiing, fishing, and exploring. The lakes are stocked with trout, but the best fishing here is for largemouth bass, with some big fish taken every year.

Those who tow boats on trailers or who arrive in the area by boat will find moorage at the marina. Some people fish and crab from the docks here, but there's much better pier fishing and crabbing across Grays Harbor at Westport. During the summer season, a passenger ferry travels between Ocean Shores and Westport.

TOURS AND TRIPS

Westport/Ocean Shores Passenger Ferry, Marina Store; Main Float; Ocean Shores; (360) 268–0047. Operates between Ocean Shores and Westport on weekends in May; daily, June 1 to Labor Day. Departs Ocean Shores dock every one and a half hours, from 9:30 A.M. to 6:30 P.M.

GOLF

Ocean Shores Municipal Golf Course, Albatross and Canal Drive; Ocean Shores; (360) 289–3357. An 18-hole, 6,021-yard, par-71 course. Pro shop, cart and club rental and sales. Clubhouse with restaurant and lounge.

WEATHER AND TIDE INFORMATION

U.S. Coast Guard, Westport; recorded message, (360) 268–0622

TRAVEL INFORMATION

Ocean Shores Chamber of Commerce, 120 West Chance A La Mer; P.O. Box 382; Ocean Shores; (360) 289–2451 or (800) 762–3224; www.oceanshores.org

Washington Coast Chamber of Commerce, P.O. Box 562; Copalis Beach 98535; (360) 289–4552

EVENTS

March	Beachcomber's Fun Fair, Ocean Shores, (360) 289–3968
April	Associated Arts Photo Show, Ocean Shores, (360) 289–4411
May	Festival of Colors, (800) 762–3224
June	International Kite Challenge, Ocean Shores, (800) 762–3224
	Sand and Sawdust at the Shores, (800) 762–3224
July	"Color Over the Water" Kite Contest, Copalis Beach, (360) 289–4552
	Sand Sculpture Contest, Copalis Beach, (360) 289–4552
	Fire Over the Water, Ocean City, (360) 289–4552
	Kite-Flying Contest, Pacific Beach, (360) 289–4552
September	Kelper's Parade, Moclips, (360) 289–4552
	Associated Arts & Crafts Show, Ocean Shores, (800) 762–3224
November	Dixieland Jazz Festival, Ocean Shores, (800) 762–3224

FORKS

Population: 3,400

....

Location: *On U.S. 101, 105 miles north of Hoquiam, 65 miles north of Quinault, 35 miles north of Kalaloch (**Clay**-lock), 47 miles southeast of Neah Bay. Zip: 98331.*

....

Highway 101 levels off on a broad prairie between the Bogachiel and Calawah Rivers and slows through the one-stoplight town of Forks. Despite its diminutive size, Forks is the economic hub of the western Olympic Peninsula. It's also a jumping-off point for many who travel here to enjoy a great variety of outdoor recreation opportunities.

The history of Forks is the history of logging in western Washington. Evidence of the timber industry is everywhere, from the roadside clear-cuts to the Forks Timber Museum. This is a land of wool-collar workers, hard hats, calk boots, and red suspenders.

Numerous rivers and creeks drain the western slopes of the Olympic Mountains and the vast expanses of rain forest, where as much as 140 inches of rain might fall in the course of a year. Most of the land here is public, under the jurisdiction of the National Park Service and U.S. Forest Service. Hiking trails of every stripe stretch through lowland meadows and into the high country. Some meander to wilderness lakes, others to spectacular waterfalls. Many lead to broad beaches, rocky shores, coastal cliffs, and rugged headlands.

Some of the attractions listed here might seem distant or far-flung, but this is big country, with Forks the only community of any appreciable size. For the traveler, it can be a convenient headquarters for day trips into the nearby Hoh Rain Forest and the coastal stretches of Olympic National Park.

LODGING

Forks Motel, 351 Forks Avenue South; P.O. Box 510; (360) 374–6243 or (800) 544–3416. On U.S. 101, town center. Double and queen beds in 73 units with cable TV, refrigerators, and microwave ovens. A modern, well-maintained motel. Inexpensive to moderate.

Kalaloch Lodge, 157151 Highway 101; (360) 962–2271; www.visitkalaloch.com. In Olympic National Park, on U.S. 101, 30 miles north of Lake Quinault, 35 miles south of Forks. A beautiful, rustic lodge and cabins on the edge of the Pacific. Forty lodge rooms, suites, and cabins available, 12 with kitchens. Most are oceanfront with easy beach access. Good clam digging in season, excellent beachcombing, surf fishing, hiking, biking, photography, and exploring. Great getaway spot. Guided tours, gift shop, store, service station, and restaurant at lodge. Moderate to expensive.

Lake Quinault Lodge, 345 South Shore Road; P.O. Box 7; Quinault 98575; (360) 288–2900; Washington, (800) 562–6672; www.visitlakequinault.com. Two miles east of U.S. 101, 30 miles south of Kalaloch, 65 miles south of Forks, 40 miles north of Hoquiam. A grand old country inn with a variety of room and suite configurations, modern amenities, and lake view. Heated indoor pool, whirlpool, sauna, and game room. Superb restaurant and comfortable lounge on premises. Everything is stone and cedar and has the scent of fresh rain on conifers. Many hiking trails nearby. Weekends, especially in summer, can be crowded. Weekdays aren't so bad, and off-season weekdays are outstanding. One of the West Coast's great getaways. Moderate to expensive, but off-season rates and package deals offer bargain opportunities.

Manitou Lodge, 813 Kilmer Road; P.O. Box 600; (360) 374–6295; www.manitoulodge.com. About 9.5 miles west of U.S. 101. Take LaPush Road to Mora Road, then right off Mora Road on Kilmer Road. A small, rustic lodge with 5 sleeping rooms. Caters to anglers in season and functions as a bed-and-breakfast inn the rest of the year. A hearty breakfast to sustain you for recreation is served. One room has a queen bed and queen sofa bed. All others are furnished with twin beds. Near Sol Duc, Bogachiel, and Quillayute Rivers. Short drive to Rialto Beach. Moderate.

Miller Tree Inn, 654 East Division Street; P.O. Box 1565; (360) 374–6806; www.northolympic.com/millertree. At Sixth and East Division Streets, east of U.S. 101, in Forks. Twin and double beds in 6 rooms with 3 shared baths. A charming 1914 former farmhouse on three acres. Eight-person hot tub. Full breakfast and snacks. Predawn breakfast available for anglers, photographers, and others who want to be out at first light. Cleaning and freezing facilities for fish and game. Off-road parking for boat trailers. Trailer shuttle service. Inexpensive to moderate.

Olympic Suites Inn, 800 Olympic Drive; (360) 374–5400 or (800) 262–3433; www.olympicsuitesinn.com. Located within the city, but tucked away along the Calawah River, this hotel has recently undergone an extensive renovation. The very private 1- and 2-bedroom suites are spacious and feature private decks or balconies in a wooded setting that often grants views of eagles or deer. Microwaves, refrigerators, coffeemakers, some with full kitchens, all nonsmoking. Inexpensive to moderate.

Pacific Inn Motel, 352 South Forks Avenue; P.O. Box 1997; (360) 374–9400 or (800) 235–7344; www.pacificinnmotel.com. On U.S. 101, city center. A modern, comfortable motel with queen beds, refrigerators, microwave ovens, and cable TV in 34 rooms. Laundry facilities on premises. Restaurants nearby. Inexpensive.

CAMPGROUNDS AND RV PARKS

Bogachiel State Park, HC 80; Box 500; (888) 226–7688. On the Bogachiel River, 6 miles south of Forks. Has 41 campsites with tables and stoves for RVs up to 35 feet, but no hookups. Showers, tank dump, and river access. Inexpensive.

Forks 101 RV Park, P.O. Box 1041; (360) 374–5073 or (800) 962–9964. On U.S. 101 in Forks. Has 48 sites (13 pull-through) with full hookups and cable TV. Showers and laundry facilities. Inexpensive.

Hoh River Resort & Recreation Area, 175443 Highway 101; (360) 374–5566. On U.S. 101, 15 miles south of Forks. Has 20 full-hookup sites and 10 tent sites with tables and fire pits. Four cabins with kitchens. Satellite TV, showers, tank dump, firewood, store, tackle, propane, gasoline, ice, and laundry facilities. Inexpensive.

Kalaloch Campground, Olympic National Park; (360) 565–3100. West of U.S. 101, 1 mile north of Kalaloch Lodge, 31 miles north of Lake Quinault, 34 miles south of Forks. A National Park Service campground with 195 campsites, 15 picnic sites, tables, fire pits, tank dump, and 100 feet of ocean frontage. Sand beaches and rocky intertidal areas. Interpretive center open in summer. Inexpensive.

Three Rivers Resort, HC 79; Box 280; (360) 374–5300. Seven miles west of U.S. 101, via Mora Road, north of Forks. A

A foggy morning on a driftwood-strewn beach at Kalaloch

full-service resort with tent sites, full-hookup RV sites, 1- and 2-bedroom cabins, grocery store, gas station, laundromat, guide service, and a restaurant that serves the best burgers in the area and a dozen different milk shakes and malts. Inexpensive.

FOOD AND BEVERAGES

Kalaloch Lodge Dining Room, 157151 Highway 101; (360) 962–2271; www.visitkalaloch.com. On U.S. 101, 30 miles north of Lake Quinault, 35 miles south of Forks. Breakfast, lunch, and dinner daily. River and ocean view. Hearty breakfasts include eggs any style with bacon, ham, country or Italian sausage, toast, and home fries or cottage cheese; hotcakes; French toast; and eggs Benedict. Several omelettes, including the Northwesterner, with oysters and smoked salmon. Good coffee. Lunch menu includes burgers and sandwich plates, salads, chowder, and a good selection of seafood entrees: grilled trout, salmon fillet, clam strips, fish and chips. For dinner, start with baked Brie, oysters on the half shell, or seafood sampler. Chicken and steak available, but seafood is the specialty, especially salmon—served baked, broiled, poached, barbecued, or blackened, with various sauces and accompaniments. Full bar. Moderate.

Riverrun Coffee Shop, 71 Forks Avenue; (360) 374–7580. Open 7:30 A.M. to 5:00 P.M. This espresso bistro/gift and art boutique is a charming alternative to the lumberjack fare at the area's other coffee shops. Serving gourmet coffees, bagels, and pastries as well as wine and snacks, this bistro offers living room–style seating on comfy sofas. The adjoining gift shop and art gallery feature fine ceramics and local photography. Moderate.

The Roosevelt Room, Lake Quinault Lodge; 345 South Shore Road; P.O. Box 7; Quinault 98575; (360) 288–2571. East of U.S. 101, 40 miles north of Hoquiam, 30 miles south of Kalaloch. Breakfast, lunch, and dinner daily. Breakfasts include big three-egg omelettes, pancakes, waffles, a variety of egg dishes, and fresh biscuits and muffins. Among lunch offerings are soups, salads, deli-style sandwiches, fish and chips, tempura salmon or prawns, and shrimp fettuccine. Appetizers: oyster or prawn cocktail, bacon-wrapped scallops, smoked trout, or vegetable plate. Among the dinner entrees are salmon prepared as you wish (blackened, char-broiled, grilled, or baked), stuffed mountain trout, and Willapa Bay oysters. Full bar and excellent wine list. Moderate.

The Smoke House Restaurant, 193161 Highway 101; Box 5050; (360) 374–6258. On U.S. 101, just north of town. Lunch and dinner daily. Smoked salmon, other seafoods, and prime rib are specialties. The lunch menu includes omelettes, a half dozen different burgers, deli-style sandwiches, soups, chowder, alder-smoked salmon fillet, halibut steak, fish and chips, and prawns. Among the tempting appetizers are smoked-salmon spread, smoked-salmon platter with cheddar, sautéed mushrooms, and Cajun-style prawns. Dinner selections include smoked-salmon fettuccine, seafood sauté, chicken teriyaki, and several kinds of steak. Full bar. Smokehouse and cannery on premises with assorted products available. Moderate.

MUSEUM

Forks Timber Museum, Highway 101 South; (360) 374–9663. On U.S. 101 at the south end of town, next to the visitors' center. Open May through September or by appointment. Photographs and exhibits of logging equipment tell the story of western Washington's main industry. Also on display are the memorabilia of pioneer days and exhibits of local Indian culture.

TOURS AND TRIPS

Logging and Mill Tour, Forks; (360) 374–2531 or (800) 443–6757. Tours departing from the Visitors Center (1411 South

Forks Avenue) at 9:00 A.M. are offered Monday, Wednesday, and Friday, May through September (excluding holidays). Free, but donations accepted. The approximate three-hour tours, led by knowledgeable logging experts, take you to a variety of local mills and logging sites. Space is limited so advanced reservations are recommended, and often required, during the summer season.

BEACHES, PARKS, TRAILS, AND WAYSIDES

Western Olympic National Park is a narrow band of forest, bluffs, sandy beaches, and rocky intertidal areas, stretching more than 50 miles from South Beach, near Kalaloch, north all the way to Shi-Shi Beach, at the southern boundary of the Makah Indian Reservation. Just offshore, hundreds of rocks, reefs, sea stacks, and islands are resting areas and rookeries for countless thousands of sea birds and mammals, and most are part of the National Wildlife Refuge system.

As magnificent as this rugged coastline is, some of the beaches seem to have been named by the U.S. Army. Near LaPush are beaches with such unenchanting names as First Beach, Second Beach, and Third Beach. At the southern end of Olympic National Park are Beaches 1, 2, 3, 4, 6, and 7. We can only wonder why the names are so dull and unromantic and what might have happened to Beach 5.

Despite their drab names, these strands of sand and great expanses of rocky rubble join the surly surf to create some of the most magnificent seascapes in the world. This wild coastal zone attracts hikers, backpackers, anglers, artists, photographers, beachcombers, and the hardiest of surfers and sea kayakers.

To reach the beaches nearest Forks, turn west off U.S. 101 north of town on LaPush Road, which will take you to trails leading to First, Second, and Third Beaches. To get to Rialto Beach, take LaPush Road west off U.S. 101, but follow the signs for Mora. Beaches south of Forks are easily accessible via U.S. 101 and short trails leading from parking areas. Follow the Park Service's advice: Don't leave valuables in your vehicle at any of these beaches.

This vast area is laced with trails ranging in length from less than a mile to more than 20 miles. Many are easy to hike; others are strictly for experienced and fit hikers. Some stretches of beach and coastal trails are accessible only on low tides, so it's important to carry tide tables and to pay attention to the ocean at all times. Overnight use of any of the backcountry areas requires permits, available at Park Service and Forest Service ranger stations, which are also excellent sources for maps and abundant information about the Olympic Peninsula's wild west side.

WATER SPORTS AND ACTIVITIES

Although some of the beaches offer opportunities for surf fishing and good clam digging in season, the emphasis here is on trout and salmon fishing. Rivers and creeks of the western peninsula provide some of Washington's best angling for coho and chinook salmon and steelhead trout. Several guides headquartered here offer trips on various Olympic Peninsula streams.

George Ewing, Guides Unlimited; P.O. Box 932; (360) 374–3175. Specializes in drift-boat trips for spring and fall runs of salmon, summer and winter runs of steelhead trout.

Larry Scott, West Side Guide Service; P.O. Box 581; Beaver 98305; (360) 327–3671. Eleven miles north of Forks. Books drift-boat trips. Specializes in fishing for spring and fall chinook, summer and winter steelhead, rainbow trout, and sea-run cutthroat.

Sam Windle, Fishing Guide; P.O. Box 692; (360) 374–5439. Has thirty years' experience fishing and guiding on the Olympic Peninsula. Guides for spring and fall salmon, summer and winter steelhead.

TRAVEL INFORMATION

Forks Chamber of Commerce Visitor Information, P.O. Box 1249; (360) 374–2531 or (800) 443–6757; www.forkswa.com

Pacific Ranger District, 437 Tillicum Lane; Forks; (360) 374–6522

Quinault Ranger Station, USFS/NPS, P.O. Box 9; Quinault 98575; (360) 288–2444

EVENTS

July	July Fourth Old-Fashioned Celebration, (360) 374–2531
October	Hickory Shirt and Heritage Days, (360) 374–2531

NEAH BAY
Population: 1,700

SEKIU
Population: 600

Location: *Neah (**nee**-uh) Bay is on State Route 112, north of U.S. 101, 66 miles west-northwest of Port Angeles, 46 miles northwest of Forks. Zip: 98357. Sekiu (**see**-kyoo), also on State Route 112, is 15 miles east-southeast of Neah Bay. Zip: 98381.*

Tucked away on the outer edge of Washington and the north-western tip of the Olympic Peninsula, Neah Bay is home and home port to the Makah (muh-**kah**) Indians, a unique tribe unrelated to any others in the United States. These are a handsome, intelligent people who can trace their seafaring ancestry as far back as 1000 B.C.

The Makahs have traditionally depended on the sea for most of their food—today mainly as commercial fishermen and charter operators, in the past as fishermen, shellfish gatherers, and whalers. As whalers, they showed unparalleled courage and skill, venturing forth in canoes to hunt their great quarry, armed only with harpoons with points made of mussel shells.

About 500 years ago, a mud slide buried five Makah houses at the village of **Ozette,** 12 miles south of Cape Flattery. The clay earth encapsulated these houses and suspended them in time. By 1970, tides had eroded away enough earth to begin exposing the long-entombed Makah artifacts. In April of that year, a team of archaeologists, headed by Richard Daugherty from Washington State University, began a dig that was to last eleven years and produce more than 55,000 wonderfully preserved artifacts, representing 97 percent of all Northwest Coast Indian artifacts found to date. The best of these are on display at the $2.5 million **Makah Museum** in Neah Bay.

The Makah are friendly people who have a fascinating history on a spectacular part of the Washington coast. Best of all is their willingness and eagerness to share their culture and knowledge with the rest of us. In their own language, the name for their tribe means simply "people of the cape." The Salish name for them, however, was *Makah,* meaning "generous people."

Sekiu is an Indian word meaning "quiet waters." The tiny town of that name is situated on the west shore of Clallam Bay on the Strait of Juan de Fuca. The community of Clallam Bay (population 600) is about 2 miles east of Sekiu. Here and elsewhere along State Route 112, sportfishing is the main attraction, with hiking, beachcombing, photography, and wildlife watching among other popular attractions.

LODGING

Chito Beach Resort, 7639 Highway 112; P.O. Box 270; Clallam Bay 98326; (360) 963–2581; www.chitobeach.com. Located 7 miles west of Sekiu, 8.5 miles east of Neah Bay. Double and queen beds and sleeper sofas in two cottages and an A-frame cabin with fully equipped kitchens, situated on a private bay, 15 feet from the beach. Antiques and original art in all units. Bunkhouse with potbelly stove sleeps eight. Sunrise and sunset views of the strait. Communal bonfire pit on the beach. Moderate.

Curley's Resort and Dive Center, 291 Front Street; P.O. Box 265; Sekiu; (360) 963–2281 or (800) 542–9680. Has 22 units to accommodate up to 6 persons. Cable TV, some kitchens. Also 13 RV sites, full hookups, and showers. Boat and motor rental, diving equipment and charters, launching and moorage, bait, tackle, and ice. Inexpensive to moderate.

Straitside Resort, 241 Front Street; P.O. Box 135; Sekiu; (360) 963–2100; www.straitsideresort.com. In town. Five rooms and suites and two large cabins with twin, double, and queen beds. Cable TV, full kitchens, view of the strait, and beach access. Inexpensive to moderate.

CAMPGROUNDS AND RV PARKS

Coho Resort, 15572 Highway 112; Sekiu; (360) 963–2333. One mile east of Sekiu. Has 108 RV sites with picnic tables, full hookups, showers, and laundry. Tent sites available. Boat launching and moorage, 800-foot breakwater, rental boats and motors, bait, tackle, gas, ice, and fish storage. Inexpensive.

Sekiu on Clallam Bay and Strait of Juan de Fuca

Snow Creek Resort, Highway 112; Marker 691; P.O. Box 248; Neah Bay; (360) 645–2284 or (800) 883–1464; www. snowcreekwa.com. Four miles east of Neah Bay. Has 95 campsites: 22 with full hookups, 38 with water and electricity, and 35 tent sites. All sites with tables and fire pits. Cable TV available. Rental trailers available sleep up to six. View of the strait and beach access. Rest rooms with showers. Bait, tackle, and snack shop. Boat launch, 30 mooring buoys, and dock moorage for 30 more boats. Scuba-tank air. Charters for salmon, halibut, bottom fish, wildlife cruises, and whale watching. Inexpensive to moderate.

Van Riper's Resort Motel & RV Park, 280 Front Street, P.O. Box 246; Sekiu; (360) 963–2334 or (888) 462–0803; www.vanripersresort.com. North off State Route 112 on Front Street. Has 80 RV sites with full hookups. Showers. Firewood available. Boat moorage, boat and motor rental, tackle rental, bait, tackle, and ice. Charter service. Also 10 motel units with kitchens. Inexpensive to moderate.

MUSEUM

Makah Cultural and Research Center, Bayview Avenue, Highway 112; Neah Bay; (360) 645–2711; www.makah.com. Summer: daily, 10:00 A.M. to 5:00 P.M. September 15 through May 31, closed Monday and Tuesday. An exquisite, pleasingly de-signed museum exhibiting well-preserved artifacts from the famed

Ozette dig and other archaeological sites. The 23,000-square-foot museum has 10,000 square feet of gallery and 200 square feet of wall space for traveling or temporary exhibits. Also on display are many fine photographs depicting the Makah culture, full-scale reproductions of canoes, and a longhouse large enough for several families. Many handmade replicas on exhibit are for actual hands-on examination. Classified a *must-see.*

BEACHES, PARKS, TRAILS, AND WAYSIDES

Neah Bay lies just east of Cape Flattery, the most northwesterly point of land in the continental United States. To reach the cape, drive west from Neah Bay 8.5 miles on a good gravel road; then hike the half-mile trail for a view of the Pacific, the **Strait of Juan de Fuca,** and **Tatoosh Island.** The trail is partly planked and has several cedar observation platforms, but some parts have been left in their natural state and can be quite muddy after a rain. So don appropriate footwear and watch your step, even on the planks, which get slippery when wet.

The road to Cape Flattery also leads to **Koitlah Point,** which is 2.7 miles west of Neah Bay. There is an excellent view of the strait, **Vancouver Island,** and **Neah Bay.**

Hobuck Beach is 4.1 miles southwest of Neah Bay by paved and gravel roads. This is a good spot for a picnic and for hiking and photography. Just 2 miles beyond Hobuck Beach is a 3-mile trail leading to **Shi-Shi Beach;** a half mile beyond is the **Makah National Fish Hatchery,** which is open to visitors.

When hiking on beaches in the Makah Reservation, respect the Makahs' wishes: Leave all shells and shellfish where they are and pack out your trash.

WATER SPORTS AND ACTIVITIES

Fishing is the main activity along State Route 112, and the productive Strait of Juan de Fuca is the reason. Chinook and coho salmon are the species most sought, but these waters also give up some huge halibut and lingcod as well as many other species.

Seasons vary, so check regulations. Phone charter operators and resort owners to inquire about local conditions and season openings.

The chinook season opens as early as February in the Sekiu area, with fish then running between six and twenty pounds, occasionally to thirty or more. Bigger fish begin showing in May. Cohos follow in mid-June, with the biggest fish taken from mid-August through September.

Most bottom fish can be taken any time of the year, weather and water conditions permitting. There are special seasons for halibut, and both halibut and lingcod are regulated in the Neah Bay region.

Anglers find good freshwater fishing in the streams and lakes of this area, particularly for rainbow and cutthroat trout. On the Makah Reservation, two rivers and several lakes are open to the public for angling by permit. Freshwater and saltwater fishing permits are usually available at several places in Neah Bay.

Big Salmon Fishing Resort, P.O. Box 204; Neah Bay; (360) (360) 645–2374 or (800) 959–2374. Next to the Makah Marina. Bait, tackle, fuel, moorage, and launch ramp. Eight boats run charters for salmon, halibut, and bottom fish, as well as wildlife cruises and whale-watching trips. Operates from April 1 through September 15.

Makah Marina, P.O. Box 137; Neah Bay; 645–3015. On the waterfront, in town. Water and electrical hookups at 200 commercial-size slips with a capacity of 400 boats. Vessel pump-outs, rest rooms, and showers. Float-plane docking. Monthly and transient moorage available all year.

TRAVEL INFORMATION

Clallam Bay/Sekiu Chamber of Commerce, P.O. Box 355; Clallam Bay 98236; (360) 963–2339; www.sekiu.com and www.clallambay.com

Makah Fisheries Management Office (permits and information); (360) 645–2201, ext. 423

Neah Bay Chamber of Commerce, P.O. Box 115; Neah Bay; (360) 645–2201

EVENTS

| July | Clallam Bay/Sekiu Fun Days, Sekiu, (360) 963–2346 |
| August | Makah Days, Neah Bay, (360) 645–2201 |

PORT ANGELES

Population: 18,500

Location: *On U.S. 101, 63 miles east-northeast of Forks, 48 miles west of Port Townsend, and 17 miles west of Sequim, on the Strait of Juan de Fuca. Zip: 98362.*

Port Angeles is a shortening of the original name, for which we all can be thankful. In 1791 Spanish explorer Lieutenant Francisco Eliza named the natural harbor Porto de Neustra Senora de los Angeles, or "Port of Our Lady of Angels." Subsequently, the name was shortened to Porto de los Angeles and ultimately to its present form. Meanwhile, the city has grown to become the largest on the north Olympic Peninsula.

So many chambers of commerce tout their towns as "gateways" to one thing or another that the term has become a cliché. Nevertheless, it's difficult to resist discussing Port Angeles in such terms. For visitors arriving from Canada, the city is certainly their gateway to the Pacific Coast and the rest of America. For those heading north, Port Angeles can be the gateway to Canada and Alaska. And for most, this is the threshold of **Olympic National Park,** with headquarters located in town.

For a variety of reasons, Port Angeles has become a popular retirement spot and is gaining favor among travelers. The climate is pleasant, and the rainfall is relatively low. The Olympic Mountains are only a few miles south, and the Strait of Juan de Fuca laps at the city's northern limits. Naturally, opportunities for outdoor recreation abound.

The city is also emerging as the cultural center of the area. It supports an excellent historical museum and a fine-arts center. It has its own symphony orchestra, light opera company, and a theater group that offers a year-round program.

183

Although the waterfront area is heavily industrialized, improvements in recent years have made it kinder to the eye. The award-winning **City Pier** offers an excellent vantage point for the waterfront photographer. It has a picnic area, promenade deck, and observation tower. It also provides short-term moorage for boats and seaplanes. The Fiero Marine Laboratory is on the pier, and a sand beach is adjacent.

The Landing, an attractive mall, is just west of City Pier. HarborTowne Mall is across the street from it. The visitor center and Black Ball Ferry Terminal are nearby. Downtown shops, galleries, and restaurants are within walking distance.

Victoria, British Columbia—one of North America's most beautiful cities—is but 18 miles across the strait from Port Angeles. You can be there in ninety minutes via ferry, which docks in downtown Victoria, a short distance from the famed Empress Hotel. So plan to spend a day or more there seeing the sights, many of which are within walking distance of the ferry dock.

LODGING

Best Western Olympic Lodge, 140 Del Guzzi Drive; (360) 452–2993 or (800) 600–2993. On the south side of U.S. 101, east of downtown, adjacent to Peninsula Golf Course. Queen and king beds in 105 rooms and deluxe suites with cable TV, HBO, microwave ovens, and refrigerators. Heated outdoor pool and spa. Great view of Olympic Mountains. Moderate to expensive.

Lake Crescent Lodge, National Park Concessions; 416 Lake Crescent Road; HC 62; Box 11; (360) 928–3211; www.lakecrescentlodge.com. On the shore of Lake Crescent, 20 miles west of Port Angeles, via U.S. 101. Open May 15 to November 1. Choice of rooms with shared bath in main lodge, modern motor-lodge rooms with private baths, or cozy cottages with private baths and fireplaces. Excellent accommodations in a lovely setting on the largest and deepest lake in Olympic National Park. Lodge dining room serves breakfast, lunch, and dinner and will pack box lunches. Cocktail lounge and gift shop on premises. Moderate to expensive.

Sol Duc Hot Springs Resort, P.O. Box 2169; (360) 327–3583; www.northolympic.com/solduc. A full-service lodge in Olympic National Park, 28 miles west of Port Angeles, 12 miles south of U.S. 101. A variety of accommodations, including cabins, motel rooms, RV spaces, and campsites. Cabins and motel rooms have double beds. Cabins have full baths, motel rooms only half baths. Kitchen units available. RV spaces have water and electricity. Dump station available. Day use available for pool and mineral springs. Restaurant on premises, serving breakfast, lunch, and dinner daily. Gift shop, grocery store, mineral hot springs, swimming pool, massage, and hiking trails. Moderate.

The Tudor Inn Bed & Breakfast, 1108 South Oak Street; (360) 452–3138; www.tudorinn.com. Built in 1910 and completely restored and furnished with antiques. Has 5 rooms, 1 private and 2 shared baths. Full breakfast served. Winter cross-country ski packages offered. Summer salmon charters, backpacking, and bike rentals. Moderate.

CAMPGROUNDS AND RV PARKS

KOA Kampground, 80 O'Brien Road; (360) 457–5916 or (800) 562–7558; www.koa.com/where/wa/47127.htm. On U.S. 101 at O'Brien Road, 7 miles east of Port Angeles, 8 miles west of Sequim. Has 90 RV sites, tent sites, and Kamping Kabins. Full hookups, cable TV, heated pool, hot tub, laundry, showers, grocery store, game room, horseshoe pits, volleyball court, miniature golf, and playground. Superb mountain view. Moderate.

Lyre River Park, 596 West Lyre River Road; (360) 928–3436; www.lyreriverpark.com. Located 20 miles west of Port Angeles, 5 miles west of Joyce, north on West Lyre River Road off State Route 112. Features sites directly on the beach. Has 15 tent sites and 60 RV sites with full hookups, fire pits, showers, tank dump, firewood, store, propane, ice, groceries, and fishing tackle. Small rental boats available, or bring your own cartopper. Small-boat ramp. Saltwater fishing for perch, bottom fish, halibut, and salmon; freshwater fishing for trout and steelhead. Children's trout pond. Moderate.

Salt Creek/Tongue Point Recreation Area, 53802 Highway 112 West; (360) 928–2448; www.olypen.com/scrv. Located 3.5 miles north of State Route 112, 19 miles west of Port Angeles and 1 mile east of Joyce. Has 80 campsites with picnic tables and fireplaces. Rest rooms, showers, and tank dump. Firewood available. Hiking trails, a 9-hole golf course, World War II bunkers, beach, marine life sanctuary, sidewalks and stairs to tide pools. A beautiful setting and one of the finest county parks anywhere, on par with the best state parks. Inexpensive.

FOOD AND BEVERAGES

Bonny's Bakery, 215 South Lincoln; (360) 457–3585. Located 3 blocks from the ferry in downtown near the library. Housed in the restored vintage firehouse building with indoor and outdoor seating. Breakfast and lunch featuring fine French pastries and American favorites; great breads, soups, Northwest coffees. Extended summer hours. Moderate.

C'est Si Bon, 23 Cedar Park Road; (360) 452–8888; www.cestsibon-frenchcuisine.com. North off U.S. 101, 4 miles east of Port Angeles. Dinner Tuesday through Sunday. Award-winning French restaurant, certainly the best on the Washington coast, some say the best in the state. Start with French onion soup or an appetizer of escargots or oysters in a special butter sauce. For dinner, select from roast duck, chicken breast in puff pastry, rack of lamb, New York steak, beef tenderloin, or other meat dishes prepared with fine and flavorful sauces. Seafoods include fresh salmon with Dungeness crab and leek sauce, prawns with garlic and tomatoes, scallops in champagne sauce. Specials every night are usually fresh seafood. Cocktails, beer, and wine. Moderate to expensive.

Downriggers, 115 East Railroad Street; (360) 452–2700. On the waterfront, at The Landing Mall, second level. Daily lunch and dinner. Great appetizers include alder-smoked salmon, shellfish sampler, apple-smoked prawns, crab and shrimp cocktails, and fresh oysters. Salads, deli-style sandwiches, fish and chips, salmon Wellington, garlic tiger prawns, rib steak, top sirloin steak, prime rib, London broil, poultry dishes, smokehouse pasta, and more. Fresh seafood brought in daily. Dine in restaurant or lounge or on the outside deck. Excellent harbor view. Full bar. Moderate.

First Street Haven, 107 East First Street; (360) 457–0352. Downtown. Breakfast and lunch Monday through Saturday, breakfast all day Sunday. Specializes in creative and unusual breakfasts, including blintzes, huevos rancheros, and a variety of egg dishes. Well known for homemade baked goods, such as cinnamon rolls, sour-cream coffee cake, raspberry bran muffins, and apricot walnut scones—all baked fresh daily. Serves fresh-squeezed orange juice and gourmet espresso coffees. The changeable menu might include such entrees as artichoke stuffed with dilled shrimp salad, cheese enchiladas, chicken fajitas, or fettuccine primavera. Or maybe a lunch-size salad of fresh spinach, crisp vegetables, bacon, Swiss cheese, and slivered almonds. Moderate.

Landing's Restaurant & Dockside Lounge, 115 East Railroad Avenue; Suite 101; (360) 457–6768. On the waterfront, next to the Black Ball Ferry Terminal. Breakfast, lunch, and dinner daily. Burgers and other sandwiches, soups, chowders, and salads. Fish baskets with fries and coleslaw, as well as other baskets: oysters, clams, calamari, shrimp, scallops—even catfish. Kids' baskets, carry-out service. Beer and wine. Inexpensive to moderate.

SHOPPING AND BROWSING

Joyce General Store, 50883 Highway 112; Joyce 98343; (360) 928–3568. Located 20 miles west of Port Angeles on State Route 112 in Joyce. Not much has changed since the early 1900s—false front, oiled wood floors, same fixtures. A true old-fashioned general store, stocking everything from groceries, bait, and fishing tackle to clothing, hot food, souvenirs, and Indian arts and crafts.

Port Angeles Antiques and Collectibles, 123 West First Street; (360) 452–5411 or (360) 452–2582. Downtown. Tuesday through Saturday, 10:30 A.M. to 5:00 P.M. Depression glassware, jewelry, clocks, prints, English and American furniture, and a good variety of other antiques and collectibles.

MUSEUMS

The Museum of the Clallam County Historical Society, 223 East Fourth Street; (360) 452–2662. Downtown. June through August: Monday through Saturday, 10:00 A.M. to 4:00 P.M. Rest of the year, Monday through Friday. Historical collection housed in a 1914 Georgian-style courthouse. Exhibits of logging and fishing industries, agriculture, pioneer settlement, and Indian artifacts.

Port Angeles Fine Art Center, 1203 East Lauridsen Boulevard; (360) 417–1590; www.portangelesartcenter.com. Thursday through Sunday, 11:00 A.M. to 5:00 P.M. Exhibits the works of prominent Northwest artists. Wheelchair access. Free admission.

BEACHES, PARKS, TRAILS, AND WAYSIDES

The natural deepwater harbor at Port Angeles was formed by a long spit, known as Ediz Hook. It was created centuries ago by silt and sand washed downstream by the Elwha River, west of town. The spit is popular with joggers, bikers, and anglers. To reach it and **Ediz Hook Park,** follow Marine Drive west and north around the port.

Hurricane Ridge, Olympic National Park

Of course, the main attraction of the area is **Olympic National Park,** with 900,000 acres of mountains, meadows, forests, rivers, creeks, lakes, and rugged Pacific coastline, and containing seventeen campgrounds within its boundaries.

South of Port Angeles, at 3002 Mount Angeles Road, is the **Pioneer Memorial Museum and Visitor Center,** which houses park exhibits and a small theater for programs on the park. This is also the place to get park maps and literature. It has a good selection of books on the park, peninsula, and coast.

The road to mile-high **Hurricane Ridge** extends into the park 17 miles from Port Angeles. As the road climbs through forested mountains, a number of parking areas offer splendid views of the alpine country and the Strait of Juan de Fuca.

Hurricane Ridge Lodge serves sandwiches and light meals and beverages. There's also a small gift shop on the premises. The lodge is open daily from Memorial Day through September, weekends through mid-October. In winter, when the area opens for skiing, the lodge opens on weekends and holidays. For the schussing set there are ski rentals, rope tow, and Poma lift.

West of Port Angeles, access to the park is along the Elwha River and in the Lake Crescent area. To the northwest, a road leads southwest off State Route 112 to the village of **Ozette** and parklands along the coast. Farther along U.S. 101, a number of roads lead into the park west and south of Forks.

The park offers hikers and backpackers more than 600 miles of trails in varied terrain. Those most easily reached from Port Angeles are in the Hurricane Ridge, Elwha River, and Lake Crescent areas.

Abundant wildlife in the park includes many species of songbirds and raptors as well as small mammals, amphibians, and reptiles. Rest easy—there are no poisonous snakes in the park.

Large mammals include black-tailed deer, Roosevelt elk, mountain goat, cougar, and black bear. Bears can be dangerous and should be avoided. Even those that don't pose a threat can be a nuisance to campers who don't take the necessary precautions to hang food in trees, well out of the reach of bears.

The park service offers naturalist programs in the summer at Hurricane Ridge Lodge and elsewhere. Check site bulletin boards for details. Seminars are offered through the Olympic Park Institute. Get information at visitor centers or park headquarters.

WATER SPORTS AND ACTIVITIES

Olympic National Park offers outstanding trout fishing in its many lakes and streams. Although no license is required in the park, a salmon and steelhead punch card is necessary in waters where those species are taken.

Rainbows are the most popular and abundant trout in the park. Cutthroat and brook trout are other park residents. Lake Crescent is the only place on the planet where anglers can catch Beardsley trout, a race of rainbow, and Crescenti, a race of cutthroat trout.

Minutes from port, saltwater anglers can catch coho and chinook salmon as well as halibut, lingcod, rockfish, Pacific cod, and other species of bottom fish. From shore, fishermen take perch, greenling, cabezon, rockfish, sole, flounder, and lingcod, as well as salmon, steelhead, sea-run cutthroat, and Dolly Varden.

Olympic Raft & Kayak, 123 Lake Aldwell Road; (360) 452–1443 or (888) 452–1443; www.raftandkayak.com. Guided river trips that include rafting on the Elwha River and inflatable kayak trips on the Hoh River, Lake Alwell, Lake Crescent, and Freshwater Bay. Kayak and canoe rentals available.

TOURS AND TRIPS

MV *Coho* (ferry to Victoria); (360) 457–4491; www.north olympic.com/coho. On the downtown waterfront at the foot of

Laurel Street. Four trips every day in the summer, once a day in winter, to Victoria, British Columbia. Trip takes about ninety minutes aboard the 342-foot, twin-diesel MV *Coho*, which carries 100 cars and 1,000 passengers.

Victoria Express, P.O. Box 1928; (360) 452–8088 or (800) 633–1589; Canada, (250) 361–9144; www.victoriaexpress.com. Passenger ferry service between Port Angeles and Victoria, British Columbia. Vessel cruises at 20 knots and makes the crossing in one hour. Operates from late May to early October, departing twice a day from each port early and late in the season, three departures a day from late June to early September.

GOLF

Peninsula Golf Club, P.O. Box 628; (360) 452–6856. An 18-hole course with driving range, complete pro shop, and resident pro. Private club that accepts reciprocal memberships.

OTHER ATTRACTIONS

Arthur D. Fiero Marine Laboratory, (360) 417–8035. On the Port Angeles City Pier at the downtown waterfront. Summer: daily, 10:00 A.M. to 8:00 P.M. Winter: weekends, noon to 4:00 P.M. A working lab used in local high school and college marine biology courses and research. More than eighty species collected from nearby waters live here, including sculpins, wolf eels, octopuses, sea slugs, anemones, tube worms, sea stars, crabs, and sea urchins. Touch tank for hands-on examination.

WEATHER AND TIDE INFORMATION

U.S. Coast Guard, Ediz Hook; recorded message, (360) 457–6533

TRAVEL INFORMATION

Olympic National Park; (360) 452–0330 or (360) 565–3130; www.nps.gov/olym

Port Angeles Chamber of Commerce, 121 East Railroad Avenue; (360) 452–2363; www.cityofpa.com or www.port angeles.org

Port Angeles Victoria Tourist Bureau, 115 East Railroad #2; (360) 452–1223

EVENTS

April	Jazz in the Olympics, (760) 452–2363; www.jazzolympics.com Port Angeles Kayak Symposium, (360) 452–1443
May	Juan de Fuca Festival, (360) 457–5411
July	Old Fashioned Fourth, (360) 452–2363
August	Clallam County Fair, (360) 457–3963

191

SEQUIM

Population: 4,200

Location: *On U.S. 101, 17 miles east of Port Angeles, 31 miles west of Port Townsend. Zip: 98382.*

Sequim (skwim) grew out of a small cluster of farms in the Sequim/Dungeness Valley, some of which date as far back as 1851. The area is known for its unusually warm, dry climate, so dry in fact that pioneers found cacti growing on the lowlands. They couldn't raise crops without irrigation provided by the Dungeness River. While western portions of the Olympic Peninsula get drenched each year with as much as 140 inches of rain, the Sequim/Dungeness Valley lies in the dry shadow of the Olympic Mountains and gets a mere 10 to 18 inches.

Today, Sequim is famous for its Dungeness crab and fields of growing lavender. The pleasant climate and nearby recreational opportunities have recently attracted enough new residents to make this one of the fastest-growing areas on the peninsula. Although it's largely a retirement community, in recent years it has become much more tourist oriented, with new motels, bed-and-breakfast inns, and restaurants.

LODGING

Best Western Sequim Bay Lodge, 268522 Highway 101; (360) 683–0691 or (800) 622–0691. Two miles east of Sequim. Queen beds in standard rooms, minisuites, and 2-room suites—all with cable TV and coffeemakers. Minisuites have refrigerators. Other suites also have wet bars. Fireplaces, spas, and hot tubs available. Heated pool and 9-hole putting green. Restaurant and lounge on premises. Special golf packages available. Moderate to expensive.

Dungeness Bay Motel, 140 Marine Drive; (360) 683–3013 or (888) 683–3013; www.dungenessbay.com. On Dungeness Bay,

7 miles north of Sequim. Six kitchen units with views of the bay and mountains. Near golf courses, wildlife refuge, and a superb seafood restaurant. Nonsmoking. Moderate.

Great House Motel, 740 East Washington; (360) 683–7272 or (877) 683–7272. North side of U.S. 101, in town. Twin, double, and queen beds in 20 rooms with cable TV and HBO. Inexpensive to moderate.

Juan de Fuca Cottages, 182 Marine Drive; (360) 683–4433; www.juandefucacottages.com. North of Sequim, on Dungeness Bay and the Strait of Juan de Fuca. Six units with double and queen beds, complete kitchens, TVs, VCRs, free movies, tea, and coffee. Bay or mountain view. Two-room cottage has whirlpool and fireplace. Five cottages overlook Dungeness Spit and Dungeness National Wildlife Refuge. Moderate to expensive.

CAMPGROUNDS AND RV PARKS

Diamond Point RV Park & Campground, 294 Industrial Park Way; (360) 681–0590. Three miles north of U.S. 101, via Diamond Point Road, between Sequim Bay and Discovery Bay. Has 25 tent sites and 32 RV sites with full hookups, showers, tank dump, laundry, kitchen shelter, beach access, and boat ramp. Breakfast served on weekends in summer; dinner served on Saturday nights—usually salmon dinner and dessert, all you can eat for a modest charge. Hiking trails, ten minutes to the beach. Fishing, beachcombing, and clam digging. Moderate.

Sequim Bay State Park, 1872 Highway 101 East; (360) 683–4235 or (800) 452–5687; www.parks.wa.gov/sequim.htm. West side of U.S. 101, 4 miles southeast of Sequim. Has 60 tent sites and 26 RV sites with full hookups, showers, and tank dump. In a beautiful wooded setting with hiking trails. Picnic area with 4 kitchen shelters, tennis courts, playground, horseshoe pits, and ball field. Boat launch, mooring floats and buoys, and loading dock. Fishing, crabbing, clam digging, scuba diving, and waterskiing are main attractions. Inexpensive.

FOOD AND BEVERAGES

Chinese Garden, 271 South Seventh Street; (360) 683–4825. In town, south of U.S. 101, across from Safeway, behind McDonald's. Daily lunch and dinner. Appetizers include fried wonton, egg roll, barbecued pork, and deep-fried prawns. Typical deluxe dinner: barbecued pork, moo goo gai pan, almond chicken, sweet and sour prawns, pork fried rice, and fortune cookies. Outstanding Szechuan and Cantonese cuisine. Inexpensive to moderate.

The Salish Room, 270756 Highway 101; (360) 683–7777 or (800) 458–2597. At the Seven Cedars Casino, on the south side of U.S. 101, east of town. Dinner nightly. Big buffet, soup and salad bar, French dip, burgers, halibut fish and chips, baked salmon, grilled oysters, and fried shrimp—in generous portions and at good prices. Microbrews and domestic and imported wines. Full bar. Moderate.

The 3 Crabs Restaurant & Lounge, 101 Three Crabs Road; (360) 683–4264. Located 4.5 miles north of U.S. 101 on Sequim-Dungeness Way, then right on Three Crabs Road a half mile. Lunch and dinner daily. Award-winning seafood restaurant, among the best on the Washington coast. Start with oyster shooters, smoked-salmon appetizer, or jumbo-prawn cocktail. Then feast on such house specialties as crab Louis, crab sandwiches, crab and shrimp omelettes, cracked crab, oysters, scallops, prawns, salmon, or halibut. Cocktails, beer, and wine. Moderate.

CASINO

Seven Cedars Casino, 270756 Highway 101; (360) 683–7777 or (800) 458–2597. On the south side of U.S. 101, east of town. A beautiful casino, owned and operated by S'Klallam Indians, offering craps, roulette, blackjack, poker, bingo, lightning bingo, pull tabs, and keno. Bingo hall seats 600. Northwest Native Expressions art gallery features the works of 200 Indian artists. Restaurant, deli, and full-service lounge on premises.

MUSEUM

Museum and Arts Center, 175 West Cedar; (360) 683–8110; www.sequimmuseum.org. One block north of U.S. 101. May 1 to October 1: Wednesday through Sunday, noon to 4:00 P.M. Rest of the year: weekends, noon to 4:00 P.M. A variety of historical exhibits. Some excellent old photographs depicting the settlement of the Sequim/Dungeness Valley. Most fascinating is an interpretive exhibit of mastodon remains discovered on a nearby farm.

John Wayne Marina

OTHER ATTRACTIONS

Open Aire Market, Cedar Street and Sequim Avenue North. Downtown. Open every Saturday, mid-May through mid-October, from 9:00 A.M. to 3:00 P.M. Popular farmers' market featuring fresh local produce, plants, cut flowers, soaps, lavender products, freshly baked breads, quality local arts and crafts, and live music.

Purple Haze Lavender Farm, on Bell Bottom Road; (360) 683–1714; www.purplehazelavender.com. One of several farms in the area. Seven-acre organic farm with gift shop and U-pick produce. Open daily, May through September, 10:00 A.M. to 5:00 P.M.

WATER SPORTS AND ACTIVITIES

Admiralty Charters, (360) 683–1097 (business) or (360) 683–1097 (residence). Fish year-round aboard the 34-foot charter boat *Scamp* for halibut, salmon, shark, and a variety of bottom fish. Also winter river steel-heading.

John Wayne Marina, 615 West Sequim Bay Road; (360) 417–3440. North off U.S. 101, east of Sequim. A beautiful marina, first envisioned by actor John Wayne and built mainly on land donated by the actor's family. Will eventually have a capacity of 422 moorage slips, protected by a gracefully curved breakwater that blends well with the environment. Showers, laundry, boat ramps, fuel facilities, public beach, and picnic areas. Restaurant on premises.

GOLF

Dungeness Golf Course, 491-A Woodcock Road; (360) 683–6344 or (800) 447–6826; www.dungenessgcc.com. North of U.S. 101, west end of town. An 18-hole course with driving range, pro shop, clubhouse, resident pro, and restaurant on premises.

Sunland Golf & Country Club, 109 Hilltop Drive; (360) 683–8365 or (888) 289–4314; www.sunlandgolf.com. North of U.S. 101, between Sequim and Dungeness. An 18-hole course with driving range, pro shop, and coffee shop.

TRAVEL INFORMATION

Sequim-Dungeness Valley Chamber of Commerce, P.O. Box 907; (360) 683–6197; www.cityofsequim.com

EVENTS

May	Irrigation Festival, (360) 683–6197
July	Independence Day Picnic and Celebration, (360) 683–8110
August	Rotary Salmon Bake, (360) 683–6840
December	Annual Grange Christmas Fair, (360) 683–4431

PORT TOWNSEND

Population: 8,200

Location: *13 miles northeast of U.S. 101, on State Route 20; 48 miles east of Port Angeles, 31 miles east of Sequim, and 6 miles, via ferry, west of Whidbey Island. Zip: 98368.*

Port Townsend, located on the northeast tip of the Quimper Peninsula, grew from a single log cabin (built in 1851) to a Victorian-era boomtown in the 1880s. It flourished as Washington's "Key City" and swelled with a population of 20,000. It functioned as the port of entry for Puget Sound, its waterfront a dense forest of great sailing-ship masts.

The city's prosperity and promise were both real and anticipated, its future dependent upon the railroad. Townspeople, businessmen, and speculators assumed that Port Townsend would become the northwestern terminus of the transcontinental railway system. But their dreams were dashed when the rails stopped at Seattle, assuring that town's future as Washington's capital of commerce. By 1893 Port Townsend had gone bust and would languish where it lay for more than half a century.

In the 1960s Port Townsend's Victorian charm was rediscovered, and since then many of its beautiful old brick buildings have been restored and now house interesting shops, galleries, taverns, and restaurants. Most of its stately old houses and mansions also have been refurbished; a number of them function as bed-and-breakfast inns.

In some communities the terms uptown and downtown are used interchangeably, and the districts aren't always easy to distinguish. In others downtown is the business district, uptown the residential area. Port Townsend is both typical and unique. Downtown is clearly the lower section, comprising the waterfront and Water and Washington Streets, as well as the streets connecting them.

197

Uptown is situated on a bluff overlooking downtown and is mainly residential. Amidst the uptown houses and churches, however, another small business district grew in the latter part of the nineteenth century, so the wives and daughters of the town's menfolk would have a place to shop and stroll without having to associate with sailors, prostitutes, and other denizens of the waterfront. So uptown has its own downtown.

The rabble and riffraff are long gone, and nobody hesitates going to the waterfront now. In fact it's one of Port Townsend's main attractions: a shaped-up, compact area that is perfect for walking. It's the town's main shopping area, with a variety of stores, antique shops, and art galleries. Here, too, are the favorite eateries and watering holes, some with splendid waterfront views.

State Route 20 carries travelers right into downtown and to the ferry terminal. Motels and marinas are nearby, uptown inns only a short distance away, with shopping centers and drive-in restaurants on the outskirts.

Port Townsend Paper Company, a kraft-paper mill, is a major contributor to the town's economy, as are the many marine services and facilities located along the waterfront. Boat building and repair are big business here. So are commercial fishing and fish processing.

Water sports and recreation are important too. Port Townsend bills itself as the "Wooden Boat Capital of the World" and hosts an annual festival during which visitors can see wooden boats of all kinds and sizes, from skiffs to schooners. The three-day event attracts thousands of people with its boats and booths of nautical hardware and abundant literature and information on boat building and allied topics.

Although food and lodging are a bit more expensive here than elsewhere on the Olympic Peninsula, prices aren't outrageous, as they often are in the larger metropolitan areas. And the Port Townsend people are a friendly lot who welcome travelers. So Washington's Victorian Waterfront, as it's known, is certainly worth a visit.

LODGING

Aladdin Motor Inn, 2333 Washington Street; (360) 385–3747 or (800) 281–3747. On the waterfront, just south of downtown. Queen beds in 32 waterfront rooms with remote cable TV, refrigerators, and microwave ovens. VCR and movie rentals available. Guest laundry. Easy beach access. Moderate.

James House Bed & Breakfast, 1238 Washington Street; (360) 385–1238 or (800) 385–1238; www.jameshouse.com. One block above Water Street, overlooking the harbor and ferry dock. A fine Victorian mansion, built in 1891, with 12 guest rooms and suites furnished with antiques. Private and shared baths. Walk to shops and restaurants. Continental breakfast. Moderate to expensive.

Manresa Castle, P.O. Box 564; (360) 385–5750; Washington, (800) 732–1281; www.manresacastle.com. At Seventh and Sheridan, west off State Route 20, on a hill overlooking the city and waterfront. Turreted castle built in 1892 as a private residence but abandoned when the local economy slumped. Now a restored Victorian-style hotel with 40 rooms and suites with private baths, cable TV, and HBO. Double, queen, and king beds available. Dinner restaurant on premises. Moderate to expensive.

Palace Hotel, 1004 Water Street; (360) 385–0773 or (800) 962–0741; www.olympus.net/palace. Downtown. A fine old Victorian inn, built in 1889 and fully restored. Has 15 Victorian units, from bedrooms with shared baths to suites with kitchens and private baths. Cable TV, in-room coffee and tea, continental breakfast. Moderate.

Ann Starrett Mansion Bed & Breakfast, 744 Clay Street; (360) 385–3205 or (800) 321–0644; www.starrettmansion.com. At Adams and Clay Streets, 4 blocks above the waterfront. Eight guest rooms in a fine example of classic Victorian stick-style architecture in a stunning 1889 building with interior wall and ceiling frescoes, octagonal tower, and spiral staircase. View rooms available. Open for tours. Full breakfast. Nonsmoking. Moderate to expensive.

James G. Swan Hotel, 216 Monroe Street; P.O. Box 856; (360) 385–1718; USA, (800) 776–1718; Canada, (800) 458–7926. On Monroe at Water Street. Four cozy cabins with queen beds and private baths. Five suites, including a penthouse that sleeps 12. Boat launch across the street. Walk to downtown shops and restaurants. Inexpensive to moderate.

The Tides Inn, 1807 Water Street; (360) 385–0595 or (800) 822–8696; www.tides-inn.com. On the waterfront, downtown. Used in the filming of the 1981 smash hit *An Officer and a Gentleman.* Has 21 rooms with queen and king beds, private decks and patios, cable TV. Also offers a waterfront view, whirlpool, and continental breakfast. Kitchen units available. Moderate to very expensive.

Vacation Housing, Fort Worden State Park; (360) 344–4400;

Ann Starrett Mansion Bed & Breakfast

www.olympus.net/ftworden. At the northern city limits—follow the signs off State Route 20. Offers 23 refurbished and unrefurbished houses with completely furnished kitchens, linens and towels provided. The houses, built a century ago for commissioned and noncommissioned officers, have from 2 to 6 bedrooms. Most have fireplaces. One of the best family or group lodging values on the coast. Reservations essential, booked a year in advance. Moderate.

CAMPGROUNDS AND RV PARKS

Fort Worden State Park, P.O. Box 547; (360) 344-4400; www.olympus.net/ftworden. About 1.5 miles from downtown—follow the signs off State Route 20. Has 3 tent sites and 50 RV sites with tables, stoves, firewood, full hookups, showers, kitchen shelter, boat launch, mooring floats and buoys, beach access, hiking and biking trails, and tennis courts. Reservations accepted all year. Moderate.

FOOD AND BEVERAGES

Lonny's Restaurant, 2330 Washington Street; (360) 385-0700; www.lonnys.com. Southeast of Route 20 (Sims Way), about 1½ blocks, via Benedict Street, then left on Washington Street. Dinner daily, except Tuesday. Award-winning restaurant with an impressive menu of gourmet foods. Choose from more than a half dozen appetizers, including grilled eggplant with mozzarella, chargrilled prawns with mango salsa, and oysters Florentine. Fresh oyster stew, Tuscan mushroom and tomato soup, and dinner-size salads. Pasta dishes, chicken, duck, lamb, pork, beef, and seafood entrees. Italian, French, and domestic wines. Moderate.

Manresa Castle Restaurant & Lounge, P.O. Box 564; (360) 385–5750 or (800) 732–1281; www.manresacastle.com. At Seventh Street and Sheridan, on a hilltop overlooking the city and waterfront. Serves dinner and light supper daily, except during winter when it's closed Monday and Tuesday. Elegant Victorian restaurant and bar with good view. Appetizers include steamed shellfish, chicken tenderloin satay, seafood cocktails, and various smoked seafoods. Light suppers include bouillabaisse, stir-fry, and seafood marinara. Dinners include New York steak, Cajun beef and scampi, breaded pork schnitzel, poached salmon, spicy crab cakes, and cashew chicken. Manresa's mixed grill includes loin lamb chops, beef tenderloin, chicken breast, fresh salmon, and apple pork sausage—charbroiled and served with black-bean sauce, green-peppercorn sauce, and gingered lobster sauce; potatoes and vegetable included. Full bar. Moderate to expensive.

The Public House, 1038 Water Street; (360) 385–9708; www.thepublichouse.com. In the downtown waterfront area. Vintage-style eatery boasts casual seating, wooden floors, Lincrusta ceilings, wainscoting, kayak decor, and a cozy bar with Victorian bar front. Open for lunch and dinner daily, 11:00 A.M. to 10:00 P.M. (until 11:00 P.M. on weekends; a late-night menu is available). Great salads, sandwiches, pasta, and stews for lunch; dinner offerings include grilled beef, chicken, and fish and house specialties from gumbo to linguine. Wine and beer. Moderate to expensive.

The Wine Seller, 940 Water Street; (360) 385–7673; www.winespt.com. Downtown. Daily, 10:30 A.M. to 6:00 P.M.; Sunday, 11:00 A.M. to 5:00 P.M. Good selection of wines and beers, case-lot discounts, coffees, teas, cheeses, chocolates, wine tasting, and espresso bar.

SHOPPING AND BROWSING

Bergstrom's Antique and Classic Autos, 809 Washington; (360) 385–5061. One block above Water Street, downtown. Open Monday, Thursday, Friday, Saturday, and sometimes Sunday, 10:00 A.M. to 5:00 P.M. Historic garage built in 1917 and formerly used as Ford and Buick dealerships, now used for restoring vintage and classic cars and trucks.

Earthenworks, 702 Water Street; (360) 385–0328 or (866) 466–4411; www.earthenworksgallery.com. Downtown. Daily, 10:30 A.M. to 5:00 P.M. A pleasing gallery displaying wood sculptures, carvings, pottery, kaleidoscopes, wall hangings, jewelry, and limited-edition prints.

Port Townsend Antique Mall, 802 Washington Street; (360) 379–8069. One block above Water Street, downtown. Open Monday through Friday, 10:00 A.M. to 5:30 P.M.; Saturday, 10:00 A.M. to 6:00 P.M.; Sunday, 11:00 A.M. to 5:00 P.M. Large selection of antiques and collectibles, including oak furniture, Victorian furniture, clocks, lamps, guns, decoys, nautical items, dolls, glassware, baseball cards, musical instruments, and old paintings. A *must* for collectors and noncollectors alike. Don't miss the display of Chinese artifacts uncovered in 1990 during excavation for the Antique Mall lower level.

MUSEUMS

Commanding Officer's House, Fort Worden State Park; P.O. Box 574; (360) 379–9894 or (360) 344–4431. North of town—follow the signs off State Route 20. April to October: daily, 10:00 A.M. to 5:00 P.M. Phone for winter hours. A two-and-a-half story, fully restored Victorian structure with cross-gabled roof and great veranda. Has 5,979 square feet of living space, all beautifully decorated with period furnishings and memorabilia.

Jefferson County Historical Museum, 540 Water Street; (360) 385–1003. Downtown. Monday through Saturday, 11:00 A.M. to 4:00 P.M.; Sunday, 1:00 to 4:00 P.M.; closed weekdays in January and Febuary. Located in the rear of Port Townsend's city hall, built in 1891. A fine museum on four levels, displaying Indian, military, pioneer, and maritime artifacts. Early fire-fighting equipment, Victorian furnishings, toys, collections, and more than 6,000 cataloged photographs. Don't miss the city jail on the lower level—a chamber of horrors where author Jack London is said to have spent a night on his way to the Klondike gold fields in 1897.

Rothschild House. At Taylor and Jefferson, 2 blocks above Water Street; (360) 385–1003. Open May 1 through September 30, 10:00 A.M. to 5:00 P.M.; weekends only in November; closes for the season December 1. A family house built in 1868 and maintained by the State Parks and Recreation Commission. Contains many original family furnishings, original carpeting, and even original wallpaper. Fine craftsmanship. Many interesting antiques. Nominal admission fee.

BEACHES, PARKS, TRAILS, AND WAYSIDES

Port Townsend is the seat of a county that has 271 miles of saltwater shoreline. Visitors to the area should have no difficulty finding beaches to hike. Near town, **Point Wilson** and **Fort Worden State Parks** offer beaches and trails to hike and a former military reservation to explore.

At the tip of Point Wilson is the beautiful Point Wilson Light with an octagonal tower that stands 46 feet tall. This lighthouse, with its beacon flashing alternating red and white signals, is critically important to Puget Sound shipping and navigation. It also warns mariners away from nearby shoals and serves as a guide light to the Port Townsend harbor.

Fort Worden occupies lands adjacent to Point Wilson. This is one of three forts built a century ago as part of a major coastal fortification effort to guard the entrance to Puget Sound. The other two are Fort Flagler on Marrowstone Island and Fort Casey on Whidbey Island.

The fort was first occupied on May 3, 1902, by the 126th Coast Artillery Company and was deactivated in 1953. Counting the gun emplacements, Fort Worden has ninety-nine buildings on 339 acres. Many of its buildings have been refurbished. Some are used as dormitories and vacation housing. Others are used for conferences. A few hold local businesses.

The fort is now a beautiful, immaculately maintained state park that certainly ranks as a *must-see* attraction. First-time visitors may attribute any déjà vu to the popular movie *An Officer and a Gentleman,* which was filmed here and starred Richard Gere, Debra Winger, and Louis Gossett Jr. To get to Fort Worden and Point Wilson, simply follow the signs off State Route 20.

GOLF

Chevy Chase Golf Course, 7401 Cape George Road; (360) 385–0704 or (800) 385–8722. North off State Route 20 at Four Corners Grocery. A 9-hole course with pro shop, club rental, pull-cart rental, and snack bar with beer available.

Port Townsend Golf Course, 1948 Blaine Street; (360)

385–4547. Off State Route 20 on Kearney to Blaine, in town. A 9-hole course with driving range, pro shop, resident pro, rental carts and clubs. Clubhouse restaurant and lounge. Full breakfast and lunch menu. Beer and wine.

TRAVEL INFORMATION

Port Townsend Visitor Information Center, 2437 East Simms Way (State Route 20); (360) 385–2722 or (888) 365–6978; www.ptguide.com

EVENTS

February	Shipwrights Regatta, (360) 385–3628
March	Victorian Festival, (360) 385–7911
May	Rhododendron Festival, (360) 385–0712
June	Classic Mariner's Regatta, (360) 385–3628
July	Fireworks and Jefferson Days, (360) 379–5380
August	Jefferson County Fair, (360) 385–1013
September	Wooden Boat Festival, (360) 385–3628
November	Christmas Arts & Crafts Fair, (360) 379–3813

⋆ OAK HARBOR
Population: 20,000

COUPEVILLE
Population: 1,700

Location: *Whidbey Island is 6 miles, by ferry, northeast of Port Townsend. Zip: 98277. Coupeville is about 4 miles north of the ferry landing, via county road; Oak Harbor lies 10 miles north of Coupeville, via State Route 20. Zip: 98239.*

Whidbey Island is the largest of more than 600 islands that punctuate the Washington coastline. At 64 miles tip to tip, it's also the longest island on the West Coast.

Pleasing climate and relatively low annual rainfall first attracted the Northwest's greatest concentration of Indians and later led to settlement of the island. While Seattle gets about 36 inches of rain a year, and more than 100 inches drench western portions of the Olympic Peninsula, south Whidbey Island gets only about 25 inches, and a mere 18 inches dampen the central and north island.

Oak Harbor is Whidbey's largest city. From the mid-1800s until the early 1900s, this area was settled mainly by people of Irish and Dutch extraction. The same climate that attracted others also led the U.S. Navy to pick the Oak Harbor vicinity for a major air installation in 1942—the weather is good for flying.

The explorer Captain George Vancouver named Whidbey Island after shipmaster Joseph Whidbey of HMS *Discovery*. Whidbey discovered Deception Pass and thereby proved this to be an island after all. Coupeville was named after another sea captain, Thomas Coupe, who was the only man ever to sail a full-rigged ship through the pass.

Captain Coupe's house, built in 1853, still stands in Coupeville, as do a number of other historical buildings, many of which have been carefully restored. Downtown, Front Street is itself a historical area, with interesting shops, galleries, and restaurants situated behind Victorian facades, along both Front and Main Streets. A "Walking Tour" brochure with a map of the historical

205

Deception Pass, located north of Oak Harbor

buildings is available at the museum.

A trip to south Whidbey Island will take you through forests, meadows, and agricultural lands to a variety of parks, island hideaways, and some fine bed-and-breakfast inns. The southernmost community is Clinton, which is the western terminus of the Mulkiteo–Clinton ferry.

Langley lies on the southeast shore of the island, east of State Route 525, via Langley Road (4 miles north of Clinton) or Bayview Road (5 miles south of Freeland). This quaint and quiet village is a favorite stop for travelers. It's an artsy little hamlet with studios and galleries tucked among shops, restaurants, and taverns. It's also headquarters for the Island Arts Council and home to several theater groups that perform at the old Clyde Theater and the Whidbey Island Center for the Arts.

With its easy pace, rich history, miles of parklands, and interesting towns, as well as land-based and waterborne recreation, Whidbey Island is great for day trips, weekend getaways, or full and fulfilling vacations.

Ferries connect the island with Port Townsend in the west and Mulkiteo in the east. Those traveling I–5 should exit west at Mount Vernon and take State Route 536 to State Route 20, or near Burlington at State Route 20. From Bellingham, follow State Route 11 (scenic Chuckanut Drive) south to State Route 237 and on to State Route 20, which leads west and south to the island.

LODGING

Auld Holland Inn, 33575 State Route 20; Oak Harbor; (360) 675–2288 or (800) 228–0148. Nine miles south of Deception Pass, north end of town. Queen and king beds in 52 rooms with cable TV. Kitchen units available in adjacent mobile park. Pool, sauna, whirlpool, tennis courts, basketball, playground, and laundry facilities. Varied decor. Rooms furnished with some antiques. Flowers in window boxes. Restaurant and lounge on premises. Moderate.

Captain Whidbey Inn, 2072 West Captain Whidbey Inn Road; Coupeville; (360) 678–4097 or (800) 366–4097; www. captainwhidbeyinn.com. Off Madrona Way, north of Coupeville. Twin, double, queen, and king beds in 32 rooms, suites, and cottages. Room rates include continental breakfast. Kitchen units available. Rustic inn built of madrona logs in 1907. Inn rooms with shared baths, antiques, and feather beds. Lagoon rooms have private baths and waterfront views. Restaurant and lounge are on premises. Expensive.

Coachman Inn, 32959 State Route 20; (360) 675–0727 or (800) 635–0043. In town, on Goldie Road at Highway 20. Queen beds in 100 rooms with cable TV, including 30 kitchen suites, 7 Jacuzzi suites, and a 2-bedroom penthouse suite. Excellent accommodations. Moderate.

Fort Casey Inn, 1124 South Engle Road; Coupeville; (360) 678–5050 or (866) 661–6604; www.fortcaseyinn.com. Next to Fort Casey State Park, less than a mile from Keystone Ferry Terminal. Ten duplex units are refurbished World War I officers' quarters with 2 bedrooms, living room, bath, and country-style kitchen, built in 1909. Fruit and cereal provided for breakfast; bring your own groceries for other meals. No radio or TV (bring your own). Two bikes provided. Trails to beach. Good location for walk-on ferry traffic. A good lodging bargain. Moderate.

Guest House Log Cottages, 835 East Christenson Road; Greenbank 98253; (360) 678–3115; www.guesthouse logcottages.com. West off State Route 525, 10 miles south of Coupeville, 1 mile south of Greenbank, 16 miles north of Clinton. Three cottages, a log lodge, and a suite in a 1920s farmhouse on twenty-five acres of meadow and woods. Private baths with some in-room Jacuzzis, fireplaces, stained glass, antiques, TVs, VCRs, outdoor pool, and spa. Full breakfast served at the farmhouse. Breakfast makings provided at cottages and lodge. Expensive.

The Inn at Langley, 400 First Street; P.O. Box 835; Langley 98260; (360) 221–3033. At the north end of town, overlooking Saratoga Passage. Each of the 24 rooms has a view, fireplace, refrigerator, coffeemaker, TV, and Jacuzzi tub. Easy walk to everything in town. Complimentary continental breakfast daily. Five-course Northwest dinners on Friday and Saturday evenings. Two-night minimum on weekends. Expensive to very expensive.

CAMPGROUNDS AND RV PARKS

City Beach Park, City Beach Road; Oak Harbor; (360) 679–5551. On the waterfront on 90th Street. Has 56 RV sites, plus overflow area. Bathhouse, swimming pool, tennis courts, playground, and ball fields. Good place for July Fourth fireworks. Moderate.

Deception Pass State Park, 5175 North State Route 20; (360) 675–2417. Ten miles north of Oak Harbor on State Route 20. Has 246 campsites with picnic tables and stoves, as well as 5 primitive sites. Lake and saltwater fishing, boat launch, mooring floats and buoys, beach access, hiking trails, showers, wheelchair access. Moderate.

Fort Casey State Park, 1280 Fort Casey Road; Coupeville; (360) 678–4519 or (360) 678–5632. Three miles south of Coupeville, off State Route 20, adjacent to the Keystone Ferry Terminal. Has 35 campsites with picnic tables and 3 primitive sites. No hookups. Showers, firewood, rest rooms, and wheelchair access. On the beach. Boat launch nearby. Underwater park for scuba divers. Old fort to explore. Inexpensive.

Fort Ebey State Park, 395 North Fort Ebey Road; Coupeville; (360) 678–4636 or (360) 678–3195. Eight miles south of Oak Harbor, off State Route 20. Has 50 campsites with picnic tables and 3 primitive sites. Showers. Inexpensive.

Island County Fairgrounds, P.O. Box 172; Langley 98260; (360) 221–4677. Has 50 RV sites with full hookups and an open tent area. Showers and tank dump. Near town. Closed mid-August to month's end for county fair. Inexpensive.

South Whidbey State Park, 4128 Smuggler's Cove Road; Freeland 98249; (360) 331–4559. West off State Route 525 on Smuggler's Cove Road, 15 miles southwest of Coupeville, 7 miles northwest of Freeland. Has 54 campsites with picnic tables and stoves and 6 primitive sites. Showers, tank dump, and firewood. Inexpensive.

FOOD AND BEVERAGES

Captain Whidbey Inn, 2072 West Captain Whidbey Inn Road; Coupeville; (360) 678–4097. Off Madrona Way, north of Coupeville. Breakfast, lunch, and dinner daily. Great breakfasts include apple-nut pancakes or French toast with raspberry butter, biscuits and gravy, and Hangtown Fry. Design your own omelettes with a choice of forty fillings. Soups, hearty lunch salads, sandwiches, and such entrees as Cajun crab cakes for lunch. Appetizers include smoked salmon and onion cheesecake, smoked quail, and ginger-steamed mussels. Clam chowder, warm duck salad. Dinner entrees include New York pepper steak, pecan chicken breast, poached salmon or oysters, and blackened rockfish. Cocktails, Northwest and imported wines, and two dozen domestic and imported beers. Moderate to expensive.

Christopher's, 23 Front Street; Coupeville; (360) 678–5480. Downtown. Serves lunch and dinner, Wednesday through Sunday. Appetizers: bagels with smoked salmon, tomato, provolone; pesto cheesecake; steamed Penn Cove mussels. Soups and chowder. Various salads, including shrimp-stuffed avocado and chicken salad with wild rice. Lunch offerings include Cajun seafood crepe, sautéed prawns with strawberry chutney, peppered beef strips with merlot sauce. For dinner, choose from oyster scampi fettuccine, pork medallions with orange-tequila sauce, baked chicken with blackberry and walnut stuffing, among others. Beer, wine, espresso, and other coffees. Daily specials. Moderate.

Kasteel Franssen Restaurant & Lounge, 33575 State Route 20; Oak Harbor; (360) 675–0724. Adjacent to Auld Holland Inn. Dinner daily. European-French cuisine. Start with Chuckanut Bay oysters, Penn Cove mussels, Zuiderzee herring, or any of a half dozen other appetizers and soups. Dinners include steaks, veal, chicken, and seafoods such as mahimahi, prawns, lobster, salmon, and halibut. Great desserts such as baked Alaska, peach melba, chocolate mousse, and English trifle. Piano bar and lounge. Moderate.

Mario's Pizza, 531 Southeast Midway Boulevard; Oak Harbor; (360) 679–2533. Open for lunch and dinner most days; call ahead for hours. Advertises "old-fashioned" pizza and is certainly not exaggerating. Pizzas made from scratch and from the freshest ingredients. Fresh dough made daily. Free delivery. Moderate.

SHOPPING AND BROWSING

Penn Cove Antique Mall, 12 Northwest Front Street; Coupeville; (360) 678–2986. Summer, 10:00 A.M. to 5:00 P.M. daily; winter, closed Tuesday. Glassware, jewelry, furniture, cameras, English imports, and other antiques and collectibles of twenty dealers on display.

Penn Cove Gallery, 9C Northwest Front Street; P.O. Box 1662; Coupeville; (360) 678–1176. Winter, 10:00 A.M. to 5:00 P.M. daily; summer, open till 6:00 P.M. A cooperative displaying and selling the works of eighteen local artists and artisans. Good selection of original paintings, prints, photographs, sculpture, jewelry, and more.

Whidbey Island Antiques, 799 Suzanne Court; Langley 98260; (360) 221–2393. Second Street at Anthes Avenue. Daily, 10:00 A.M. to 5:00 P.M. A good selection of antiques, including fine oak furniture and fixtures.

Whidbey's Greenbank Farm, 2832S 780th East; Greenbank 98253; (360) 678–7700; www.greenbankfarm.com. Ten miles south of Coupeville on State Route 525, 18 miles north of Clinton Ferry Terminal. Daily, 10:00 A.M. to 5:00 P.M. (cafe closed Monday). A beautiful berry farm where Whidbey's Liqueur is made and sold, along with Chateau Ste. Michelle wines, jellies, and gifts. Self-guided tour and tasting room.

MUSEUM

Island County Historical Society Museum, 908 Northwest Alexander; P.O. Box 305; Coupeville; (360) 678–3310. North end of town, overlooking the waterfront. Seasonal hours; call ahead. A beautiful museum, first open to the public in July 1991, it houses artifacts from the island's rich history and seafaring heritage. Also on display are canoes, paddles, baskets, fishing equipment, and tools used by the Coast Salish Indians. A fine museum.

OTHER ATTRACTIONS

Meerkerk Gardens, just off Highway 525 at Resort Road; Greenbank; (360) 678–1912; www.meerkerkgardens.org. Open daily from 9:00 A.M. to 4:00 P.M. Colorful woodland garden maintained by the American Rhododendron Society and other volunteers. Ten acres of display gardens on the forty-three-acre forest preserve. Spectacular spring blooms, summer perennials, and autumn foliage.

BEACHES, PARKS, TRAILS, AND WAYSIDES

Fort Casey State Park, adjacent to the Keystone Ferry dock, was one of three forts built in the area a century ago to protect the Puget Sound entrance and to ward off foreign invasion of the Bremerton Navy Yard and other likely targets. Troops occupied the fort until shortly after World War I, when the installation was mothballed and its great 10-inch guns melted down for scrap. The fort was reactivated as a training center during World War II, but it was again placed in caretaker status and ultimately sold to Washington State.

Visitors to the park are free to roam the concrete gun emplacements; to the delight of most, there are guns to inspect that are similar to the fort's original artillery. In 1968 the park acquired two 3-inch rapid-fire guns and two 10-inch guns on disappearing carriages from the Philippines.

Also in the park proper is **Admiralty Head Light,** which was deactivated in 1927. The state acquired the land and converted the beautiful old lighthouse into an interpretive center. Shutterbugs will find this to be one of the most photogenic lighthouses remaining on the West Coast.

At the north end of Whidbey Island and the south end of Fidalgo Island is **Deception Pass State Park,** with 2,500 acres of forest and miles of hiking and biking trails. The park has a freshwater lake and saltwater beach. Trails lead to many spectacular vistas of mountains, islands, and Puget Sound.

Park and walk out onto **Deception Pass Bridge** for a dizzying view of the chasm that narrows to 200 yards. Watch tides boil and rip in an eight-knot current, and imagine Captain Thomas Coupe navigating the gorge under full sail.

WATER SPORTS AND ACTIVITIES

With 135 miles of shoreline, Whidbey Island offers abundant opportunities for all kinds of water-related recreation. Fishing is a popular year-round sport, both from shore and boats, with chinook and coho salmon the most popular species. There is some clam digging on the island, and crabbing is good from docks, piers, and boats.

Sailing and island cruising are popular pastimes, and Whidbey Island serves as a good stopover port between Seattle and the San Juan Islands. Several marinas are here to serve those arriving by water and others who tow their boats and need to use launching facilities.

Deception Pass Marina, 5191 North Cornet Bay Road; Oak Harbor; (360) 675–5411. East off State Route 20, about 8 miles north of Oak Harbor. Fishing tackle, bait, ice, beer, licenses, fishing information, charter fishing, launching facilities, and moorage.

Oak Harbor Marina, 8075 Catalina Drive; Oak Harbor; (360) 679–2628. East side of town, near the seaplane base. A full-service marina with 130 open and 183 covered slips for boats up to 50 feet, dry storage for 104 craft to 24 feet, largest launch ramp in the Northwest (usable on any tide), and 8,000-pound-capacity launching crane.

TRAVEL INFORMATION

Greater Oak Harbor Chamber of Commerce, P.O. Box 883; Oak Harbor; (360) 675–3755; www.oakharborchamber.org

Central Whidbey Island Chamber of Commerce, 107 South Main Street; P.O. Box 152; Coupeville; (360) 678–5434; www.centralwhidbeychamber.com

Langley Chamber of Commerce, 124½ Second Street; P.O. Box 403; Langley 98260; (360) 221–6765; www.whidbey.com/langley

Clinton Chamber of Commerce, P.O. Box 317; Clinton 98236; (360) 341–3424; www.whidbeynet.net/clinton

Freeland Chamber of Commerce, P.O. Box 361; Freeland 98249; (360) 331–1980; www.islandweb.org/freeland

Whidbey Island Web site: www.whidbey.net

EVENTS

March	Penn Cove Mussel Festival, Coupeville, (360) 678–5434
April	Holland Happening, Oak Harbor, (360) 675–3755
May	Annual Art Show and Sale, Greenbank, (360) 678–5434

	Memorial Day Parade, Coupeville, (360) 678–5434
June	Annual Art Show and Sale, Langley, (360) 221–6765
	Annual Fine Arts Show, Coupeville, (360) 678–5434
July	Chochokum Arts Festival, Langley, (360) 221–7494
	Old-Fashioned Fourth of July Celebration, Oak Harbor, (360) 675–3755
	Whidbey Island Race Week (regatta), Oak Harbor, (360) 675–3535
August	Arts and Crafts Festival, Coupeville, (360) 675–7116
	Island County Fair, Langley, (360) 221–4677
September	Annual Fall Art Show and Sale, Langley, (360) 221–6765
	Annual Open Artists Studio Tour (all island), (360) 221–6422
October	Harvest Festival, Coupeville, (360) 678–5434
November	Christmas Boutique Craft Fair, Oak Harbor, (360) 675–3755
December	Greening Day, Coupeville, (360) 678–5434
	Self-Guided Holiday Tour (south island), (360) 221–6765

LA CONNER

Population: 760

Location: *About 5 miles south of State Route 20, via La Conner-Whitney Road. Junction is 6.4 miles west of I-5 (exit to State Route 20 at Burlington or State Route 536 at Mt. Vernon), 39 miles northeast of Keystone Ferry Terminal (to Port Townsend) on Whidbey Island. Zip: 98257.*

Tiny La Conner has more to offer the visitor than many towns ten times its size. Located on Swinomish Channel, it began as a trading post in 1867 and was known then as Swinomish. In 1869, John and Louisa Anne Conner bought the trading post and established a post office. John named the town after his wife by joining her first two initials to their last name.

Settlers ditched, diked, and drained thousands of acres of Skagit River delta and adjacent wetlands to create some of the most fertile farmlands in the world. Bumper crops of grain and hay turned La Conner into a thriving shipping center. Fishing, freight, and farming attracted people to the area, until La Conner residents numbered about 1,000 by the early 1900s.

The town flourished until the arrival of railroads in the Pacific Northwest. The Great Depression and decline of the fishing industry then further hastened the deterioration of La Conner's commerce.

Although a number of the region's artists and writers discovered La Conner in the 1940s, the town languished until the mid-1970s. As the oldest settlement in Skagit County, La Conner had many historic commercial buildings and some fine examples of Victorian architecture still intact. When owners began refurbishing the old buildings and setting up new businesses, tourists flocked to the town.

Agriculture is still a major industry in the Skagit Valley; in fact, it's one of La Conner's greatest attractions. Each spring, nearby fields become the stuff of artists' and photographers' dreams, as bulb farmers' crops of tulips and daffodils bloom, transforming acre upon acre into scenes worthy of canvas and Kodachrome.

The charming community is now a year-round attraction and one of the most popular spots in the Northwest. About 75 percent of the businesses are engaged in retail, food, and lodging enterprises. Summers, of course, are bumper-to-bumper busy, but autumn also draws Christmas shoppers to the many interesting and unusual shops.

LODGING

The Heron in La Conner, 117 Maple Avenue; P.O. Box 716; (360) 466–4626 or (888) 883–8899; www.theheron.com. The classic architecture belies this small hotel's age: It is a modern hostelry, built in 1986. All 12 rooms have full baths and cable TV; some have fireplaces. The honeymoon suite has a whirlpool tub. Complimentary continental breakfast is served in the dining room. Moderate to expensive.

Hotel Planter, 715 South First Street; P.O. Box 702; (360) 466–4710 or (800) 488–5409; www.hotelplanter.com. This historic hotel in the heart of town, built in 1907, was completely restored in 1989. It now features 12 cozy, comfortable, custom-furnished rooms with double and queen beds, private baths, ceiling fans, and armoires. Outside is a lovely courtyard garden and gazebo with a hot tub. Whirlpool suite available. Moderate.

La Conner Channel Lodge, 205 North First Street; P.O. Box 573; (360) 466–1500 or (888) 466–4113; www.laconner lodging.com. On Swinomish Channel, at the north end of town. This is La Conner's only waterfront hotel. All rooms have beamed ceilings, decks or balconies, and fireplaces. Some have whirlpool tubs. Complimentary breakfast served in the morning room. Expensive.

La Conner Country Inn, 107 South Second Street; P.O. Box 573; (360) 466–3101 or (888) 466–4113; www.laconner lodging.com. In town, just south of Morris. This rustic, country-style inn features fireplaces in each of its 28 rooms, brass beds, and complimentary breakfast served each morning in the library. Restaurant on premises, well known for sumptuous pasta dishes. Moderate.

Rainbow Bridge

CAMPGROUNDS AND RV PARKS

Bay View State Park, Bayview-Edison Road; (360) 757–0227. About 9 miles west of Burlington and north of La Conner. From State Route 20, follow the signs for Bayview and Padilla Bay National Estuarine Research Reserve. Has 99 campsites with tables and 1,300 feet of frontage on Padilla Bay. Hookups available. Beach access. Minus tides nearly empty the bay. Good beachcombing and birding. Wildlife includes bald eagles, herons, waterfowl, and harbor seals. Abundant Douglas fir, cedar, and alder. Near estuarine reserve, interpretive center, and nature trails. Inexpensive.

FOOD AND BEVERAGES

Calico Cupboard Bakery & Cafe, 720 South First Street; (360) 466–4451. South end of downtown La Conner. Open 8:00 A.M. to 5:00 P.M. daily, for breakfast, lunch, and English-style tea. Delicious homemade breads and desserts. Hearty breakfasts, great soups and sandwiches, fresh salads. Wholesome and healthful foods made from the freshest ingredients. Moderate.

Kerstin's Restaurant, 505 South First Street; (360) 466–9111. Open for dinner and lunch in downtown La Conner. Cozy bistro decorated with antiques. Bottom level hosts a popular wine bar featuring an impressive wine list from California and Washington. Upstairs is the elegant and intimate candle-lit dining area, where delicacies ranging from Samish Island oysters to fresh wild Troll King salmon are served for dinner. Luncheon specialties feature some of the entrees served at dinner, gourmet salads, and unusual treats such as bay shrimp, chives, capers, and Neufchâtel cheese broiled on focaccia. Outdoor patio with views of the harbor. Moderate to expensive.

La Conner Seafood & Prime Rib House, 614 South First Street; (360) 466–4014; www.laconnerseafood.com. In the heart of La Conner's shopping district. Open daily for lunch and dinner. Large selection of seafood, sandwiches, pasta, soups, salads, appetizers. Fish and chips, Cajun chicken, mariner's plate, salmon, prawns, king crab legs, steaks, and prime rib. Waterfront dining, inside or outside. Washington wines featured. Full bar. Moderate to expensive.

SHOPPING AND BROWSING

Earthenworks, 713 First Street; P.O. Box 702; (360) 466–4422; www.earthenworksgallery.com. Downtown. Open daily, 11:00 A.M. to 5:00 P.M. A good selection of top-quality artwork displayed in a pleasant, tasteful gallery. Excellent variety of types and media: porcelain pottery, metal sculpture, watercolors, batiks, *goyotaku*, basketry, jewelry, and more.

Nasty Jack's Antiques, 103 East Morris; P.O. Box 251; (360) 466–3209; www.nastyjacksantiques.com. At the north end of town. Open daily, 9:00 A.M. to 6:00 P.M. A big store with a huge selection of top-quality oak furniture and other antiques. A *required stop* for every antiques buff.

Tillinghast Seed Company, 623 East Morris Street; (360) 466–3329 or (800) 320–3329. Open Monday through Saturday, 9:00 A.M. to 5:30 P.M.; Sunday, 11:00 A.M. to 6:00 P.M. The oldest seed company in the Northwest, but much more. It's a general store with a garden center, kitchen shop, and Christmas attic, featuring a large selection of kitchen gadgetry, dinnerware, cookware, coffee beans, candies, condiments, spices, herbs, gourmet foods, and more.

The Wood Merchant, 709 South First Street; P.O. Box 511; (360) 466–4741. Open daily, 10:30 A.M. to 5:30 P.M. Billed as "a gallery of fine woodworking," it's certainly more than that, with a great variety of exquisitely finished wood products and works of art at good prices. A second-floor loft displays fine handmade furniture. Downstairs is the work of about seventy Northwest artists and woodworkers: beautiful carvings, marquetry, jewelry boxes, desk accessories, hand-turned bowls, decoys, and much more. From letter openers to rocking chairs, these are some of the best works in wood to be found in the Northwest.

MUSEUMS

La Conner Quilt Museum, 703 South Second Street; (360) 466–4288; www.laconnerquilts.com. Open Wednesday through Saturday, 11:00 A.M. to 4:00 P.M.; Sunday from noon to 4:00 P.M. Winter hours are Friday and Saturday, 11:00 A.M. to 4:00 P.M. and Sunday, noon to 4:00 P.M.; closed the first two weeks in January. The only quilt museum in the Pacific Northwest and one of only ten in the United States, the museum is housed in the historic Gaches Mansion. The first floor retains the mansion's turn-of-the-century decor; the second floor holds the quilt exhibits, which change every two to three months. Small admission fee.

Museum of Northwest Art, 121 South First Street, P.O. Box 969; (360) 466–4446. Open Tuesday through Sunday, 11:00 A.M. to 5:00 P.M. The work of Mark Tobey, Margaret Tompkins, Clayton James, and other outstanding artists of the Pacific Northwest are on display. The museum also sponsors shows by Northwest artists in a variety of media.

Skagit County Historical Museum, 501 South Fourth Street; P.O. Box 818; (360) 466–3365. Open Tuesday through Sunday, 11:00 A.M. to 5:00 P.M. On display are exhibits of kitchen utensils and housewares from early pioneer days, fishing gear, logging tools, and mining equipment. Two popular exhibits are a blacksmith shop and a general store. There are Northwest Coastal Indian displays and historic photographs.

BEACHES, PARKS, TRAILS, AND WAYSIDES

Compact La Conner is a walker's town, so park the car and hoof it. As you investigate the downtown area, keep watch for the pleasing gardens and walkways that show up in surprising spots. Here and there, you'll find benches and picnic tables—some in quiet corners, others amid the bustle of the business district.

At the south end of town, near the east end of Rainbow Bridge, is Pioneer Park, with plenty of room for picnics. Although much of the literature says overnight camping is allowed here, it hasn't been for several years.

During the Tulip Festival, it's best to find a place to park and either use the shuttle service, or walk or bike to the flower fields. The wide lanes along the berm are for bikers and walkers. Those who park vehicles there get ticketed.

The Padilla Bay Shore Trail starts just north of State Route 20 and takes hikers and bikers 2.2 miles to Bayview. It then joins a trail extending about 4 miles to the Breazeale Interpretive Center.

In the same vicinity, Bay View State Park is a popular spot for hiking, beachcombing, kite flying, and picnicking, as well as watching and photographing birds and other wildlife.

OTHER ATTRACTIONS

Padilla Bay National Estuarine Research Reserve and Breazeale Interpretive Center, 1043 Bayview-Edison Road; Mount Vernon 98273; (360) 428–1558. About 4 miles north of State Route 20, via Bayview-Edison Road. Reserve trails open daily. Interpretive center open Wednesday through Sunday, 8:30 A.M. to 5:00 P.M. An 11,000-acre reserve, which includes 2,600 acres of Padilla Bay mudflats, eelgrass beds, and coastal wetlands. The reserve sponsors many nature activities. At the interpretive center are saltwater aquariums and information about estuaries in general and Padilla Bay specifically. Part of the National Estuarine Reserve System.

TRAVEL INFORMATION

La Conner Chamber of Commerce, 313 Morris Street, Box 1016; (360) 466–4778 or (888) 642–9284; www.laconnerchamber.com

EVENTS

February	Smelt Derby, (360) 466–4778
April	Skagit Valley Tulip Festival, (360) 428–5959
May	Opening Day Boat Parade, (360) 466–4778
July	Waterfront Fireworks Display, (360) 466–4778
August	Pioneer Picnic, (360) 466–4784
October	Festival of Family Farms, (360) 428–4270
November	Art's Alive Festival, (360) 466–4778
	Lighted Boat Parade, (360) 466–4778

BELLINGHAM

Population: 67,171

Location: *On I–5, 21 miles south of the Canada border, 89 miles north of Seattle, 26 miles north of State Route 20, via State Routes 237 and 11. Zip: 98225–27.*

In 1904 a handful of communities scattered along the shores of Bellingham Bay were consolidated into one city and named after the bay. The city has grown and absorbed the individuality of the earlier towns and tied them together in an occasionally troublesome tangle of thoroughfares.

One of the early townsites, Fairhaven, remains a relatively distinct district within the city. Its charming collection of old brick buildings and attractive Victorian houses will continue to attract visitors, so long as Fairhaven can resist the ravages of progress.

Like their neighbors to the southwest in Port Townsend, Fairhaven speculators, gambling that the area would become the western terminus of the Great Northern Railroad, built the town in the 1890s. When the railroad went south, Fairhaven went bust. The area remained in a state of decline well into the twentieth century. In 1970 a developer bought a number of buildings and renewed Fairhaven's vitality.

Another historically significant area is the "Old Town" district near the waterfront and Whatcom Creek. This is where the first white settlers came ashore in the mid-1800s and where Henry Roeder built a sawmill in 1853. A number of historical buildings still stand here, including the magnificent New Whatcom City Hall, which is now the Whatcom Museum of History and Art. Several interesting galleries, antiques shops, and restaurants add to the enjoyment of an Old Town tour.

The Eldridge district's residential area is characterized by some fine old houses built in the late nineteenth and early twentieth cen-

220

turies. In the Sehome district, near the Western Washington University campus, are more vintage houses and other buildings. "Walking Tour" guides and maps of all these areas are available at the convention and visitors bureau.

Arriving at and departing from Bellingham via the north, it's difficult to avoid I–5 and its frenetic freeway pace. But to the south, you have a much more pleasant and scenic alternative. A stretch of the old coast highway—State Route 11 (Chuckanut Drive)—clings to sheer coastal bluffs above Bellingham and Samish Bays, commanding splendid views of Rosario Strait and the San Juan Islands.

You can pick up State Route 11 off I–5 south of Bellingham at Burlington. From Whidbey Island, take State Route 237 north 9 miles off State Route 20 to State Route 11. Chuckanut Drive leads into the Fairhaven district. From Bellingham head south on Chuckanut Drive, take exit 250 west off I–5, and follow Old Fairhaven to Chuckanut.

LODGING

Best Western Heritage Inn, 151 East McLeod Road; (360) 647–1912 or (888) 333–2080; www.bestwestern.com/heritageinn bellingham. Just east of I–5, via exit 256 or 256A, near Bellis Fair Mall. Queen and king beds in 90 roomy and comfortable rooms and suites with coffee and tea makers, hair dryers, cable TV, and HBO. Complimentary daily newspaper and continental breakfast. Pool and whirlpool. Moderate.

DeCann House Bed & Breakfast, 2610 Eldridge Avenue; Bellingham 98225; (360) 734–9172; www.decannhouse.com. About 3 miles west of I–5, via Lakeway and Holly Street, exit 253. Two guest rooms with private baths, decorated with family heirlooms. Century-old house overlooks Bellingham Bay and San Juan Islands. Moderate.

North Garden Inn Bed & Breakfast, 1014 North Garden Street; Bellingham 98225; (360) 671–7828 or (800) 922–6414; www.northgardeninn.com. West of I–5 at exit 253, Lakeway to Holly, then left on North Garden. Ten guest rooms have a view of Bellingham Bay. Near the university, shops, and restaurants. Continental breakfast. Moderate.

Schnauzer Crossing Bed & Breakfast, 4421 Lakeway Drive; Bellingham 98226; (360) 733–0055 or (800) 562–2808; www.schnauzercrossing.com. Three miles east of I–5 at exit 253. Inn overlooks Lake Whatcom and has 2 guest rooms. One room

Antiques and collectibles found in Bellingham

with private bath and queen bed. Master suite with king bed, private bath with whirlpool tub and double shower, sitting or child's room, and TV. Use of canoe and sailboat. Private tennis court. Sumptuous breakfasts of quiche, berries, muffins, fruit parfaits, bagels, and freshly ground coffee. Moderate to expensive.

CAMPGROUNDS AND RV PARKS

Larrabee State Park, 245 Chuckanut Drive; Bellingham 98226; (800) 233–0321 or (800) 452–5687; www.parks.wa.gov. Seven miles south of Bellingham on State Route 11. Has 61 tent sites, 25 RV sites with full hookups, and 3 primitive sites. Tables, stove, picnic area, kitchen shelter, showers, and tank dump. A beautiful park on 1,886 wooded acres with 3,600 feet of shoreline on Samish Bay. A great area for exploring tide pools at low tide. Good hiking trails. Fishing and scuba diving are other popular attractions. Inexpensive.

Wildwood Resort, 990 South Lake Whatcom Boulevard; Sedro Woolley 98284; (360) 595–2311; www.wildwood-resort.net. Located 11 miles southeast of Bellingham, 5.6 miles northeast of Alger, east of I–5 on west shore of Lake Whatcom. From north, exit 253; from south, exit 240. A 15-acre campground with full-hookup campsites, tent sites, and cabins. Store, marina, fishing tackle, groceries, beer, wine, and souvenirs. Boat launch, moorage, gas dock, and rentals. Moderate.

FOOD AND BEVERAGES

Archer Ale House, 1212 10th Street; (360) 647–7002. In the Fairhaven district. Opens at 3:00 P.M. Sunday through Friday and 1:00 P.M. Saturday. One of Bellingham's most popular pubs, offering a good selection of seasonal American microbrews and imported bottled beers. Ten taps turn out fresh bock, pale ale, special bitter, stout, lager, and pilsner. Superb pub food includes hearty soups, pizza, sandwiches, salads, and smoked salmon. Among the daily specials are shepherd's pie, Cornish pasties, and a variety of ethnic foods. Beer-battered oysters are the special on the second Friday and Saturday of the month, oyster stew on the last Friday and Saturday of the month. Moderate.

Boundary Bay Brewery, Bistro & Taproom, 1107 Railroad Avenue; (360) 647–5593; bbaybrewery.com. West of I–5, via exit 253, between Maple and Chestnut, across from the Bellingham Farmers Market. Lunch and dinner daily. A microbrewery that features a half dozen freshly brewed ales and lagers, including porter, bitter, and India pale ale. Appetizers include steamers in ale, smoked-salmon hot pot, and blue-cheese salad. For lunch, mushroom ragout with polenta, burgers, and hearty sandwiches. Dinner selections include lamb-and-pepper goulash, eggplant-and-mushroom lasagna, and paprika schnitzel. Inexpensive to moderate.

Chuckanut Manor Restaurant, 302 Chuckanut Drive; Bow 98232; (360) 766–6191. South of Bellingham, west of I–5, on State Route 11. Lunch and dinner Tuesday through Saturday, brunch and dinner Sunday. Friday smorgasbord includes all the roast chicken, beef, oysters, poached salmon, and salads you can eat. Sunday brunch features baked goods, fruit, eggs, quiche, oysters, omelettes, and complimentary champagne or sparkling cider. Other house specialties include fresh Samish Bay oyster dishes, Penn Cove mussels, poached or grilled salmon, prime rib, veal, and New Zealand lamb. Good wine list, featuring Northwest and California wines. Offers more than seventy-five domestic and imported beers, including Northwest microbrews. Moderate.

Colophon Cafe, 1208 11th Street; (360) 647–0092; www.colophoncafe.com. In historic Fairhaven at Village Books. This legendary bookstore cafe offers award-winning soups and giant desserts, as well as sandwiches, salads, and quiches. The bakery prepares all its creations from scratch, ranging from decadent cheesecakes to all-natural fruit pies. Deli, dining room, and outside patio seating. Moderate.

Mannino's, 130 East Champion Street; (360) 671–7955.

Downtown. Lunch and dinner daily. Italian and continental cuisine. Start with prosciutto and melon, antipasto, steamed clams, deep-fried mozzarella, stuffed mushrooms, shrimp scampi, or fried calimari appetizer. Then pick from a large selection of pasta dishes and such entrees as chicken, veal, steak, seafood, sausage and peppers, or the Peasant Dish: chicken and homemade Italian sausage, served with bell peppers, onions, tomatoes, potatoes, and garlic. Full bar. Moderate.

Sadighi's Fine Food Restaurant, 921 Lakeway Drive; Bellingham 98226; (360) 647–1109. Off I–5, exit 253, across from the Fred Meyer store. Dinner Wednesday through Monday, closed Tuesday. Carefully prepared international cuisine, some Cajun, some Chinese, some Northwest. Select from a half dozen appetizers, including shrimp and avocado salad, hot spinach salad, and smoked salmon. Entrees include blackened New York steak, lamb chops, veal sautéed in butter and brandy, stuffed sole, seafood Creole, sockeye salmon fillet, and chicken Dijon fettuccine. Homemade desserts. Cocktails and domestic beers and wines. Moderate.

Skylark's Hidden Cafe, 1308-B 11th Street; (360) 715–3642. Located in historic Fairhaven, the tiny cafe is hidden down a quaint cobblestone alleyway. It is decorated in oak and stained glass. Open at 7:00 A.M. daily and serving breakfast, lunch, and dinner. Breakfast features griddle treats, a hearty organic granola, and a variety of omelettes. For lunch check out the homemade soups and generous sandwiches. Dinner entrees range from jumbo prawns to baked salmon. Moderate.

SHOPPING AND BROWSING

Bellis Fair, 1 Bellis Fair Parkway; (360) 671–5654; www.bellis fair.com. At I–5 and Meridian, east of the interstate, via exits 256-B and 258. Monday through Saturday, 9:30 A.M. to 9:00 P.M.; Sunday, 11:00 A.M. to 6:00 P.M. A large mall with five major department stores—The Bon Marché, JCPenney, Mervyn's, Sears, and Target—as well as more than 150 specialty shops and fifteen restaurants.

Jody Bergsma Gallery, 1344 King Street; Bellingham 98226; (360) 733–1101; Washington, (800) 445–5639; elsewhere, (800) 237–4762. East of I–5, next to the visitor information center, exit 253. Open Monday through Saturday, 10:00 A.M. to 6:00 P.M., and Sunday, 11:00 A.M. to 6:00 P.M. Original artworks, plates, figurines, and limited-edition prints. Mail-order catalog available. The gallery cafe serves lunch from 11:00 A.M. to 2:00 P.M.

Indian Street Pottery, 1309 Indian Street; Bellingham 98225; (360) 733–3432. West of I–5, exit 253, Lakeway to East Holly to Indian Street. Wednesday through Saturday, 11:00 A.M. to 5:00 P.M. Large selection of pottery, raku, stoneware, lamps, masks, vases, planters, and wall hangings.

MUSEUMS

American Museum of Radio, 1312 Bay Street; (360) 738–3886; www.antique-radio.org. Located in downtown. This one-of-a-kind museum is a tribute to the history of radio in America, with many exhibits, some interactive. The museum houses a fine collection of vintage radios and broadcast technology from the early twentieth century. Open Wednesday through Saturday, noon to 5:00 P.M.

Whatcom Museum of History & Art, 121 Prospect Street, Bellingham 98225; (360) 676–6981; www.whatcommuseum.org. West of I–5, via exit 253. West on Lakeway to East Holly to Prospect. Tuesday through Sunday, noon to 5:00 P.M. An elegant Victorian building erected in 1892, which served as city hall until 1939, now houses permanent and changing exhibits of regional history and Northwest art. Exquisite, well-lighted interior complements displays of Indian artifacts, logging equipment, nautical items, and furnishings and fixtures from the Victorian era. Ranks among the best such museums on the coast. Classified a *must-see*. Free admission.

WATER SPORTS AND ACTIVITIES

Island Mariner Cruises, No. 5 Harbor Esplanade; Bellingham 98225; (360) 734–8866 or (877) 734–8866; www.orcawatch. com. On Bellingham Bay waterfront. Whale-watching and nature excursions, as well as dinner cruises in the San Juan Islands aboard the 83-foot former Coast Guard cutter *Rosario Princess*.

San Juan Islands Shuttle Express, 355 Harris Avenue; (360) 671–1137 or (888) 373–8522; www.orcawhales.com. At the Bellingham Cruise Terminal. Passenger service, day cruises, and whale-watching excursions from Bellingham to Orcas, Lopez, and San Juan Islands. Operates daily from late May to the end of September.

Victoria–San Juan Cruises, 355 Harris Avenue #104; (360) 738–8099 or (800) 443–4552; www.whales.com. At the Bellingham

Cruise Terminal. Day cruises and overnight packages booked for the San Juan Islands and Victoria, British Columbia. Phone for brochure and current schedule.

OTHER ATTRACTIONS

The Bellingham Farmers' Market, Railroad and Chestnut; (360) 647–2060; www.bellinghamfarmers.org. Held April through October, 10:00 A.M. to 3:00 P.M. Wander and shop for fresh produce, plants, great food, arts, and music—all found within fifty-seven booths and with more than one-hundred vendors in a festive atmosphere.

GOLF

Sudden Valley Golf Course, 2145 Lake Whatcom Boulevard; Bellingham 98226; (360) 734–6435. East of I-5, southeast of Bellingham. From the north, take exit 253, from the south exit 240. An 18-hole, par-72, 6,553-yard course.

TRAVEL INFORMATION

Bellingham/Whatcom County Convention & Visitors Bureau, 904 Potter (I-5, exit 253); Bellingham 98226; (360) 671–3990; www.bellingham.org

EVENTS

May	Ski to Sea Festival, (360) 734–1330
June	Airfest, (360) 676–2500
July	Seafood & Wine Festival, (360) 756–1998
August	Bellingham Festival of Music, (800) 335–5550
November	Home for the Holidays, (360) 676–1891
	Whatcom Artist's Studio Tour, (360) 734–9472
December	Holiday Festival of the Arts, (360) 676–8548
	Lighted Boat Parade, (360) 734–1330

BLAINE
Population: 3,770

BIRCH BAY
Population: 5,123

Location: *Blaine is on I–5 at the Canada border, 21 miles north of Bellingham; Birch Bay is about 6 miles south of Blaine via county roads or west off I–5 at exit 270. Zip: 98230.*

B laine is a small border town that has several decent eateries, watering holes, and overnight digs. Charter boats take anglers to nearby fishing grounds for salmon and bottom fish. Peace Arch Park has attractive formal gardens, a pleasant picnic area, and a picturesque arch standing between northbound and southbound lanes of I–5 as a monument to the peaceful border between the United States and Canada.

The area's main attraction, though, is a posh resort at the tip of Semiahmoo (seh-mee-*ah*-moo) Spit, across Drayton Harbor from Blaine. The $200 million complex includes an inn with three restaurants and 200 guest rooms, a 250-slip marina that's expandable to 800 slips, a golf course designed by Arnold Palmer, a complete fitness center, shops, homesites, and town house condominiums. To reach Semiahmoo, take Blaine Road south to Drayton Harbor Road, which follows the south shore and connects with Semiahmoo Drive.

South of Blaine, on the shores of Birch Bay, is a small resort community of the same name. This is a popular area for water sports and activities. The bay is shallow, and the summer sun warms its waters enough for wading and swimming. Because the bay is so shallow, minus tides expose miles of tide flats, making this one of the best areas on the Washington coast for digging big horseneck and butter clams. Along the south shore of the bay is **Birch Bay State Park** with fine campgrounds, a beautiful picnic area, and a long stretch of sandy beach.

LODGING

Driftwood Inn Resort Motel, 7394 Birch Bay Drive; (360) 371–2620 or (800) 833–2666. Exit 266 west off I–5, then 8 miles to Jackson, north 2 miles to Birch Bay Drive, and left 3 blocks. Has 14 motel rooms, cottages, and condominium suites, 1 to 3 bedrooms, some with kitchens. Cable TV, heated pool, playground, bike rental, boat and canoe rentals, beach access. Moderate.

Resort Semiahmoo, 9550 Semiahmoo Parkway; (360) 371–2000 or (800) 770–7792; www.semiahmoo.com. A $33.5 million inn at the 800-acre resort complex. Washington's largest resort hotel, with 200 rooms and suites featuring all the expected amenities. View rooms and fireplaces available. Walk to shops, galleries, marina, charter craft, beach, and bike rentals. Fitness center includes indoor and outdoor pools, indoor and outdoor tennis courts, indoor track, squash and racquetball courts, fully equipped weight room, spa, saunas, steam rooms, and tanning booths. Also at the inn is a gourmet dining room called Stars Restaurant, and, for more casual dining, Packers Oyster Bar and Lounge. Moderate to very expensive.

Water's Edge Bed & Breakfast, 7379 Birch Bay Drive; Birch Bay; (360) 371–2043. Six miles south of Blaine, take Birch Bay/Lynden Road west off I–5 at exit 270, then south (left) on Birch Bay Drive. King beds in two spacious, comfortably appointed, upstairs guest rooms with cable TV, half baths, and shared shower room. Water's Edge Suite has wet bar, refrigerator, microwave oven, and private balcony overlooking the bay. Living room with fireplace. Coffee, tea, and cold drinks available all day. Full breakfast. Moderate to expensive.

CAMPGROUNDS AND RV PARKS

Birch Bay State Park, 5105 Helwig Road; (360) 371–2800. Ten miles south of Blaine, via Blaine Road and Birch Bay Drive, or exits 266 and 270 west off I–5. Has 147 tent sites and 20 RV sites with water and electric hookups, picnic tables, stoves, firewood, showers, tank dump, and picnic area along the bay. Access to a beach. Store and cafe nearby. Reservations accepted. Inexpensive.

FOOD AND BEVERAGES

Harbor Cafe, 295 Marine Drive; Blaine; (360) 332–5176. Unassuming green cafe looks out over the harbor and serves the best seafood—direct from the fishermen—in the area. Open daily, 7:00 A.M. to 9:00 P.M.; lounge open until midnight, Friday and Saturday. The lunch and dinner specialties are fish and chips and salmon and chips, but the cafe also features a variety of locally caught fresh-fish dishes, as well as burgers and sandwiches. Breakfasts are ample with traditional country fare. Moderate.

Packers Oyster Bar & Lounge, 9550 Semiahmoo Parkway; Blaine; (360) 371–2000 or (800) 770–7992; www.semiahmoo. com. At the Resort Semiahmoo. Daily, 11:00 A.M. to 10:00 P.M. Cold foods, hot foods, and sandwiches include seafood sampler, oysters on the half shell, steamed clams, clam chowder, hot wings, Caesar salad, Asian noodle salad, Alaskan cod and chips, cioppino, salmon sandwich, sirloin-steak sandwich, and burgers. Full bar.

Stars Restaurant, 9550 Semiahmoo Parkway; Blaine; (360) 371–2000 or (800) 770–7992; www.semiahmoo.com. At the Resort Semiahmoo. Dinner nightly. Such appetizers as alder-smoked salmon, curried oysters, wild-mushroom and goat-cheese strudel, and prawn cocktail. Soups, salads, and pasta dishes. Such entrees as alder-plank roasted salmon, grilled halibut, wok-charred sea scallops, Dungeness crab cakes, roast duckling, Northwest venison, rack of lamb, roast pork tenderloin, filet mignon, and prime rib with Yorkshire popover. Chef's specials each evening and desserts fresh from the inn's bakery. Wine list and full bar. Moderate to expensive.

SHOPPING AND BROWSING

Peace Arch Factory Outlets, Birch Bay/Lynden Road; (360) 366–3127. Just west of I-5, via exit 270, 6 miles south of Blaine, 15 miles north of Bellingham. Monday through Saturday, 9:30 A.M. to 8:00 P.M.; Sunday, 10:30 A.M. to 7:00 P.M. Discount prices on top-name brands at twenty-eight stores. Fine porcelain and china, glassware, appliances, men's and women's apparel, children's clothing, cookware and cutlery, fragrances and cosmetics, and much more—even a duty-free shop.

WATER SPORTS AND ACTIVITIES

Passenger Ferry *Plover*, Blaine; (360) 332–5742. At the Blaine Marina, on Marine Drive, just past the Visitor Information Center, or at Semi-ah-moo Resort. May 30 to Labor Day: Friday and Saturday, noon to dusk; Sunday, 10:00 A.M. to 5:00 P.M. Historic restored wooden passenger ferry, listed on the National Park

Mount Baker rises above Semiahmoo Marina

Service's National Register of Historic Places. Owned by the What-com Maritime Historical Society and operated as a working museum display. Runs between Blaine and Resort Semiahmoo. Leaves Blaine Harbor on the hour and carries up to seventeen passengers, with limited space for bicycles. Links bicycle/pedestrian paths on both sides of Drayton Harbor. Westbound trip, about 15 minutes, through Blaine harbor, past commercial fleet. Departs eastbound about 20 minutes later and takes a different scenic route. No charge, but donations are appropriate.

Semiahmoo Marina, 9540 Semiahmoo Parkway; (360) 371–5700 or (800) 770–7992; www.semiahmoo.com. A 300-slip marina that will eventually expand to 800 slips. Features yacht maintenance, thirty-five-ton haulout capacity, full hookups and phone lines, showers, laundry, boat repairs, and supplies. A short walk to the inn, shops, galleries, and restaurants.

GOLF

Semiahmoo Golf and Country Club, Resort Semiahmoo; (360) 371–7005 or (800) 770–7992; www.semiahmoo.com. An 18-hole, par-72, 7,000-yard course laid out in a beautiful forested setting. When course designer Arnold Palmer saw the finished course, he said, "It looks like it's been here for a hundred years." Complete facilities. A semiprivate course, open to the public. Phone for tee times.

OTHER ATTRACTIONS

Peace Arch State Park, P.O. Box 87; Blaine; (800) 233–0321; www.parks.wa.gov. Peace Arch State Park lies on the boundary between the United States and Canada, making it a favorite entryway for international travelers because of its beautiful gardens and picturesque setting. Peace Arch stands as the first structure of its kind in the world and was built with volunteer labor from both the United States and Canada as a symbol of lasting peace between the two countries. The 67-foot monument is situated so that one of its two feet rests in each country. It is inscribed with the words "Children of a Common Mother." The gardens surrounding the arch are planted with more than 200 perennials and 55,000 annuals. More than 500,000 visitors tour the Arch each year and place a foot in each country. It is one of the few landmarks in the world listed on the National Historic Registries of two countries.

TRAVEL INFORMATION

Birch Bay Chamber of Commerce, 7806 Birch Bay Drive; Birch Bay; (360) 371–5004; www.birchbay.net

Blaine Visitor Information Center, 215 Marine Drive; P.O. Box 4680; Blaine; (360) 332–4544 or (800) 624–3555; www.cityofblaine.com

EVENTS

May	Blessing of the Fleet, Blaine, (360) 332–4544
June	Peace Arch Celebration, Blaine, (360) 332–4544
	Skywater Festival, Blaine, (360) 332–4544
July	Discovery Days, Birch Bay, (360) 371–5004
	Fireworks Show, Blaine, (360) 332–4544
	Sand Castle Contest, Birch Bay, (360) 371–2070
September	Peace Arch Anniversary, (360) 332–7165,
December	Christmas Lighting Celebration, Blaine, (360) 332–4544
	Christmas Sail-by, Blaine, (360) 332–4544

OREGON INDEX

WASHINGTON INDEX

ABOUT THE EDITOR

Kathy Strong, a native southern Californian, has lived and traveled extensively on the West Coast for more than forty years. Strong has also authored the popular guidebooks *The Seattle Guidebook, Recommended Bed & Breakfasts California, Recommended Island Inns: The Caribbean,* and *Southern California Off the Beaten Path,* all published by the Globe Pequot Press. Kathy and her family reside in the Palm Springs area, where she writes travel and other features for various magazines and has a regular travel column for *Desert Magazine.*